Chris Woolston is founder and Chairman of the strategy consultancy forward thinking inc. Established in 1998, the firm has since supported many of the world's most admired organisations.

He is the author of the companion book On Strategy, first published in 2020.

First published in Great Britain as a hardcover original in 2023

Editing and publishing by UK Book Publishing

www.ukbookpublishing.com

Watercolour portrait illustrations by Jon Elworthy

Design and typesetting by Zoe Edwards

Typeset in Book Antiqua and Century Gothic

ISBN: 978-1-916572-21-8

ON REFLECTION

CHRIS WOOLSTON

For Gilly, George, Rory, Michael, Charlie and Mum

With thanks to Trevor, Ruth, Jon and Zoe

CONTENTS

INTRODUCTION

Over the course of a long career people accumulate a wealth of knowledge, not only about the technical nature of their jobs but about the many aspects of work and life which they need to master to become successful. As time goes by they will impart much of that knowledge to younger colleagues and many become very skilled at imparting it.

The value of that experience is considerable, not the kind of knowledge which can be learned from a textbook or taught easily at a university where the teachers are often career-long academics. It is soft knowledge and the more powerful for that.

Several years ago I interviewed one or two senior clients whom I admired, suggesting to them that they might enjoy reflecting on the thirty years or more of their careers to that point and the knowledge they had accumulated. I asked them questions about their business experience and their companies, the people who had influenced them and those they had learned from early on in their careers. We talked about episodes that had been meaningful and influential in shaping their perspectives and their careers, about what they enjoyed most about their jobs, how they coped with adversity, how they juggled work and home lives, and what they thought were some of the key lessons they had learned along the way. At the time I turned the articles into occasional features for our consultancy's newsletter and the response was always very positive. Readers found the articles engaging and easy to read and seemed to enjoy the natural flow of the stories as they unfolded. And so the idea behind this book was formed. I set out to interview people from a range of backgrounds and professions with an interesting story to tell and who might exhibit a contrasting mix of learnings and perspectives. In the end I managed to put together a pleasing cocktail. A leading scientist and former SAGE member, co-founder of one of the UK's most successful companies, a Board member at Foster + Partners, an advisor to the Bank of England, a Charity CEO, a senior executive from the BBC and Oxford Said Business School, and a blend of business leaders from sectors ranging from Property to Banking and Advertising.

When I began I was not sure that the busy executives concerned would find it a valuable use of their time to sit with me and a voice recorder for two or three hours. What was pleasantly surprising was that not only were they prepared to give up their time but actually really enjoyed the experience. My guess is that busy senior people do not always find it easy to set aside time to reflect on things in this way. It turns out that my interviews were cathartic. Those interviewed who have since retired enjoyed the chance to take stock, consider what they had achieved and how they did it. Perhaps the ones still busy working used the opportunity to reflect and reset for the final chapters of their careers.

If you are interested in finding out more about and reflecting on the accumulated experience of others, understanding people and what drives and forms them, then I think you will enjoy the book as something to dip in and out of. I hope you do and that perhaps some of their experience will be of value to you as you chart your own lives and careers.

For the most part I will let the stories speak for themselves but if you look carefully there are a number of recurrent themes. The importance of a parent's influence, early insecurities driving a will to succeed, the role of mentors and the 'sweet spot' where natural abilities intersect with opportunity to propel a career.

INSPIRATION

I've always been interested in other people. It's why I tend to read biographies more than novels and in conversation I hope I am a good listener. I'm more interested in finding out about the person I'm talking to than talking about myself. Learning from the experience of others selectively is more valuable to me than reading a textbook, someone else's distillation of knowledge and experience. You can choose for yourself the bits that particularly resonate with you.

As a young man I read two books which have always stayed with me and perhaps inspired me to write a book based on the real-life experiences of others. One, "Akenfield", by Ronald Blythe, first published in 1969, is a collection of individual interviews with the residents of a fictional Suffolk village based on Akenham. Each has their own story and together they paint a vivid and engaging picture of a place with a rich history caught at a moment in time when many things in the world were changing. It's a beautiful book. As I write this book we are about to experience a new monarch and a new Prime Minister, appointed within days of each other. A new era and a great deal of change ahead, so it feels like a good time to reflect on past experiences as we all look forward to what happens next in our lives.

The second is a book entitled, "In The Long Run", which I first read when I was fourteen. It's the biography of a today little remembered marathon runner called Jim Peters. The title had and has particular resonance and meaning in the context of this book because our lives represent a long race. Unlike a sprint, they require endurance, changes of pace and often strength of will is a more important determinator of success than physical or intellectual prowess. Peters was a case in point. He looked like a civil servant and ran in plimsolls but in the 1950s broke the marathon world record four times! His final race was in 1954 at the Empire Games in Vancouver. He entered the stadium 17 minutes ahead of the next runner but began to struggle, fell to the ground, rose, collapsed again and again, managing to cover 20 metres in 11 minutes. He was eventually carried off on a stretcher and never raced again. He ended his career working as an optician in Surrey. I was struck by the extraordinary determination he portrayed, making the most of his assets in forging an unlikely world class athletics career.

RONALD BLYTHE

Born in 1922, grew up in Acton, Suffolk, the eldest of six children. He worked as a librarian in Colchester and founded the Colchester

Literary Society. He later worked for Benjamin Britten at the Aldeburgh Festival. He published his first book in 1960 entitled, "A Treasonable Growth", a novel set in the Suffolk countryside, and later, "The Age of Illusion", a set of essays examining English social history between the wars. He said about himself, "what I basically am is a listener and a watcher. I observe, without asking questions, but I don't forget things".

JIM PETERS

Born in Hackney, London in 1918, he began racing after the Second World War at the age of 27. At 28 he became English six-mile champion. Selected for the 1948 Olympics, he was lapped by the winner and wanted to retire. His coach Jimmy Johnson persuaded him to carry on but switch to the marathon. He trained part-time for three years while working as an optician. Peters won his first marathon in 1951, beating veteran champion Jack Holden. In 1952 he broke the world marathon record by an astonishing five minutes. He entered the next Olympics as favourite but failed to finish.

Prior to the Vancouver Empire Games he broke the world record three more times. Vancouver was to be his last race. In his biography, he remembers "I actually had a lead of nearly three and a half miles in the final stages, if I'd known that I could have stopped at the last fuelling station, had a good sponge down and run in slowly". He continued: "I set off fast in the heat, but that was always my way, to destroy the field."

“

I have a very visual brain, but have always been dyslexic. I'm unusually good at visualising things. I can look at a system and analyse it, see how it works. In my mind's eye I have a picture of molecules interacting in the same way that parts of a clock operate.

PETER OPENSHAW

INTERVIEWED 5TH JANUARY 2021

Peter is an expert in lung diseases and immunology, leading the Infection Theme of the Biomedical Research Centre at Imperial College London. Growing up with a Quaker background, he followed both his parents into medicine. After working as a clinician he made the decision to focus on scientific research.

Today he is part of a global academic community pushing the boundaries of immunological research. During the 2009 influenza and the 2020 COVID pandemics he became well known for this frequent appearances on radio, TV and in the written media.

Can we start with you talking to me about your current role and then perhaps we'll explore the journey which led to it.

I am professor of experimental medicine at Imperial College London and I lead a research team that's currently working predominantly on COVID-19. I have studied the immunology of respiratory viruses for about 30 years now.

I am really an immunologist, somebody who looks at the way in which a body responds to lung infections, how it defends itself against invasion by viruses and bacteria. The immune system does some other things as well, but to my mind defence against infection is what the immune system is for.

If I might ask, what led you to specialise in the area?

I qualified in medicine in 1979 and spent five years being a front-line clinician. In my last year of being a medical registrar it struck me how we were dealing with a tide of diseases, the causes of which were largely obscure. We were trying to mend people once they were broken rather than looking at why they were sick in the first place.

I became convinced that for many of the diseases we see in hospitals, infection might trigger them but we did not really know exactly how. We knew infections might be at the root of some common chronic diseases but the suspicion was that this was more widespread than currently understood and that we usually did not know what the trigger was. In asthma, I knew from my personal experience as a lifelong asthmatic that most exacerbations are triggered by viral infections. But did viruses have a role in initiating my disease in childhood?

I just felt, that rather than standing in front of a rising tide of disease in a district general hospital, it would be better if I tried to work out some way of preventing the tide from coming in.

That makes sense.

Yes. Even if there was only a remote hope of succeeding, it would be better than tinkering around with doses of insulin and inhalers for the rest of my career. It was the hope of finding something fundamental about the relationship between infection and diseases that drove me to do a PhD.

Tell me about that.

As soon as I got into the lab, I became hooked on the excitement of doing research. It satisfied my need to understand things.

I'd like to come back to your PhD and career track from there, but can I first ask whether you always had that urge to explore?

Yes, I have always been very experimental in my approach to life. From an early age I always liked taking things apart and working out how they functioned, whether it was messing around in woods, out in the fields or damming up streams; whatever I did was always experimental. I liked finding out how things worked and how to fix them. Sometimes I just broke them, but that's part of being curious.

So, from a relatively early age, you felt you would end up in science or medicine in some capacity?

Yes.

Were your parents doctors or scientists, out of interest?

They were both first-generation doctors. My mother came from a long line of Quakers and I guess that my upbringing was influenced by Quakerism. I went to Quaker schools, my friends and family had a Quaker heritage.

What are the characteristics of Quakerism?

Liberal, egalitarian, anti-authoritarian. Corporal punishment has never been part of Quaker education. I don't know if you know anything about Quaker meetings, but basically there is no minister. Anyone can stand up and speak, and everyone is regarded as being equal. Quakerism has always given women an equal voice, for example.

Do you still follow the religion?

I am a member of the Society of Friends, but not a theist.

But, the principles, and some of the ideas, and thoughts about life have adhered over the years?

Yes.

Was your father also a Quaker?

He became an attender but he never became a member. He came from the North, which you might guess from the name Openshaw. It's a Mancunian name; his family were fishmongers and were antagonistic towards his decision to go to university and not carry on in the fish trade.

My father fell out with his father who felt that he was turning his back on a decent trade. It was insulting that he wanted to go off to become a doctor.

Have you got brothers and sisters?

I have one brother who's a retired solicitor who lives in Glastonbury and another who died in a climbing accident.

Were you similar to either of your brothers?

My younger brother was never interested in science and was always more cautious than me. I was much closer to my older brother who was a mathematician.

I'm sorry that your older brother died. Do you want to talk about it?

He was 19, I was 17; we were climbing together with a friend, Pete Godsell, on sea cliffs in Cornwall. They both fell and were killed but I somehow survived. It had a profound effect on my family. My brother Tom was the academic one; I was not very sure that I wanted to become an academic. Tom got a scholarship at sixteen to go to Cambridge, a bit of a mathematical genius and a very nice person. His death was very influential for me, perhaps making me want to step into his role as the older child and as an academic.

Take up the torch?

Yes.

Did your parents encourage you? Were they also high achievers, ambitious people?

My mother was. She was the outgoing one, very energetic and high profile in Glastonbury. She was Mayor a couple of times, on the county council. She was a very active liberal politician at the same time as working as a GP. She had lots of ideas, many of which had to be moderated by the more sensible members of the family!

My father became the anchor who kept things reasonable. He was a very practical man, good with his hands, loved orthopaedics and had a real natural way with people. He had a sure touch and a reassuring, calm voice.

I'd like to come back and talk about your family influences again later but for now to maintain the chronological thread can we return to how your career started? The PhD?

I spent three years at the National Institute for Medical Research funded by the Medical Research Council, and then was awarded a Wellcome Trust Senior Fellowship in clinical medicine, which you could not do now. You could not go straight from a PhD, but I had already done a lot of research in lung physiology and had some publications which allowed me to fast-track from doing a PhD straight into being a lab head. After about 10 years of being funded by the Wellcome Trust I was taken on by Imperial as a full Professor.

Did you study at Imperial originally?

I did my medical degree at Guy's. At a time when there were just 110 people in the year. It was a very elite but friendly medical school with talented teachers, some of whom inspired me to become interested in infection.

That's a good link, one of the questions that I like to ask everybody is if there were one or two people who particularly inspired them. Were there for you?

At medical school one of the people who inspired me most was a chap called Cedric Mims, a microbiologist. He'd spent some time in New Guinea, working on Creutzfeldt-Jakob disease, trying to work out whether prions were infectious. He had worked with a Nobel Prize winner called Carleton Gajdusek. Cedric was a very entertaining lecturer.

In clinical medicine, my main inspiration was Margaret Turner-Warwick who was at the Brompton. A very intelligent, lively, bird-like woman who was respected universally for being at the forefront of lung inflammation, both clinically and in research. She subsequently became the first female President of the Royal College of Physicians. A remarkable woman.

For my PhD I went to work with another remarkable woman, Dr Ita Askonas FRS. Her family were Viennese-Jewish who had left Europe with the rise of Hitler. She did her PhD in Toronto and then became the head of immunology at the National Institute for Medical Research at Mill Hill. She was internationally very well connected and had a very critical mind.

Her method of teaching was to try to take apart any argument that you made and show you how wrong it was, which is not the way that you would do it these days. But once I'd worked out that she did that as a kindness, as a way of trying to sharpen your thoughts,

I realised that this was her expressing her concern for you and for your career. Her criticism was an act of love, in a way. That made it easier to bear.

Do you do the same?

I have at times. I think what I learned from her was the absolute importance of having controls for every experiment. The importance of only moving one thing at a time in an experimental setting so that you can really determine whether that single thing is making a difference. Like in rock climbing, only move one point of attachment at a time.

Isolating cause and effect?

Yes, establishing what causes what. She was brilliant in that way, but some people found her very challenging because she was so argumentative and would almost never allow you to suggest anything without trying to pick it apart.

My clinical training helped me deal with that because I'd learnt to deal with some awkward (and stressed) patients and relatives and had to try and understand why it was that they were being so difficult. Once I started treating her like a difficult patient, it was much easier.

We talked about patience earlier. Are you a patient person?

Patient but impatient. I absolutely hate putting off until tomorrow something which I can do today.

It strikes me that your lab work must require a certain patience, it's very methodical.

You need to be patient in research. I think coming from clinical medicine into science one of the major contrasts is that in clinical medicine, you have a patient engagement that lasts about 10 to 40 minutes, and at the end of it there is a conclusion. You have achieved something palpable, whether it's prescribing a medicine or making someone feel better by being listened to.

In medicine, you are rewarded by a series of immediate satisfactions, whereas in science you may work on the topic for a year or more before you begin to see what's going on. There was one topic that I got interested in back in 1987 which I didn't publish on until 1996. Science is a very long game, but you have to savour little successes every day.

You have patiently and painstakingly built your career with quite a narrow focus. Have you ever found that restricting?

Not at all. I find the detail fascinating. One of the times when I was happiest was when I was focused on one of the proteins of respiratory syncytial virus (a common cold virus) called glycoprotein G. For several years I was just working on what a particular 32 amino acid stretch of that protein did. Happy days!

Knowing more about a specific field than anyone else can be very satisfying. In a scientific career you need to establish yourself a niche. People think, "If I want to know about X, Y is the person to go to."

When you are as absorbed as you are in that kind of endeavour, do you find it difficult to switch off?

Once you find something that you are most interested in, it doesn't feel like work. You don't think, "thank goodness it's five o'clock, I can stop doing this now and go home." Instead, you think, "thank goodness it's eight o'clock, it's quiet and nobody's bothering me. Now I can now finally just concentrate on the things that I really, really want to do!

Do you have a family, Peter?

Yes, I have somehow acquired six children.

And how does your desire to spend most of your time thinking about work balance with the conflicting requirements to interact with the family?

You would have to ask my family. I married Clare Vaughan who was in the year below at Guy's; she was a contrast to me, not very science-y; she became a GP. She was extraordinarily bright, creative and artistic. In some ways not dissimilar from my mother, she was full of ideas and needed somebody to act as a bit of a sheet anchor. She desperately wanted children.

I remember thinking just before I made the decision to do a PhD that I was not sure that I wanted a big family because I was so enjoying my work. But she became inconsolable with the idea of not having kids. So, we had one. Then, we thought, "well, two can't be too much more trouble," and we had a second. Then Clare wanted a girl, so a third came along. Fortunately, female.

Did your wife maintain her career when the family arrived?

Yes, Clare was a GP but had much more of a strict work / life division, she needed to be able to switch off because she found work quite stressful. I never found clinical work stressful. I enjoyed it, and I still did up until lockdown. But unfortunately, Clare developed breast cancer.

Oh, I'm very sorry to hear that.

She died in 1996. Our daughter was only five and the boys were 10 and 12.

How did you cope with that?

Not too well, but you can't go back and do it better. One of Clare's best friends, Evelyn Welch, was our neighbour and had three children. Evelyn lived just four doors away. As my wife became increasingly ill, Evelyn would come round with meals and help me with the kids. She would cook a supper for her family and cook an extra meal for us.

Then, after Clare died, Evelyn and I very quickly became closer. I remember at the time feeling like a limpet without a rock; we very quickly merged our families. Her ex-husband, Nick, is still a good friend; we have always got on very well. Together we've managed to bring up the six of them. They are all a remarkable set of individuals, and I am so proud of them all.

Evelyn is very different from Clare but there are many ways to make a good relationship. I would say that listening, kindness, tolerance and good humour are key.

Are any of your children scientists or doctors?

My eldest son did a PhD at Cambridge and ended up teaching science, now he's a biology teacher. I think he could have been a lab scientist but he loves teaching. My second son did archaeology and anthropology and is now a writer and an artist. My daughter is becoming a GP. My stepson is a biologist and film maker, and my stepdaughters are very bright and creative. One is a singer- and a very good one!

Going back to a slightly earlier thought, what drives you. Are you competitive?

I think I probably am competitive, but I avoid direct competition as much as possible. If it looks like somebody else is going to succeed in something, I won't redouble my efforts. I will back off and find something else to do.

I love seeing a solution to a problem, it's one of the things I've most enjoyed about science. As a PhD student I would come in and read the results from the day before, whatever it is, and you plot them. By coffee time, a new 'vista' has been revealed that nobody else has seen. It's like coming over the top of a mountain range and looking into a hidden valley that is an undiscovered terrain with new plants and terrain. It is so exciting when you find something that you have been looking for which no one else has seen.

Can we go back and talk a little more about your current work?

When I stopped being President of the British Society for Immunology, I became one of Imperial College's consuls. Imperial has these unusual roles, where 50% of your time is taken up by sitting on or Chairing disciplinary committees or promotions panels. The consuls are the only elected members of senior management, elected by your peers. There are two of us for each of the three Faculties, six consuls in all and one senior consul. Having spent three years as a consul for medicine, I was elected as senior consul, which I have been doing for two years. The consuls are described as the 'conscience' of the college.

The conscience?

Yes, you try to maintain good standards of ethics and behaviour and make sure that across Imperial there is alignment in terms of the standards and behaviours.

Just talk to me a little bit more about the other 50% of your time.

Well, I was doing some clinical work, outpatient clinics, and enjoying that, but found it was distracting me from all the other things I do, such as running grants when the pandemic struck in 2020. I am also the infection lead for our Biomedical Research Centre, supported by a £90m award which allows us to do research in the Imperial hospitals.

What else? I am currently on a lot of different committees for COVID, and for immunological research and spend quite a bit of time talking to journalists about science. It's very varied.

That's a very large responsibility and quite clearly you have achieved a great deal in your chosen field. Is there anything in terms of your career that you look back on and wish might have been different?

In my early days in immunology, we were focused on antibody and T cells, the so-called 'acquired' immune responses. We knew almost nothing about what we now call the innate immune system which is made up of in-built design features of immunity that recognise dangerous elements or patterns that suggest infection. These include size, shape and charge of particles - common features that signify the presence of a pathogen.

Those were only described in the 1990s. I guess if in the 1980s I'd known how important those were, I would've taken more notice of them. But there are still things that we really do not understand which are clearly crucial. In the experiments that we did a few years ago, we infected volunteers with respiratory syncytial virus and we gave them all exactly the same dose. Roughly half of them became infected and developed symptoms, and the other half just resisted infection. We had a paper which came out in the journal Science which shows that variation in outcome was not to do with antibodies or T cells, but to do with something mysterious which we still don't understand about the lining of your nose.

I think it would've been wonderful to have been able to have a crystal ball and to be able to say, in 2002, whether SARS would be defeated or not. We were terrified, we thought this was going to be a global pandemic with a 10% mortality, and it almost was. It was just about defeated by public health because it lacked the ability to infect that this new coronavirus has. I suppose it would've been lovely to have known that all the avian influenza viruses that we were agonising over for many years, none of which actually took off and became a pandemic with a high mortality rate.

It would've been so helpful to have known that SARS-CoV-2 was going to get out of China and spread around the world and mutate so radically. We didn't quite anticipate the ability to mutate into new variants.

Did you believe that the vaccine could be developed so quickly?

No, astonishing. I mean, it's fantastic that it's happened, and an extraordinary tribute to the global scientific effort that's been put into this but the real surprise is, that it's possible to generate such strong protective immunity. We didn't know that that would happen. There's no other vaccine that's ever been developed that depends on injecting RNA. It's been an extraordinary, exciting, bobsleigh ride.

What is your analysis of why the UK academic community has been so successful in contributing to the vaccine breakthrough?

There was a lot of investment put into infection research during the 1920s,'30s, and ever since then research in this area has been something that we did well in the UK. In the period just after the Second World War, people like Peter Medawar worked on transplantation and trying to understand tissue grafts in injured airmen, trying to graft tissue onto people who'd been burnt or maimed.

He was very influential in building up the National Insititue at Mill Hill and also, amongst his cohort, building the Imperial Cancer Research Fund, which was in Lincoln's Inn. The cadre of people who trained at those two institutions and then were seeded around university departments in the UK and globally were very important.

Some of those scientists were very influential in the formation of things like the Medical Research Council. The person who first really put lymphocytes on the map, Jim Gowans, was head of the MRC for a while, back in the 1970s. All of that investment in immunology has been critically important. A few key charismatic individuals have made a difference; they ensured that funding was in place and managed to inspire other people to work on understanding immunology.

But as I understand it the UK is very much part of a global effort. How does that work?

Anyone can have a thought today and by tomorrow, it's all around the world. Ideas just fly in every direction, often via Twitter. Twitter is such a good way of keeping up with science currently.

Really?

Yes, the first time I ever came across Covid-19 was on Twitter. Most of the stuff that's happening I first see on Twitter. It's a marvellous medium for science, because it links you to the original research. You can then go and read the articles, but they're handles that lead you into discovery of the latest publications. I hope Twitter carries on being such a good source of information.

I hadn't expected to hear that.

Yes, it's true, Twitter is very valuable in our community.

How has digital communication impacted your efficacy and your enjoyment?

Well, I do miss being in the lab, miss being with people, and I also very much miss my global community. My real friends, my true friends, are people who have studied the same things that I have and with whom I meet on the conference circuit. I counted up recently how many different conferences I'd been at over the past three years up until lockdown, and I'd been to about sixty meetings.

And you enjoy that travelling and interaction?

Yes, I used to do a lot of my slide preparation and thinking on flights, and in airport lounges. I can just sit at a conference as part of the listening audience while I wait to go up on stage, it's where I do some of my best thinking. Ideas collide. It's a valuable time to reflect. You'd see colleagues presenting their latest thinking and because you're sitting a few yards from them you really have to concentrate on what they're saying and make notes which you can then bring back to your own research team.

I can see that.

It focuses you on the science, whereas sitting here at my computer, meeting and giving lectures, I can nip into three different conferences around the globe in 24 hours, deliver my content, but then log out, and very rarely stay on and listen to what my friends have to say.

Of course, you don't get the chance meeting in the bar afterwards or going out for a meal in Barcelona with a small group and really getting to know people. It feels like this remote way of working might be sustainable for a short time, but over time we're losing that sense of community and natural interaction which is so valuable and rewarding.

You've had a real depth of experience and worked with a wide array of colleagues and friends. Can you remember any particularly good advice relating to your professional life that has resonated?

Yes, one thing I always remember was at the start of my career. I was a houseman and there was a lady who needed to have a repeat chest X-ray and couldn't be discharged unless she'd had that done. I was asked to arrange that on a Friday. When we went round on the Monday, it hadn't been done, and I explained that I'd personally gone up to the X-ray department with the form which I'd handed to the radiographer, I'd told them how important it was, and it wasn't my fault that it hadn't been done. I remember the consultant looking at me and saying, "Well, next time, make sure it is your fault." The message from that was, that if something is important, you just don't give up until it's been achieved. You can't just say, "I've handed this on, I've delegated it."

In terms of general learning, I would say trying to understand what people can contribute, and what their strengths are. I try to build a diverse team with different qualities. It's also important to be able to articulate a passion for whatever it is that your group is pursuing and bring ideas to the group from the outside world, because they may be quite blinkered, sitting in the lab.

They may not be that aware of the global trends in science that need to be brought into the lab in order to develop that bigger picture. The bigger picture is really what you need to contribute as a leader, and to make sure that people are motivated, but not intimidated.

Intimidated?

Yes, too much intimidation in a lab will drive research fraud. Research fraud is one of the most destructive things that can happen in a research group. If people start to falsify data to produce the result that the lab chief is desperate for, that's disastrous. That falsification of data can hold back fields for years and can be very hard to detect.

A leader who is too demanding is a big problem. The way that they conduct themselves, making it very clear that there is only one result that is acceptable.

That's different from the intimidating behaviour of the professor that you admired?

In its impact, yes. I think my PhD supervisor's behaviour might be regarded as bullying these days and that could be career-ending, but people need to understand that science is tough, and standards must be high. It's very hard to do that without treading into the territory that would, these days, be described as bullying.

A lot of things have changed over the years that we have worked. I've discussed at some length with other interviewees the impact of digitisation because it is impacting every field. What about in science and medicine? Do you see big changes?

Yes, it transforms every year. It's just extraordinary how it's changed. When I started in science, and at medical school, we didn't have computers. We had a Casio calculator that was held in the professor's drawer, and if you wanted it rather than your slide rule or tables, you had to go and ask his permission, then sit in his office under supervision while putting your numbers into his calculator!

One of my early contributions to the research group in 1972 was working out that we could discover the area under the curve instead of by counting squares on a trace, by using nail scissors to cut out the piece of paper and weigh it on a very sensitive balance. I explain this to people these days and they can't believe how primitive science was then.

It's hard for people to understand just how little we understood about the immune system in the 1980s.Now we really have got an enormously complex picture of how it works, which has led to our ability to make vaccines within a year of a pathogen first being characterised. It's just wonderful to see the way that science has advanced and the way in which the ability to handle large data sets is producing completely unanticipated insights. Every day, new things are discovered that just are amazing.

Are younger colleagues today very different in their approach to your own generation?

There has been a change in PhD students. It used to be an absolute vocation and a huge privilege to be able to devote yourself 100% to just doing a project, not have to worry about all the other stuff that is going on in life, and that you wouldn't flinch from coming in at night or weekends.

There's been a change in some of the new generation of PhD students. Some seem to feel that you are there to provide them with a PhD, and that as long as they turn up between 9:00 and 5:00, they are then entitled to the post-nominal. That's not all the students, but it's commoner than it used to be.

But there are others who are fantastic. Amongst those, there are great young scientists who can go all the way and will certainly be leading lights in the future. It is so wonderful to find junior colleagues who are bright, energetic, creative and kind. It just lights up my days that there are people like that in the lab.

How else has digitisation impacted your field?

Well, at the start of my career, we had no need to use 'kits' bought from companies. We would design an assay, optimise it, and then run the assay in the lab using some pretty basic reagents, often generating our own serum by immunising rabbits. These days people hardly know how that's done.

They just buy a kit from a supplier and it comes with a set, a pack of reagents, and it costs thousands of pounds, but actually in terms of how it works, they often have little interest, because what they want to do is get the data, and then plug it into a large database array, and start to crunch some numbers. A lot of the effort is in number crunching and large data sets, rather than in the optimisation of what you do in the lab. I don't particularly think that we ought to be going back to mixing up our own reagents, but things are just different now.

How about in Telemedicine, has remote analysis via computer transformed things in the clinical world?

Absolutely, and I think that as doctors we were very antiquated in the way we held face-to-face consultations, people sitting in the waiting room for hours, waiting for their slot. Being able to do consultations online is the way we ought to have done it years ago, it was almost prevented by the anxiety in the NHS around confidentiality. I think it was all a load of nonsense, really.

I can't see us ever going back to the way that we used to do it. The other big thing that has happened was that we used to do things almost blindly according to 'expert' opinion. So many things that I did as a junior doctor I did because people who were regarded as 'expert' had decided on first principles that this was the right drug to use or procedure to perform, and not that much had really been subjected to controlled clinical trial.

Nowadays, so much of what we do medically has been through rigorous clinical testing in a properly organised, usually double-blind, trial. Lots of things we used to do are being proved to be completely useless, and things that we didn't think were worth doing have proven to be enormously beneficial.

Give me an example.

A current one would be the use of steroids for treatment of patients with Covid-19. Many of us thought that because steroids had a bad history in SARS, they would be detrimental in Covid. I wasn't sure, I felt it was likely that steroids were going to be harmful and that therefore, should be withheld.

A trial at Oxford called RECOVERY came up with the stunning results that the survival of patients, particularly most severely ill patients with hypoxia, patients on ventilators, was improved by 20 to 30% if they were given steroids. A fantastic result. I didn't think it would be anything like more than a marginal benefit. I even thought it might be harmful.

Then, in the same study, they tried things with antivirals which everyone thought, "Well, of course, it's a viral disease. Inhibit the virus and patients will get better." They made not a jot of difference! These big trials, rapidly organised, adaptive clinical trials have shown not only what is beneficial, which is steroids, but what is harmful, which is all the other stuff.

Avoid the pointless and embark on what is good for people where survival improves. Survival is so much greater now than it was back in the first wave because of all this clinical research.

Is there any merit in intuition in your world at all?

I think it's okay as a motivation for doing a study. Hypotheses and preconceptions are vital in driving your design of an experiment, but you just can't assume the outcome until you've done it many times and observed it with your own eyes. There's nothing to replace that empiricism.

We're coming towards the end of our interview. I'd like to ask you some more general questions about your life and career. Thinking back, what would you say you're most proud of?

I would say my children, my two wives and the people who've been through my lab. The careers of those I have mentored are something which I am really delighted by. I was at a conference just before the pandemic where there were about 200 people in the room, and I could trace my mentorship line through to more than half of them. That was a great moment for me.

Do you have a sense of purpose for your life and work more broadly?

That is an interesting question. I think on the whole, what I have done is to try to do whatever I'm working on each day to the best of my ability, and to find where it leads me next. My career has been organic rather than strategic. I've never set out to be a professor or to achieve a particular career aim. The environment in which I work has been moulded over a long period to be of a shape that suits me very well.

Do you feel like your best work is done or not nearly done? Do you have a burning ambition to achieve more?

I think my best work in the lab certainly was done some years ago. I used to enjoy the physical, practical detail of how to make sure the experiment was laid out well, every single reagent was added in the right order that it all worked, I found that immensely satisfying. It is almost like building a piece of Meccano and then winding the handle and seeing everything doing what it should do.

Over the past decade and a half, I've been much more in the role of supervising people, trying to build the careers of other scientists. When I became President of the British Society for Immunology, I did leadership training and undertook root and branch reform of the Society and completely new governance; I found that extremely satisfying. So, in a way, my current roles are much more based on that, rather than actually doing the science myself.

One of my other interviews was with Grant Booker, a Director at Foster + Partners. I was asking him a question about the future he planned and any thoughts about retirement. He said, "An architect never stops working." How about you? Do you always envisage yourself working?

I can't imagine anything that I would enjoy more than what I do. I can well do with less of it, but I really do look forward to doing the work. There are some aspects which are more stressful and time consuming than others. I absolutely detest red tape and the meaningless obstructions that are put in the way of doing interesting things. I am quite enjoying no longer working within the NHS.

The training you need to do to tick boxes is so frustrating and unproductive. It's not improving your skills, just meeting someone's daft targets.

You were talking about the benefits in career terms of narrow focus and being seen as the go-to person in your field. Are you motivated by recognition?

I think I just love finding things out. That's my prime motivation, discovering an explanation or aspect of the truth that gives me a new insight into why things are as they are.

Are you a sociable person or do you prefer to work by yourself?

If I am in a room with a group of people, I normally focus on maybe one person in the room at a time but I do enjoy giving lectures and being in front of a big audience. I find that energising, exciting, and I don't feel nervous. And as I said, I enjoy interacting with a global community that I'm lucky enough to be part of.

And you are a good lecturer or presenter?

Yes, I think so. I'm not the cleverest person in the room and I realise that having to work things out for myself means that I can lead people through an argument in a way that maybe people who are cleverer might be less good at.

I must understand something in order to remember it. That means I need to explain my chain of thought in everyday terms, which I think is a good basis for being an effective communicator.

Has that feeling, that approach and perhaps your dyslexia caused you any concerns as you've progressed through university and your professional career?

Well, yes it was always just there but it has also helped in many ways.

What is your key talent?

I think, if I'm objective, what I'm unusually good at is visualising in my head. I can look at a system and analyse it, see how it works. In my mind's eye I have pictures of molecules interacting in the same way that parts of a clock operate.

How interesting. Have you always been able to do that?

Yes, I am not so good at reading but have a visual brain. My dyslexia means I read slowly. I enjoy reading, but short books, poetry, short stories. I enjoy those very much, but a long, rambling book is not for me. I tried to make myself read Emma as a teenager and it was an absolute torment. I hated it.

I've found our conversation very rich. It's great to get a perspective from the world of science since the majority of the interviews are with businesspeople. It is a different world which to me at least is fascinating.

One final question. If you were addressing a room full of 20-year-olds and drawing on your own life experience, what advice would you give them as they set out on their different careers?

Find a partner, a social group, friends that you love to be with. The most important thing is to be happy in your personal life. That gives you the freedom to throw yourself every day into doing work that you enjoy so much that it doesn't even feel like work. That's the ideal way to live.

“

As a Bureau Chief we were constantly working in a pressure cooker setting, because everything that you do is to a deadline, there is nothing that is comfortable or slow. Then you add to that all the circumstances of working in a war zone or an earthquake zone. Everything is pressured. That's when you see at what point people crack and you have to be the one that doesn't crack, the resilient one.

”

SARA BECK

INTERVIEWED 23RD AUGUST 2022

Sara was most recently Chief Operating Officer at Oxford University's Saïd Business School, a role which spanned a noteworthy time in the school's development. She worked with the Dean, Professor Peter Tufano, and the Chair of the School Board and ex-Unilever CEO, Paul Polman, to define the school's purpose and strategic direction and also managed operations through the extraordinary challenges of the Covid-19 pandemic.

Prior to Oxford Saïd, Sara spent 28 years at the BBC, latterly in a succession of very senior roles including Bureau Chief in Moscow, Jerusalem and Singapore and Director of BBC Monitoring. Presently she is living and working in Bangkok, training for a business coaching accreditation and undertaking freelance work whilst her partner establishes the school of Wellington College International in Thailand.

Tell me a bit about your childhood and where you grew up.

Youngest of three, very happy, stable, not too eventful of a childhood really but part of a very loving family.

Whereabouts were you growing up?

I was born in West Yorkshire, in a place called Bingley, as in The Bradford and Bingley Building Society. When I was about eight, we moved to Leeds. And that was it. Both parents worked in education. Dad was a lecturer and a football player and my mum was a teacher and then a head teacher and educational advisor.

In state schools?

Yes, my dad worked at what is now called Leeds Met but it was Leeds Polytechnic then. He was a senior lecturer at Carnegie College, one of the elite physical education colleges, he was an FA coach as well and coached the England colleges team. In his spare time, he was a manager of a local football team in the Yorkshire League, a quite rough and competitive sub-division football league and he was a kind of 'thinking man's manager'. Football was a big thing in our house.

What kind of a character was your father?

Very grounded, confident. All my friends say he's a bit zen and very calm with a quiet confidence, a thoughtful man.

Does he sound like a Yorkshireman?

He's not a Yorkshireman. I'm the only Yorkshire person in the family. He's from Norfolk. My mum is from Lincolnshire.

You had a brother and a sister?

Yes, my sister is four years older than me and my brother six years older, so they were always off doing other things. I was the younger one trailing along. I was very into sport like Dad, I spent a lot of time with him. He coached me when I was younger in gymnastics. I was very keen until I was about 13 or 14 and then I turned to netball.

What have your brother and sister gone on to do?

My sister ended up working in a bank, for HSBC, but stopped working when she got married. My brother was a lecturer. He lectured in Business Studies at Sheffield Hallam; he's retired now.

What influence do you think your parents have had on you?

A huge influence. The thing that is really striking about our family is that it's very close and very loving, I only have happy memories. Mum and Dad are an absolutely ideal couple and that means the pressure is on for the rest of us in terms of the standards they set [laughs]. They're demonstrably in love, we could never play one off against the other. I don't think I have ever heard them argue once.

Any advice that you can remember from either of them?

No, they'd never been directive, although it was very clear what the rules were in the house and we had very clear boundaries on what was acceptable and what wasn't. Even though we were '60s and '70s kids it wasn't a laid-back hippie house [laughs]. The work ethic was really strong. I remember my parents both sitting and working in the evening, always. The more senior they became, the more obvious it was that they would do whatever it took. They were professionally very proud and conscientious. Growing up I watched people that really cared about what they did and went the extra mile.

Were they ambitious for you as children?

We were talking about this during the summer. I think they were very careful about fairness. We went to an ordinary school, the local comprehensive. My mum told me that there was a point where the school suggested that I should go to the fee-paying school, and they decided that it wasn't fair for the other two if I were to do that. So, I stayed at the comprehensive, which was fine. They were careful about being fair but there was never any pressure. They didn't really need to pressurise me because I was quite motivated! They had a harder time with my sister who was more wayward [laughs], but they didn't push in any way. It wasn't a 'follow us' or 'you need to do what we do'. It was 'you need to do what you're interested in'. So, it was fine that I was interested in languages and it was obvious from a very early age that I was leaving there and going abroad as soon as I could. And that's what eventually happened.

Let's come back to that, but right now I'm interested to know what kind of girl were you?

I was rather quiet early on, I remember. Because school was quite rough, I know that when we moved to Leeds I was about eight or nine and there was a bit of bullying and I didn't speak up. My parents had to find out that it was happening. I was resolute that it didn't matter and nobody was going to upset me, so they had to prise it out of me. I was quiet and self-reliant. I spent a lot of time playing tennis against the wall [laughs]. I became a bit more confident in my early teens and I had a good friendship group but probably never really felt that I was in 'my group' until I went to university.

Have you kept in touch with any of your friends from school?

Yes, a couple. A couple of school day boyfriends [laughs].

Oh right! What are they doing?

One of them is a well known journalist, he's the one that I keep in touch with and one of them is in Australia.

You mentioned that you had thought about living abroad early on. Where did that come from, the desire to live abroad as a young girl?

I went to France when I was about twelve and liked it. My dad used to travel when he was coaching the England colleges side. They'd go to quite exotic places. I was always really intrigued when he came back, I used to pump him for all the information about the places he'd been to. I remember he went to Bulgaria, Iran, and Mexico. We weren't a family that went away much on exotic holidays, we used to go to Scotland and Cornwall mostly. I always was interested in going further and then Mum and Dad took me to Texas, we had an uncle in Texas, I was probably 14 or so.

Let's talk about your time at university, what subject did you study?

Russian and French.

Had you studied Russian at comprehensive school? Quite unusual back then I would imagine?

Yes, I had a great Russian teacher. It was really unusual, and God knows they don't do it now. They alternated a second language option, so it was just fate that I landed in the Russian year rather than the

German year. I had a very, very good teacher, one of those teachers who was a one-man department. He fired my imagination about the country. I found it fascinating and that fuelled a long-term interest in Russia for me, which explains how my later career unfolded.

Where did you go to university?

Bristol.

Tell me a bit about your time there.

For me that was finding my own tribe. I met people that I just instantly was in-sync with. It was a fantastic time. A great time to be in Bristol. There was a great music scene, a lot of socialising - too much socialising! My conclusion for university is that I really wasted the chance to hurl myself into the studies, but came out of it with a brilliant network, a set of friends that I've never lost so I can't be regretful. I just can look at it in hindsight and think 'you could have done it slightly differently' [laughs].

You say you enjoyed the music scene, what was the music in Bristol in the late '80s?

Bristol had a really good club scene. I used to go to clubs in Yorkshire as well, so I just carried on. We had friends that were DJs and so we would be out a lot. It was just before Massive Attack rose to prominence. It was a really, really good time.

Did you practise gymnastics or play netball when you were at university?

I was in the first team for netball, eventually. That reflects my relative lack of confidence at the time, we had a very strong school team and I'd had trials for Yorkshire, but when I went to Bristol I just presumed that I wouldn't be good enough, I didn't trial in the first year.

You got into the netball team in your second year?

I did, I was just thinking 'how did that happen?' [Laughs]. I can't quite remember what provoked me, but maybe by the second year I felt more calm and more confident about giving it a try. I played in the second and fourth year and in the third year I was abroad.

Where did you go?

I went to Paris; I went to the Sorbonne. When you do joint languages, it's quite hard because you need more time than you actually get for language practice. So, I did a rather unsatisfactory French language course at the Sorbonne and lived in Paris. That was really hard because we had to find somewhere to live ourselves. In the end, I had to pull in a favour from my boyfriend's mother, whose business partner gifted us an apartment in the centre of Paris! [Laughs] All these other students were living in little half-rented houses somewhere far from the city and I got to live in the apartment of a French Count! It was great, but I used to go back a lot to the UK, sneakily on night trains from Paris. After Paris I was supposed to go – this becomes relevant – I was supposed to go to Kyiv, but the year before, Chernobyl had exploded, so they weren't putting anybody through Ukraine at that point. Instead, I went for three months to a place called Krasnodar in southern Russia. It was like a door swung open for me, it was like going through the wardrobe into Narnia, into this completely different world and I found it fascinating.

What was it like?

It was a provincial Soviet town that had rarely seen Western foreigners. There was no reason for anybody to go there. It's famous for two things: its Cossacks and having a wide river! And then all of a sudden it was invaded by a party of British students. The local authorities were trying to keep control of us but we were finding ways to get out of the hotel accommodation and meet local people and do the things that you want to do in an exciting new place.

What were your impressions of the culture and the people?

I befriended a couple of teenagers. I had my 21st birthday there, which was not the best place to have your 21st birthday because food was limited and there was very little alcohol. They used to lock the alcohol in a special room in the hotels so that the staff didn't take it! It was hard to get drink because of Gorbachev's alcohol laws (which were deeply unpopular). I befriended a teenage boy because most of the people my age were in the army. And it was really hard to make friends with any working people because it would have been difficult for them, they weren't encouraged to talk to foreigners. So, I just used to talk to this teenage boy – he was maybe 15 or 16 years old – to get my Russian practice. I used to spend a lot of time walking around town with him talking, and then we did some secret overnight missions to places that we weren't supposed to go to on the train. We pretended to be locals, which was obviously quite hard because we clearly didn't look like locals, but we didn't get caught.

Were there aspects of the politics or life there that you found interesting or attractive at all?

All of it. I just wanted to know more about everything. It was absolutely without reference points from anything else that I'd ever done. I was absorbed by it and everything was crazy, everything was difficult, everything was different. I found it fascinating, even though it wasn't the most interesting town, it wasn't Moscow. I came away thinking how could I get back to Russia? Eventually, I managed to get myself a placement in the Easter holidays, this time in Leningrad.

How did that work?

You had to apply to be part of what was called a 'cultural exchange'. These were limited – you couldn't just go to the Soviet Union, you had to be part of a controlled entry and exit into the country. I was accepted on a programme and shared a room with a woman from Cambridge who was doing the same thing. We were at an Institute in the centre of Leningrad. We lived in this really mouldy student accommodation just off Nevsky Prospect, but it was brilliant as well. I was prepared to do anything, I went with no friends, knowing nobody.

When you came back and finished your degree, and as you were approaching the end, what were you thinking then about what you wanted to do workwise?

All I wanted to do was go back to the Soviet Union and try and think of a way to use my Russian, which wasn't easy then. So, I moved to south London with my three best friends. One of us was working at Virgin Records and one was a journalist at 'The Face' so we had a good line straight into the London clubs too. I got a job in a direct marketing agency in Kennington but all the time I was looking for ways to get back to the Soviet Union. And then there was a tiny little job ad for a local rep for a Virgin joint venture with Intourist, the state tourist agency. Branson had set-up a venture with the Soviets in Yalta, and I thought 'that's a way of getting back' and for some reason I ended up getting the job and I was the only Westerner living and working in the Crimea as the Soviet Union fell apart!

You were a holiday rep for British tourists going to the Soviet Union?

Exactly, and can you imagine how disappointed they were when they turned up and found out that it was somewhat limited on the food front and the service levels weren't quite the same as Western Europe…?

It's interesting to know that you had such determination to get to Russia, what was it about Russia that was so compellingly appealing for you?

It's really hard to explain it to others who hadn't experienced that period, and now of course it's gone. I had a recent conversation with someone who was in Beijing in the '80s and she said the same thing, it was like stepping into a completely different world and you were welcomed into that world. There was no hostility, just completely normal people trying to do very normal things and it busted all the myths about what the Soviet Union was when you started dealing with ordinary people. At the same time, because I could eventually speak the language, I got a real high from being able to communicate and be understood and accepted in a different world. The deeper you went into it, the more you got to understand it, the more compelling it was. I suppose it was the exoticism of being somewhere so different and also seeing on a human level how absolutely grinding it was for people. To make friends with Russians or Ukrainians and try to help them in some way. The union was absolutely on the brink of the collapse. In the hotel I used to sit in the foyer and they had a little telly there because so much was happening in the Duma at the time, in the Parliament, they had this telly on permanently. They were trying to keep across what was happening and what the debate was and where the politics was going, which was unprecedented. There was this sense that something was coming. Gorbachev had opened things up, they were starting businesses, people could own foreign currency, they could do things that they hadn't been allowed to do for decades. You could tell that something was about to happen and I suppose I was drawn to that.

What were your thoughts on Gorbachev?

I mean, living through that time in the country - because it was later when I was more involved journalistically - you could see that it was going to come off the rails. You could sense what he was trying to do was in the right direction, but it was too hard to control. Essentially it was a really exciting time, I was comfortable and happy there. And culturally it was incredibly rich and interesting. Linguistically, it was fantastic for me in terms of really getting to grips with the language. All I missed were my friends, although some did come to visit me.

What were characteristics or traits of Russian people that you grew to admire?

Well, in Crimea, it was every type of Soviet citizen and there aren't clear national traits. The main thing as a young foreigner was that people were very generous. I suppose those are the things, having lived in other places since, with which to contrast that experience. It was incredibly open and generous and you were quickly part of somebody's life or family. It was a 'come on in' culture, which made it easy to be there on my own. It wasn't risky, it was virtually danger free, there was somebody watching over me all the time anyway so nothing could have happened to me. I was recorded and followed and all those things, but I didn't care about that because I wasn't doing anything wrong so it didn't really matter. They were wasting their time.

How long did you do the holiday rep job for?

For a year.

Living where?

Living in a fancy hotel! Well, as fancy as they got then. It was built in the early 1900s, a famous Tsarist hotel, where people came to take the waters of the Crimea, on the Esplanade with the sea opposite. It didn't look like most images of the Soviet Union, put it that way.

And what happened at the end of that year?

I jumped on a plane and for 30 roubles, which was about £20, I went around the whole of Central Asia and the Caucasus on my own, visited all of these wild and wonderful places like Tashkent and Bukhara. I had a young Russian who was quite soft on me, who came with me, we got arrested in Central Asia and had all sorts of adventures!

What were you arrested for?

Because he shouldn't have been travelling with a foreigner. So, we attracted the attention of the local authorities.

What happened when you were arrested?

They just threatened us and threatened to leave him in the desert somewhere and he wouldn't be heard from again.

Did he go back home?

Yes. They put him on a plane back to Leningrad and then I flew back. As I'm talking to you, Chris, I realize that I really was not worried about going anywhere and seeing what happened and finding out more about the country, and maybe those are the roots of my journalistic interest because all you're doing is telling stories about a place, trying to convey what happens. And I'd already done those first years of just trying to dig as deep as I possibly could and understand things, understand the people. I came back from my trip and did some interpreting, I interpreted on the pitch at Wembley when the Russian rugby team came to the UK!

I suspect fluent Russian speakers were not so common in the UK then. So you had a rare skill.

You had other fluent Russian speakers, but fewer had been to the Soviet Union and I'd actually lived there by then for quite a long time if you added it together. Somebody put me in touch with the Russian service at the BBC, I did a freelance report for them and afterwards they offered me a job.

What was your first job?

In the Russian service? As a production assistant.

You were still there 20 odd years later! Talk to me a little about your time at the BBC.

Too many years! [Laughs] But the funny thing is that when I was at Bristol, I washed dishes in BBC Bristol as a holiday job. That was actually the very first job I had at the BBC: pot washer. I did radio production in the Russian service, I learned about radio and then I was moved to arts, I used to work on the arts programme for the World Service.

Russian arts?

No, by then I had moved to the English service and worked with a presenter called Simon Fanshawe. We got on really well and we used to go off to the Edinburgh festival and do arty programmes. That was a really good time. After that, I went out to the Moscow Bureau. I was one of the few Russian speaking producers, (by then I was quite an accomplished producer), but I hadn't worked in News. And that's where I cut my teeth in TV.

What makes a good producer?

Production is about control [laughs] and standards, it's about bringing everything together on time, delivering on time, and to the highest possible standards. You need to be able to make things happen, to be persuasive and quite directive. It strengthens those muscles in you to say 'this has to happen NOW' [laughs].

Did the BBC have a well-developed training programme for producers or did you just learn on the job?

In those days it was a brilliant training ground. I also very luckily got singled out for women's leadership training and was fast-tracked through. Production is about team-working, you only get anything done in broadcast media with the team. It's never a single job, unlike print, for example. It's not all command and control but at times you need to be pretty directive and then I really love the creative side of it and writing. Basically, what you're doing is shaping the scripts of the correspondents and getting it to the best possible place. So, it's about perfectionism and teamwork.

It sounds as if you feel it was building on some of the inherent strengths you have?

I think so, I remember becoming conscious that I could do things that other people couldn't, but I also became aware of things where I wasn't so strong as well. I could get people to do what I wanted them to do and keep the peace, and a producer really needs to be able to do that. You need to have an incredibly persuasive approach, but also get the team over the line without things falling apart. Because there will be egos in there that are inevitably bigger than the producer's. I mean, some producers have big egos too, but the whole thing hinges on whether you can get the team across the line, really.

This was radio production?

Yes, I went in as a radio producer but then I started to work with the correspondents that were doing TV and eventually ended up running the Moscow Bureau. In three years I went from being a producer to being the Bureau Chief.

What does a Bureau Chief do?

I was running a Bureau of about 100 people with Russian and expat staff. You're responsible for everything that's happening, it's the equivalent of a General Manager, with editorial added in. The BBC only created Bureau Chiefs at that time and there were five guys and me. They split the world into six regions: Washington DC, Brussels, Johannesburg, Moscow, Hong Kong and Jerusalem.

When you started in that department, were you ambitious to be in a role like that or did it happen in an unplanned way?

It wasn't planned at all, but that was my really happy time at work. It was an amazing time politically and in terms of events. We were in the middle of it. I was working with some of the best people. We were all Russian specialists. I realised that I quite liked being responsible for a group of people, I didn't mind that responsibility, whereas others that I worked with didn't want it. I think I realised at that point that I was a bit different from some others.

Thinking back to that time can you think of two or three key learnings that you could distil out of that period of your life and career?

I think everybody has to have this time where you've built your specialism, so you're not worried about what you're actually doing, because that's the thing that you really know well. So for me, at the end of my time in that role, the story and the journalism and the accuracy of what we were doing wasn't an issue, that was just a given, I'd really worked on my specialism, I was a really good producer in an area that I knew really, really well. I had a solid enough foundation to begin to acquire the next set of skills that you needed to have which for me was more managerial, the kind of skills that I hadn't understood before. I learned to speak up and be accountable to London. I was prepared to say 'this is what we've done, and if it's wrong, tell us'. I think in hindsight, you need to have that solid base before you can start adding on extra layers, before you can leapfrog from that into other areas. When I'm talking to younger people, I always say you need to get your air miles at that point, you need to have the credibility and the specialist knowledge to be very clear and credible and then your other skills can begin to show through.

In your career until then or subsequently, are there people who you particularly admired or learned from, mentors?

Well at that stage I don't think I realised, but I did have people who were sponsoring me and championing me. I was too naive to realise that's what they were doing, I would think people were just being kind. I did have managers that were particularly supportive, one of them was a woman who's still a good friend of mine. It was a very male environment then, almost exclusively male. The crews and the teams were all male. There was only one female foreign correspondent at the time, probably one female camera person. I was the only female Bureau Chief. I think that colleague recognised some of the challenges and sought to help me.

What was her role? Was she in Russia or somewhere else?

She left before me, and she's actually a COO now as well.

What was she doing in the BBC at the time?

She was the Foreign Editor, our boss, and she was very good with me, although I probably didn't realise at the time she was stretching and developing me.

Are there things that you think you learned from watching her or listening to her?

Yes. I did. I think the people that I learned from at that time were some of the editors who had good people skills. Because you're working in an industry where there are plenty of egos, what you need is somebody that cuts through all that and doesn't bring their own ego into the room. There were a couple of others who were particularly down to earth and straightforward in their leadership styles, who had humility and emotional intelligence. I wasn't planning my career and I certainly wasn't thinking, 'what do I get next?'. I probably gravitated towards people who I respected most, and it was that kind of person. When you work with some people who are quite sharp elbowed, you perhaps gravitate towards others who are more productive and collaborative. For me, I wanted to work with those kinds of people. Later on, I did work with a really brilliant manager.

What did you admire about him?

He was just very calm, always. We were constantly working in a pressure cooker setting, because everything you do is to a deadline, there is nothing that is comfortable or slow. Then you add to that all the circumstances of working in a war zone or an earthquake zone, you can't get the satellite dish up etc etc. Everything is pressured. That's when you see at what point people crack and you have to be the one that doesn't crack, the resilient one. He was very good at keeping a very controlled exterior when things were really going south.

I'm sure you became good at that. What is it within you that makes you able to do that, do you think?

I was doing that day in, day out, trying to keep creative, talented people in pressured conditions on track. So, I got used to it. I had to pull colleagues apart in arguments.You have to keep calm then.

In those stressful situations, how do you deal with it? What do you do to keep yourself calm? Is there anything you've learned over time that helps you?

I think it's probably a journalistic discipline, which is that there's a bigger picture. Whatever is happening now isn't the end of it... this is just one part and so there's a pulling back all the time. When things are really difficult, I'm always trying to think, what's coming next? What's the bigger picture? What are we missing here? Rather than focusing too much on the thing that's on fire. That's definitely something I learned from that time, just trying to remember that even if things are going really badly wrong, we have to think, what's the exit strategy and what's the next step?

Lifestyle-wise were you conscious of achieving balance? What did you do to relax and maintain an equilibrium?

No, I crashed out. I didn't achieve balance. My partner had come out with me and that relationship crashed in Moscow, mainly because I was working all the time. It's clear back then I certainly didn't know how to achieve work-life balance because it was an all-consuming environment. Everybody else worked like that, it was absolutely expected, and there was no sense of being able to say, 'I can't do this.' To be honest, I probably wouldn't have said that because it was such a compelling job. We were doing things that mattered at the time as well, but I wasn't experienced enough to be able to see where it might end and I lost an important relationship as a result.

What age were you when you got the Bureau Chief job?

30 or 31.

By the end you were exhausted, as I understand. You'd had an incredible experience, honed your skills in a pressure cooker environment, kept rising to the next challenge but to a degree that took its toll. Did you ask to come back to the UK?

Yes, I asked to come back but that was later. After Moscow I went to Jerusalem and Intifada II started and I had 12 months of working the hardest that I've ever worked. All in all, I spent nearly ten years abroad, yes. First Russia, then Israel and then Singapore.

In Israel and Singapore you were also the Bureau Chief?

Yes, I was. I think, looking back, I became the person that could be put into any situation and acquire sufficient knowledge of the region fast and get things under control. I became an experienced pair of hands. Without really realising it, you understand that people are seeing you in a different way perhaps from the way you perceive yourself, people are asking your advice.

Any particular memories of your time in Jerusalem?

That was a really incredible time when I look back at it. It was a real privilege: I had the rare combination of really enjoying the job and working to really high standards with really good people. When you're doing that work, you can hardly believe you're being paid to do it because it's just a great and interesting job. The main thoughts were, I just saw more and I probably became harder. I think I've been asked before whether the more senior or more experienced you become, do you become a less empathetic and less sympathetic person? I'd definitely seen many bad things by the time I came off the road. But I was very careful always. I saw a lot of colleagues burn out and some people had mental health issues and I managed to avoid that by saying it's time to come off the road now.

Were you travelling a lot?

When I was in Singapore, I was travelling all the time. I barely spent time in the city.

What are your memories of Asia?

I think you know this because you lived and worked in Japan and Asia for some years. We talked about this before. When you've worked in Asia you get more experience because you're making decisions that, by the time the others across the world wake up, you've already decided what you're doing and who's on the plane. You're much more independent. I became more confident in my decision-making and leadership, because there was nobody else. We just got on with it.

I was working overseas for Diageo, a large global corporation, and you for the BBC, so I suspect in other ways our experience differed quite a lot. I wonder, how is your performance evaluated when you are not assessed in terms of delivering a P&L and growing the share price? At the BBC it's not about making a revenue number!

No, it's about how much you spend most of the time. [Laughs]

How are you judged? How is your success evaluated?

You're judged on the quality of the output, the coverage. You can win awards, of course, or be known for the strength of the journalism, but it's about the team because obviously you can't do that on your own. And then you're judged on your management of the staff. I think by then I had something like 15 Bureaus that I had to manage and keep everybody on track and on board. Those are the metrics you are evaluated on, although they're not quite quantified and that's where the BBC has had difficulty because it's harder to point to metrics when it comes to equal pay, or who's the best presenter. It's very subjective, even at an organisational level. Those are the main things - and beating the competition to stories, not missing stories. That really matters.

How would you sum up the culture of the BBC for someone who hasn't worked there?

The culture of the corporation is very strong and the standards and the expectations in terms of news are very, very strong. There's a presumption of excellence and you're working with very talented people, so that's a big plus. It is very exacting in terms of its craft. The problem perhaps is that those people stay in the same organisation and so it can become insular and insulated from the rest of the world, what's moving and what's changing. Generally speaking, there is less interest in understanding what's happening around them and the need to adapt, be agile and change. After a while, you begin to realise that it's quite stifling. It was a very overwhelming atmosphere of service and purpose and understanding why you're there, but without some of the benefits of looking outside, welcoming new ideas.

Despite that inward-looking focus as you look outward, are there other business leaders or professionals that you particularly admire?

It's no coincidence but I do really admire Paul Polman, the chair of the Board at Oxford Saïd and ex-Unilever boss for what he's done and for what he's still doing. I think that's not just because I've been fortunate enough to do some work with him, but speaking out and speaking up is more and more important. And he does that so well. I think there are so few people now, if you look around, that you would want to listen to in that respect.

Let's go back to complete the loop at the BBC before you made the move to Oxford. After ten years abroad you came back. Did it feel strange? I remember when I came back after six years in Asia it seemed to me the world had stood still. I'd had six years of incredible experiences and everyone else seemed to be pretty much doing what they were doing the day before I left. Did you have a feeling like that?

Yes, I think everybody has that, don't they? They say that you need as many years as you have been away to reintegrate back in. I knew what I was doing, though, and in Asia I realized I'd had enough time away and I was missing my friends a lot. I came back to London to work for my old boss who was Head of News Programmes. He took me on as his Executive Editor. I worked with him, and was really happy, until the Savile scandal hit. The News Programmes department was responsible for the likes of Panorama and Newsnight so I had a close-up view through that period, it was a really good lesson in organisational crises and how they unfold.

Can you distil out what you learned?

I learned a lot in that period. I think the main thing that I took from it, which is something we were talking about earlier, is when you're in the middle of a crisis, trying to think about the bigger picture. I saw that some people lost their heads and they lost some of their humanity at the same time. I think they forgot that you can still treat people normally, that you need to retain your own sense of integrity and credibility through those processes. The organisation will survive, the BBC was going to come out the other side. You have to decide where you want to be in that process and remember who you are. There were some points where I said, 'is that really necessary?'. Have you been in those situations where the sands really shift quickly?

Yes, but probably not quite as extreme as the example you're using.

If you're in a company setting that might happen and you might have to replace a Board, you might have to replace a CEO. In the BBC the worst thing is that you are doing that whilst reporting on your own story. You just have to decide where your boundaries are about your own integrity and one's preparedness to throw your colleagues under the bus or not. I'm used to being extremely careful about what I say. Organisations carry through and that's fine and you have to understand when that's happening and not personalise the issues and not think that an organisation is going to do anything else other than protect itself and survive.

What happened next, career wise?

I did bigger jobs, bigger teams, more change. I began to be asked to go in and make changes. I was head of the Russian service, they asked me to come in and help change it.

What's the difference between the Russian Bureau Chief and the Head of the Russian Service, how do they interact?

The Head of the Russian Service is responsible for all the output that goes out in Russian from the UK and from Moscow. You had staff in the UK and in Moscow. The Bureau Chief was responsible for everything that was coming out of Moscow, and primarily in English, and they were responsible for all of the staff that were there and there were over a hundred of them by that point.

You were doing a series of troubleshooting roles for six months to a year, were you?

No, longer, but I would be asked 'can you go in and make changes here?'. For example, I was Head of the Russian Service which I did for maybe three years and changed it completely, changed their output and then handed over to somebody who continued the changes so they became a much more successful service. And I was in the Business and Economics Unit and started some changes there and the same when I was Deputy Head of Newsgathering.

How and when did your role as Head of BBC Monitoring come about, where we first met?

2015 I think. I went for the job and they gave it to someone else who did it for less than a year and then left and then I had to decide whether I wanted to go for it again and eventually I did.

Was it a division that you were quite aware of? From memory, not everyone in the BBC was au fait with what it did. How were you aware of it?

They had teams in the international bureaus. I knew of them because they had staff in Moscow and we used their reports.

Give us a pen picture of BBC Monitoring, what they do and what you sought to do in your time with them.

It isn't necessarily widely known as a department, although if you've worked in international news then you do generally know of it because it's like another news agency. It's an internal department within BBC News that provides an agency-like service to the UK Government and to commercial companies translating and analysing international media from the vernacular and publishing those insights in English. You are providing a service that doesn't really exist elsewhere, summarising media coverage in countries and translating that into English.

From memory when you took over they were housed in an old property somewhere out in the sticks. Talk to me about that and the overall transition you oversaw?

Well, like the rest of the BBC - there's a BBC historian, who tracks the whole of the history of the BBC and everything has its history - Monitoring has a fantastic history. It was created in the Second World War to monitor German propaganda and bring that information to the Cabinet Office so that decisions could be made about deployment. Then the service moved to the BBC and it was billeted in this Georgian mansion on the hills above Reading with a Capability Brown designed estate and a large mansion. Just one of the properties that the BBC owns! [Laughs]

Were you based there for a while?

Yes. And in its heyday it had about 700 or 800 people and they used to be shifted 24/7, they had sleeping accommodation and all sorts of things. It's really imbued in the history of Monitoring that this building and this location was all part of what they did. So I went to work in this Georgian mansion with a huge office with an antechamber and columns and all sorts of things. There were probably 200 people rattling around in the building by then and it seemed crazy to me because it was the least creative, collaborative space and it was so far from the heart of news in Broadcasting House. I knew plans to relocate had been mooted, but I was mainly tasked with a major change programme. Monitoring needed modernising and a tech update. They had the bones of what they wanted to do, but they hadn't executed it. I came in maybe a third of the way through, understood what they were trying to do and agreed with the direction, made some changes to the plan in terms of the international presence, opened some bureaus and closed some others and then executed a big change plan, which brought a new structure, closed the posts of about a third of the staff and launched new products and ways of working. There was a moment where we calculated that 1,000 years of experience left the organisation, but we did it as well as we could and it was widely accepted that it was a well-executed, well-led change programme. Monitoring is now very profitable. We turned it around to being profitable remarkably quickly really.

You did that for three years, I believe, by which time you'd been at the BBC for how long?

28 years when I left.

You left to become COO of the Saïd Business School at Oxford University.

Yes, to be honest I had begun to consider looking outside. I'd been 28 years with the BBC and was thinking that perhaps I'd like to experience something else. I spoke with my boss (we have a great relationship and she's still a friend) and I told her where my head was at and she said, "Would you be interested in this other change programme?" And I said, "I've just done one!" I decided that the time was right to try something completely new.

Tell me a little about your time in Oxford.

It was a positive experience and I suppose an ambitious transition. I remember being asked at interview about this being a three-point transition - a new sector, a new role and a new location. And I said, "I've done three- or four-point transitions before" but it was a big step. After 28 years in one organisation anything was going to be a big step! I think it was the best lily pad to land on. It was the right place. I remembered being conscious of trying to work out as quickly as possible where the commonalities were and where the synergies were and there were plenty of them, but what you had to do as well was get as up to speed with Oxford as an institution. I needed to get into the culture of the university, understand how decisions were made, what the drivers were - and they were different.

What are two or three big things that you learned from your experience at Oxford Saïd Business School overall?

I learned how important it is to listen, to engage as early as possible to hear in their own words what the issues are for staff, and their hopes for the school. We did a whole series of engagement workshops to get a sense of what was not being said openly. That then made finding shared goals, projects that people cared about and would work together on much easier. I read something recently about followership rather than leadership and it really chimed with my time at Oxford Saïd.

Also, keep your coach. [Laughs] Definitely keep a line of continuity, your own person, so when you transition you still have that person that knows you well. You can't just go straight into the new organisation and expect that they'll understand you and how you work. The ability to adapt to a new setting is crucial and it helps to have someone who knows you to support that. It gives you additional perspectives at a time when you really need it. You always need this, but at a transition this has extra value.

Was the coach someone you'd found yourself while working at the BBC?

Yes, I'd worked with her since 2015, and she's fantastic. She grounded me, she was able to remind me of things that I knew when I was beginning to say, "hold on a minute, this doesn't make sense" and she was able to draw a line of continuity. So that's one. And when I mentioned the insularity of the BBC, then Oxford is even more so. Keeping the links that I knew I had outside, including - by the way - yourself, being able to talk outside of the organisation, to listen to other opinions was extremely helpful.

I was so intrigued to understand about your early life and your time travelling the world with the BBC, an experience quite different from that of my other interviewees that we don't have much more time to dig into your experience at the Business School. I do know that you found the cultural divide between academia and running the business functions quite an eye opener and that you did some great work in the three years you were there to strengthen the focus on purpose and responsible business in the school's operations as well as its teaching. As a family you then had the opportunity to embark on another adventure with your partner this year taking

up the challenge of establishing Wellington College International senior school in Bangkok. You are using your time now to train as a coach. I wanted just to pause now to ask you to reflect more broadly on your experience thus far in your life and career. A question I have asked others is, what do you think is the single best piece of advice that anyone has given you?

I have two. One piece of advice, which I had reinforced in the leadership teaching at Oxford Saïd but which I'd always known, is that when ego leaves the room that's when the magic happens. I was almost relieved to hear this in a classroom because it is true and I'd seen it for myself on so many occasions.

The second is about remembering what you don't know. When you're working in more senior roles you need to recall what it's like coming into an organisation and the things you can't see when you're more junior. I do think being curious and talking with people across your organisation is key and not just having the same people in the room, perhaps the "yes" people. It's important to get the feel for what people are thinking and experiencing up and down the organisation. You need to make it possible to share or hear those voices, to make yourself accessible. At the Business School we created a chatbot that would send colleagues the details of a random person in the organisation and you'd set up a coffee chat with them for a chance to get to know them. I did that each week and loved it.

That sounds like a very good yet simple idea. I'd like you to think back now to those very early career years. You were the young night clubbing adventurer fresh from your fun years in Bristol and

assignments in Paris and elsewhere, keen to explore Russia and to make your mark on the world. Reflecting now, what things have you learned along the way that you would like to have understood then?

I was super trusting. I had no idea that there were big differences in how people were treated and paid. Perhaps the thing that you don't know when you're younger is about speaking up and not accepting things as they're handed down to you. Perhaps because I was of a generation where employment was more precarious there was an acceptance of how things were done and you kept your counsel when you were more junior. I think that's less of an issue now. I think young people have been encouraged to speak out more. They have had some examples to follow of others doing that.

If you were to be addressing a roomful of 18- to 21-year-olds and giving them advice on what lies ahead in their career and their lives, what advice could you offer them based on your personal experiences?

I think you've got to focus on the things that light you up. Don't take the path that everyone else may be telling you is the wise path to follow, because they are not you and no two of us are the same. Follow your intuition, follow your passions and don't be afraid to take some risks. Then when you are in a good place, where you feel you are playing to your strengths, really go for it, be the best that you can be, be a perfectionist, set yourselves high standards and follow them. Learn from the best, get involved in working with outstanding talent if you can. Watch and learn. And be supportive and act with integrity.

Looking ahead do you think what it takes to be successful in an organisation or a business today is very different from what it would have been 20-30 years ago when you started?

I do think it's different. I think the ability to speak up and challenge is much more available to one now. I remember knowing that things weren't right, that behaviour wasn't acceptable, but I wouldn't have known at some points in my career how to raise that, and I probably accepted things earlier on. I don't think younger people will now, but I think the main issue now is that there are generational differences between people in the workplace. There are different layers. It depends how you want to categorise them, but I think if you're leading an organisation today there is much more of a responsibility on your shoulders to understand those differences, it isn't just a case of saying "it's my way or the highway" - that just doesn't work. The need to engage and understand the people that are working with you is much more important today and perhaps we are now more different because people feel more able to express their differences? I think it might be fair to say there's a generation of leaders coming towards the end of their careers who grew up in different times and have not found it easy to change and adjust and who may be just getting out at the right time. Others will come in to lead in a different way.

Last question, you talked about Paul earlier and touched on purpose, this idea of there being a broader purpose and impact for an organisation to achieve, be it a for-profit organisation or the BBC where, as we discussed, impact might be measured in a different way. Give me some thoughts around that from your perspective?

I think it's about knowing why you're here, isn't it? Why you're getting up in the morning. You can understand that on an individual level or you can understand it at the enterprise level, what do you stand for and strive for? You can talk about being values-led or mission-led. In my work, when it's been really clear what we were there to do and what we stood for then that's when it's been easier to align everything else behind that. That's the best combination to get things done and be successful at the same time. When you don't have that, it's like the shopping trolley with the wonky wheel, you start to veer off in different directions, and you're constantly having to explain why things are happening. When it is aligned, and I've experienced that at different stages in my work, you really feel as if you're 'in the flow' and that has a certain, hard to define power about it.

"

I was a nightmare as a child, I had a fascination with electricity and I used to love putting knitting needles inside the sockets. My dad was a very practical man so I was always helping him, I had a very scientific background I suppose.

I think it's fair to say we were a family of high achievers and we were expected to do well. I don't know if that sounds terrible but it's how we saw it.

"

TUDOR BROWN

INTERVIEWED 12TH JANUARY 2021

Tudor grew up in the small Welsh town of Aberystwyth and after studying Physics at Cambridge, began his career as an engineer at Acorn Computers. Their BBC Microcomputer went on to dominate the UK educational computer market during the 1980s. In 1990, Tudor became one of the co-founders of ARM Holdings, going on to become President. It became one of the UK's most valuable businesses and in 2016 was acquired by Japanese conglomerate Softbank for £25billion. Here he talks about his upbringing, influences and insights into UK business and its future as a global innovator.

You grew up in Aberystwyth, tell me a bit about your background and your family.

My father was a university lecturer and started out life in Swansea which is where my parents met. My mother was a Librarian, she had to stop work as soon as she got married as was done in those days. That was in the early fifties. Then my father moved to Aberystwyth as senior lecturer of physics at the University. The department there was young and back then doing some fairly pioneering work. I grew up there as the youngest of three children, I had two older sisters and we were a very happy family. Living in the lovely coastal town of Aberystwyth, it was a simple life, quiet and clean.

Did you excel in science at school and quickly realise that it was your strength?

Well, I was a nightmare as a child, I had a fascination with electricity and I used to love putting knitting needles inside the sockets. My dad was a very practical man so I was always helping him, I had a very scientific background I suppose.

At seventeen you won a place at Cambridge to study Physics, I believe?

I did, but before that I went to school in Bath. My grandmother decided I should go away to a school there rather than stay in Aberystwyth. I loved it there, it was a place called Kingswood started by John Wesley. We were brought up in a Methodist family and in those days Methodist ministers used to move around every three years and Wesley decided he would give the offspring of ministers some stability so he started the school as a place where the sons could go when their fathers were travelling. To this day, Kingswood still has a Methodist connection. I really enjoyed my time there and it was very formative for me. It was a public school, there were a lot of very wealthy boys, also some pretty poor people too, a lot of boys whose parents really couldn't afford to send their sons to private school, I loved it.

Did the Methodist Church and your school have an impact on your life, did it influence you?

Yes and no. I'm no longer a practising Christian but very definitely the Christian roots have and still do colour my view on life. We were brought up to care about money and be frugal and that sort of thing, and I'd like to think I adhere to Christian principles.

You had two sisters who went to Aberystwyth Grammar School. Being the only son and the one that went to private school, did that make you feel like you needed to achieve something special to justify your parents' investment?

I don't think I specifically did. I think it's fair to say we were a family of high achievers and we were expected to do well. I don't know if that sounds terrible but it's how we saw it. Aberystwyth is a very interesting place because the main industry is the university, the main three employers are the university, the National Library of Wales and the hospital, and that's still true today. As a result, the cohort of kids in that town intellectually has always been quite high. I was just expected to do well, and I suppose we were quite competitive with each other as well.

Did your parents offer much advice to you in terms of university and career choices?

It was a very low touch but high impact sort of steering. In the sense that my father went to Cambridge during the war, he was the son of a Methodist minister and he had a brother who went to Oxford as well. When it was time to choose a university, we did the rounds and I got all the prospectuses and my father basically quietly said, "Why don't you apply to Cambridge if you can?" I suppose that set the bar for me and I went down that road to see what happened and I got in.

To be honest though I wasn't particularly happy there, I wasn't unhappy but I didn't really love it. I loved school but not university. There were several reasons for that, I felt Cambridge was the opposite of my school, it was full of people with their heads in the clouds and quite arrogant. There was a huge amount of over-confidence and I felt underconfident in that cohort. I did work extremely hard and I was extremely young, I was only 17 when I did my A-Levels. Looking back, I think I was too immature, if I'd taken a year out I think I might have been able to embrace some of the things that Cambridge offered, but at the time I didn't. So, I just got on with the work and didn't really partake in the bigger scene; in the end I was happy to get away from it.

And what did you do after graduation?

I went to a work for a company up in Northwich in Cheshire, a small family run electronics company.

How did you go about thinking about your career choice, did you have a very clear idea?

No, I think as with a lot of people it was accidental, you make it up as you go along. Although I started doing natural sciences and physics at Cambridge, I started to find the maths too difficult, and I'd always had this draw to electronics. So, in my third year I moved to electrical engineering, and after that I suppose my career thinking graduated towards electronics. I joined this company and it seemed interesting, I worked there for about five years and did a variety of projects. It was a very small company but I found my niche and got on well.

At that age were you very ambitious or just taking each year as it came?

More the latter. I was progressing, being given more responsibility and getting pay rises and so on, but I started to feel like I'd outgrown the company as there weren't going to be more promotions, the company wasn't going to grow that quickly.

I happened to be living in a house with a very ambitious Russian guy and a year or two before that he'd decided he wanted to leave the company and he went to Acorn. His English wasn't terribly good so I wrote his application letter for him and he got in. A year or so later he spoke to me and told me to come down and work with him at Acorn in Cambridge. Of course I didn't particularly like Cambridge at that time so I wasn't sure, but in the end with his encouragement I applied to Acorn and sure enough got a job, so I moved back down.

Talk me through the next stages of your career.

Acorn was a fascinating company full of very bright people, but it was complete chaos. You're old enough to remember the BBC computer which is where it all sprung from. Acorn went from nothing to around a £100million turnover in the space of two years and it was chaos. I was employee #468 and there were four-hundred R&D projects going on at the time, so you can do the maths on that. None of them were particularly well resourced. They were into Formula 3 racing sponsorships, there were parties all the time, it was just complete chaos. The company was doing really well but had outgrown its ability to manage itself because it had moved so quickly. Although it was fun and the work was interesting, we got very fed up when the company kept on going bust!

What happened to you then?

Let me rewind a little. I joined Acorn and at that point the BBC computer was very successful, it was a money machine for a while. Acorn then had a few technical missteps but putting that aside it was obvious that we needed to make a successor to the BBC machine. The upshot was that they decided they would design their own microprocessor called the Acorn RISC Machine, hence the name ARM. They started developing it just before I joined, and after about a year I joined that project. It was incredibly secret, we had to sign an internal NDA, which is hilarious looking back because it obviously goes against teamwork and trust, but they wanted to keep it a secret. It was undoubtedly the best people in the company that were working on it, there were about thirty of us, and without being arrogant we were the cream of the company.

Acorn kept on going bust because they had these missteps in other areas of the business but we were sort of ring-fenced. There were a couple of times we were told to bring our work home because the company might not be there after the weekend and we were really expected to fail. I think looking back there was something about Acorn which kind of imbued in us all an expectation to fail. Even though we were doing great stuff it felt like it was going to be ruined by bad management.

What was the atmosphere like in your project team?

The core group was about ten people, and the reality was we were just a fun team. Today you see the same thing in any start-up, the pioneers end up succeeding. We didn't really need much management, we knew what had to be done. We used to go out to the pub every lunch time and have a pint of beer and a sandwich, it was an extremely laid back environment but we worked very hard, long hours and so on. We were exploring and creating things that nobody else was doing and there was a certain self-generated excitement about that.

You said you were fed up with the company going bust, so did something change for you?

There were several attempts to rescue what we were doing because clearly we were creating something very interesting, but the company wasn't in a state to finance it or capitalise on it. In 1987 we finally had all the bits of the new computer together. The first computer was launched but all sorts of things had been delayed and we weren't in a position to market it properly. The Archimedes, the first ARM based computer that came out, wasn't a great success, it was the wrong market at the wrong time, but brilliant technically, even today you could argue it was way ahead of its time in many ways.

Eventually by 1990 Apple came along and wanted the technology. They were trying to build the Apple Newton and they needed the ARM technology to do it. They did a secret deal with Acorn to create a joint venture company in which Apple would have access to the technology. It was spun out into a separate group. In the new setup

Acorn didn't have the overhead of running the group anymore, and we were told to go make it successful. We expected it to fail but whatever, we were free of Acorn and on our way.

We're now in 1990?

Yes, it was the end of 1990 and we had just moved out into a new building, and we had a new CEO called Robin Saxby who became a good friend of mine. From there it was a long, long journey but eventually ARM started to become extremely successful.

At what point did you shift from being tech focussed, to interested in business more broadly?

There were four of us who were very senior technical people. One went into sales, one went into marketing, one wanted to stay a technologist and I went on to become the CTO and grew the engineering team. I quickly became de facto head of HR as well as recruiting most of the new people.

Did you enjoy managing people and building a team?

I did actually, it happened in the right way for me. I was having this conversation with my son recently and was saying, "At what point do you leave being a technician and go into management?". It struck me that it has to be the right time. If you go too early you end up not achieving your potential and if you do it too late you might stay as a technologist. Of course, that might be the right thing to do, there are still people I know today who are there working on the technology thirty years later and love it.

Between the four of you, did you somehow self-select your new roles?

We'd all been doing this technology for quite a long time, ten years or whatever, and so several of us wanted to move on. At that point I was still Head of Technology, I was still the technical guy, but gradually I became more of a manager and less of a technical chap. As I said, I did most of the hiring so I had a particular interest in finding talent.

Tell me about how you went about it?

When I look back on my career I think that recruiting talent probably was one of my biggest successes. We can be very proud of the people we brought into ARM in the early days. We created a system which hired by and large the right people.

Between us we concluded that the most important thing wasn't how brilliant someone was but whether they were going to fit into the team and play their part. We'd always have more than one person interview someone. We used to like to take people down to the pub to see how they'd fit in, and we'd do interviews at odd times like Sunday morning to test people. We'd ask people a lot about their family background and their motivation and things like that. I developed a particular trait to be nasty, to come across as disinterested and unimpressed by the person in front of me and it was up to the candidate to impress me and not the other way around. Actually, several of the people still remember the interviews. When I left, the employees all wrote comments on pieces of paper for me and several of the comments were that they still remembered the day that I interviewed them!

If I were to ask the people who you hired what you were like, how would they describe you, do you think?

I hope they would say that I was a hard taskmaster but fair. I've always tried to lead by example and I've always believed in working very hard. I believe in pushing people hard and not accepting mediocrity. On the other hand, I also try to be compassionate where appropriate.

I have a few maxims which I've developed, one of them is, "there's no smoke without fire," if you hear a rumour about something there's probably some truth to it. The other one is, "there are always two sides to a coin," if you hear about one thing it's almost certain there's something else going on. The third one is, "to succeed you must allow mistakes," you've got to push yourself and the only way to do that is to be prepared to make mistakes, so you have to construct an environment in which people can make mistakes which are not catastrophic. But I don't want them to make the same mistake again.

My last one is, "coincidences never happen". Of course in life we do find coincidences but I have found it most useful to assume if something happens or goes wrong because of two apparently random events happening at the same time, more often than not there is a common cause. If you focus on finding the common thread then you will find the true cause more effectively. Over the years I have found this a most useful thought process in understanding things!

How do you construct an environment where people can take those risks?

You've got to put in safety nets, so if you're designing a chip you have to push it to the point it might work or it might not work, but you need to have the tests to find out if it works or not. You want people to be able to play and experiment with things so that if something goes wrong it's still okay.

I was talking to a bunch of lawyers after I'd left and I was telling them the same thing, that you have to be prepared to make mistakes, and I realise that in their environment that's very difficult. In a legal environment you can't make mistakes with your customers, but you could invent scenarios and roleplay to give people the chance to learn.

I suppose the environment when you were with that small group on the 'secret project' was a bit like that, you were trusted?

Yes and no, everyone has a boss, right? We had bosses but also had direct customer contact from very early on, so there was very close collaboration. We had strict criteria to work from and were under constant pressure to make these chips and get them out quicker. I'd be doing a full day's work, take the disk drive out of my computer, come home, have dinner, start work again at 9pm, work until 1am or 2am, sleep for a bit and then go back to work again in the morning.

We're all of us unusually good at something. Often we don't realise what it is to start with or how valuable that talent is because it just seems easy to us. What is like that for you?

I'm pretty logical, some people would say I'm too logical. I'm also good at seeing things from different perspectives. I try to understand the other person's point of view, what motivates them and makes them tick. That's important if you're trying to motivate people and get them to work hard, or if you're in a tough negotiation and there's a log jam, you need to be able to understand what's causing that, resolve the issue and make progress.

What about intuition? I interviewed a scientist recently and in his field there seemed to be no room for intuition. How about with you?

It was totally the opposite. Engineering is definitely an art form. You're creating something and the question is, is it going to work?

So you're very good at logic, but also trusted your own inner voice when you had to make a leap?

Yes, let me give you an example. If you're designing logic chips then obviously, the logic has to be right, and if the logic is wrong things will fail. But will it work at a particular speed? Logic chips will work at a specific speed and you'll add it all up and see if it goes fast enough. So getting the chip right is a logical process, but getting it going fast enough is a sort of art-form.

What about the appetite for risk? I always say to people that business isn't a science, you can't always 'prove' that things are going to work, particularly if nobody's tried it before. Where are you on that spectrum?

I think in different areas I have a different profile. Financially I don't take many risks, but from a point of view of, "can we do something new, can we do something we haven't done before and risk failure?" then yes, I'm happy to take big risks and use my intuition.

Thinking about it, I always used to say with a career in engineering you're basically swapping innovation, excitement and craziness for experience. When you start out in life you think, "oh look, we can do it this way; oh look, we can do that," and then as you gain experience you know what works and what doesn't. I argue that you swap the frothiness and excitement for experience and when you think of those two curves there's a sort of sweet spot. I think that's why most people are most productive in their late twenties, you still have that excitement and craziness but you have some experience behind you.

You mentioned your involvement in negotiating. You've obviously been involved in many deals, can you tell me a bit about your experience there and what you learnt?

We were selling this technology to companies spread around the world. The first deals were in the UK then we started going to Japan which was a big culture shock for me. I didn't like Japan at first but then started to love it. I've probably been to Japan about a hundred times and I grew a huge affinity for the people. Then we started doing business with the Koreans, I found that I loved Korean people too, they were extremely loyal, they used to hold hands and this sort of thing, I was thinking, "what's going on here?"!

Having moved from the technology to being involved in negotiations, I had to be involved in them because it was a very technical sell, it's about how you can use the technology and how you can make sure it works. Then gradually I became more interested in looking after the customer, so I developed an affinity for the customer, particularly in Asia, I basically became a Eurasian. At various points I ran all the Asian offices and I suppose built up a personal following in Asia, people who trusted me as the most senior person from HQ.

How did you build that trust?

I used to really join in the culture, for example I'd be adventurous with the food, eat everything, that sort of thing goes a long way I think. I was happy to have meals with people and share experiences. When they came over to this country, my wife is an extremely good cook and we used to invite them over for dinner. We had many senior people from Asian companies to our house, and they remember that. With Huawei, which is all a bit controversial now, with them it was a case that I was prepared to take a risk on doing a deal with them when no one else would, because I could see what they were going to go on and become in the future. That's what I like about doing business in Asia, they're very loyal, I'm still friends with a lot of these people to this day.

Because of that my interest became the relationship side, which is why during my last three years in ARM I was President, which was a role largely about looking after customers and negotiating alliances of one kind or another.

Who was the CEO at that stage?

When I left it was Warren East, who is now CEO of Rolls-Royce. I have the utmost respect for Warren and we just got on very well together. He said he'd take the CEO job if I became COO which is what happened in 2001. I was his COO for a long time, I used to like going to Asia and he was much better with the Americans, so it worked out very well!

Talk me through the later stages of your career.

After a while I felt that I was getting bored and stale, and our kids at that point were pretty much finished with university. I also felt quite strongly that I was acting a bit like a glass ceiling and it was only fair to give the people I employed a route through to bigger jobs. I was fortunate to have been successful, so I didn't need to earn money. I think I was fifty-four at the time and needed something to keep me busy going forward.

I worked hard until the day I left and when I did I was in no hurry, it was nice to have some downtime for a while. It was an interesting experience at home, discovering that my wife really didn't want me in the house, everyone tells you that but it's really true. Not because I was encroaching on her, it's just that we'd always had our separate lives, so to suddenly be there all the time was quite stressful for her.

I really didn't know what I wanted to do at first, I knew I didn't want a full-time role. I left early 2012 and by December 2012 I got my first Non-Exec role at Lenovo, which is a huge international company with a Chinese-American fusion culture. Once you've got a Non-Exec job it's much easier to get more and fairly quickly after that I had opportunities to have a few more and built up a little portfolio. It kept me travelling, I spent quite a lot of time in America and the Far East. I found it a good compromise, for me it worked really well and I'm still doing that. Obviously with the virus I haven't met any of these people in over a year and I'm starting to find it difficult to keep engaged to be honest, but hopefully that will pass.

Were you keen to get involved in a British company?

No, not really to be honest. Being on the Board of ARM I discovered I don't really like how British Boards work. I found them quite formal and stuffy, a bit slow moving. The US Boards I'm on are extremely engaging and fun, the people are people you really want to talk to. It might be an unfair judgement, but I feel British companies tend to go for trophy Directors and not enough people that are actually prepared to do the work.

I read an old interview with you, conducted by the BBC. You were talking about the advantage Britain has in the area of innovation?

Yes, it's true, Britain has a long and illustrious history as a creative hub. Some of the greatest achievements in technology have come out of Britain. But after the Industrial Revolution Britain was pretty useless at manufacturing things of high quality. By and large most of the volume manufacturing has left this country, as it has left most of the Western markets. The whole drama of the last five years has come from the US trying to regain that from China, and even China's getting bored with it and moving manufacturing for items like clothing to places like Vietnam. The trouble is that you can't do that forever and there are some things that Britain would do better to do more of.

Looking at the last few years you could say there might be a bit of a sliver of light in that we are bringing things home more, what with Brexit, and there are things we need to do more of than we currently do. We have a very strong pharmaceutical industry, and in Cambridge the bio-tech industry is huge.

I think value creation is terribly important and as an inventive nation we have great scope to do that. Not just in Tech but Biotech in particular. But I do worry that those value creating jobs do not employ large numbers of people so there is an issue to resolve there. Actually, I fear that a lot of jobs which disappear during the pandemic simply will not come back and so I'm looking to the future post the pandemic and Brexit. We have great opportunities to create value, we are well placed, but the employment landscape will change. We may get back some manufacturing in some form but the value is really in intellectual property and connecting with like-minded businesses around the world to create value synergies.

If you had to distil out some of the key learnings you've accumulated over the course of your business career, what would they be?

Well as we've touched on the importance of cash, cash is king in business. A business must be able to generate cash and operate within its cash perimeters. Actually, I think oddly businesses can suffer from having too much cash and waste it because they do not have the discipline and experience of managing it adroitly. I suppose WeWork would be an obvious recent example. A business must learn its game and work within its means to be strong and capable of enduring.

What's the best piece of advice you've received in business terms and who gave it to you?

An interesting question. Here's a surprising one for you. It was a banker at Morgan Stanley who said, "Don't do business with stupid people." What he meant was don't push water uphill if the person you're dealing with is not switched on and sensible. You can waste an awful lot of time doing otherwise and it won't end well.

Are there any people you have particularly admired in the course of your career?

Yes, one I recall, he wasn't an engineer, he was actually an aeronautical scientist. His way of designing things was extremely refreshing and clean, we all learnt a lot from him. With customers, I could point to quite a few. When we used to visit LG in Korea, they were trying to grow into a market and they were so aggressive. They took motivating the workforce to a new extreme, they used to have posters everywhere with encouraging statements and you couldn't help seeing the impact of that philosophy in terms of commitment and energy.

Earlier on in the interview you talked about how you used to work early into the morning. Let's talk a bit about work life balance and how you've managed that. Did work consume you? Were you able to switch off?

I think it's fair to say work did consume me, and the reason I was able to do that is because my wife is a saint and accepted that ARM was my focus above all else. Of course I've tried to be a good father, but generally there wasn't much doubt in anyone's mind that ARM was my priority and would have to come first.

Were you able to switch off on weekends and holidays? Did you ever struggle to cope with stress?

The weird thing is I switch off by diving deep into other projects, so I've always had other projects on the go at home, building or mending cars or machines, I'm always doing something. My way of switching off from ARM was to throw myself into doing something physically constructive.

In terms of stress, there's no question I went through a period of pretty high stress, it wasn't right at the beginning, it was in the mid 2000s after ARM had gone public, had become a big success and then it all came crashing back down again. We had five or six years of really tough grind where it wasn't at all clear if we would survive. We also made a very bad acquisition at that time in America and I was heavily involved in that. Although I liked travelling a lot, at that time the travel was particularly stressful and I used to feel my blood pressure coming up.

It's partly why I changed roles and did something different. Certainly, since I left ARM I feel my personal stress levels are much, much lower.

You mentioned acquisitions, what learnings do you have about acquisitions?

Lots. Anyone will tell you any company that does lots of acquisitions gets much better at it. Companies that don't do many tend to make mistakes. It seems very hard to share the experience from one company to another. The single most important thing is culture. When you are making an acquisition, over and over again the issue is if you don't get true buy-in from the people that you're buying then it won't work.

You've also got to work out why someone is selling, quite often people are selling because they're tired and they want out. That creates a sort of malaise in the company itself, and you find people not wanting to be flexible enough to work for a new boss. If they've been near the top of the company and they're now a couple of layers down in a bigger company, they don't want that, for them it's not how it used to be and they can't make the same decisions.

Unless you really convince people of the upsides of being part of this bigger company it will fail. In the case of the big US acquisition, we did a lot of due diligence, and every time we saw something that was broken we thought that's great, we can fix that. But there ended up being too many broken things for us to fix. You have to pay attention to the due diligence and be prepared to walk away if it doesn't look good. So often in acquisitions you start out thinking it's a good idea, then you get sucked in, the bankers get involved wanting you to do the deal, and it gets harder and harder to back out. It takes a very brave man to do that, it's a bit like walking away from the altar at your own wedding.

You've had a very rich career and a wealth of experience. If you were having a quiet chat with recent graduates about to embark on their careers, perhaps drawing on your own experience, what advice would you give them?

I think it's absolutely essential that you do something you enjoy, something which motivates you. I've seen so many physics graduates go and work for banks because of the massive salaries that they give you, but they hate it. You have to do something that you're passionate about but that's not to say you should underachieve.

You need to have some aspiration otherwise you will get trodden on, but you have to do things that you enjoy. Also, there are no quick fixes in business, there are no quick fixes in your career either. I firmly believe that you can worry too much about your career progression, you've just got to do your job, and if you're in the right company you will get noticed and be given opportunities.

You've got to be flexible, perhaps willing to move location or do something you haven't done before, or whatever it is. But if you focus on doing what you're doing and do it well and you're enjoying it, then that's the best route to success.

There's also a lot of luck involved too of course. We can all go to work for companies we think are doing great but then something like Covid-19 happens and suddenly everything changes. You can only focus on the things you can control and one of the things you can control is doing a job that you're good at and passionate about.

“

To succeed collectively, people need fire in the belly, tenacity and creativity, but also the will, almost an optimism, that if you keep going you will succeed.

”

PETER DRUMMOND

INTERVIEWED 2013 AND 8TH OCTOBER 2021

Peter was for many years CEO at the leading European integrated architecture and design firm BDP (Building Design Partnership). The firm recently led the project to convert the Excel Centre into the Nightingale Hospital, designed Wimbledon No. 1 Court, the UK Headquarters for Google and AstraZeneca, and are currently overseeing the refurbishment of the Houses of Parliament. This interview was largely conducted a year before Peter retired. I have edited it slightly and added a new section at the end to include further reflections in retirement.

Peter trained as a Town Planner and first joined BDP in Preston in the 1970s. In 2004 he became Chief Executive and completed four terms at the helm. He oversaw some of the key moments in the firm's development including the opening of new studios in the Netherlands, Abu Dhabi, China and India and experienced the highs and lows of managing the firm through the fastest period of growth in its history and the challenging economic environment following the 2008 crash. He talks here about some of the lessons learned along the way.

If is often said that the first ninety days are critical for a new CEO. Can you remember yours in 2004? What was your plan and how did it work out?

I think it's true that the first ninety days are the most memorable, the most exciting. If you can't approach those first ninety days entirely energised then you're not going to start off well. I do remember them because it was a contested election which was interesting as I had a manifesto, you needed to articulate a view about what you wanted to do, a clear plan but not a detailed plan.

The plan was not to do more of the same but something quite radical for BDP - growth, which sounds odd in a business sense, but we'd always been afraid of growth. We'd always held back because 'big' in the architectural world isn't necessarily beautiful and in the '80s we grew to such a degree that we spent the first three years of the '90s pulling it back, so growth had not been an end in itself, it was something that we had to control. What you are doing in taking on people, taking on premises is accumulating risk, because BDP is in a cyclical industry. Having said that, when I took over as CEO I knew we had to grow because that's what was happening in the industry as a whole and internationally. There was definitely a sense that the leadership group wanted that as well and so the first 90 days were really spent getting that message out, not from the point of view of saying, "this is what we are going to do," it was more like, "how are we going to do this?".

I won the contest and, once in place, I employed a very good firm of consultants! I can't remember what they were called, but they helped us out enormously to produce a five-year plan. I didn't start off my time with a five year plan but the first ninety days, six months or whatever were spent putting one together.

You talked about the aspiration to grow being shared by the leadership team. How important is that kind of consensus in a partnership organisation and how do you go about managing that challenge?

It's fundamentally important actually because you need them, your partners, the other twenty-five leaders to be totally tied into your vision and doing the right things, without them you can't move forward. BDP is a more consensual type organisation than an autocratic one, so you need to have them with you.

Did you find that wearing or frustrating at all?

Yes. I suppose once you've done it for nearly ten years, you want to say, "just do it," but that's the business.

Do you remember your first boss or someone early in your career who you respected particularly and what did you learn from them?

My very, very first boss was a guy called Jeffrey Walker (an engineer and a planner) who was a partner, he interviewed me for two and a half hours at BDP in Preston, my very first job as a Graduate (Jeffrey also interviewed my parents about me!). He was absolutely through-and-through a professional, it was all about providing a level of service and it was all about the character of people. He would simply say, "you are a BDP person," and I don't know if he knew what he meant by that or if I knew what he meant by that, but it meant something – it was about character, integrity, whatever it is, and it struck me quite forcibly that it wasn't just about the business, it was about the way people were.

Do you look out for that yourself?

Yes, it's about the way people behave without a shadow of a doubt and one of the best things he did, and one of the weirdest pieces of behaviour, was that after two and a half years of me having one of the best times of my life in an office based in Lancashire, he asked me whether I had thought of leaving. I asked what he meant. He said, "I don't want you to leave but if you don't leave you will be here forever." So about three months later I got another job and he said, "You didn't have to do it so quickly! But that's great, we'll see you in a few years." In a few years I went back, but again that was all about managing my career, which I thought was just amazing.

When you say "it's about the way people behave", what kind of behaviours was Jeffrey looking for do you think?

He had an intense desire to do the right thing, for his people to do the right thing. As it turned out he was a big mentor to Roy Adams, who was my immediate predecessor as CEO – behave professionally, do the right things with your team, with colleagues, with people. He did that to the extremes sometimes because he was a devout Evangelical Christian and he would ask people very strange questions, like the first time he met my wife Sue he asked, "how long have you loved Peter?". Now that was just the way he did it and I certainly haven't done anything like that to anyone since but he just had this intense interest in the way an individual approaches their career and he also said, "you've only begun to learn, you'll never finishing learning".

What three things do you think sum up what a BDP person is?

Team focussed, respectful of others, clear thinking. Not everyone has those attributes, but these are the things I would have liked to see, they are the main things.

Those are admirable characteristics, but does a collection of people selected on those criteria make for a great business team?

I would turn the question around the other way. In the bigger scheme of life, what the hell is the point of being a horrible person in a horrible organisation? It takes up so much of your working life. If you want to be in a cut-throat organisation, behave in a cut-throat way, where you're always watching your back, then other people can have that life. I don't want that life and I don't expect other people at BDP to have that life. I also don't think that in a very people focussed business like design that clients are looking for that either, they are looking for an engagement with the team that they are going to live with for ten years. They are not just looking at what comes off of the production line, they are anticipating a life for themselves over the next ten years, so this might seem a bit philanthropic or social, but I think that's actually part of BDP's roots.

You learned from him how to respect and value people. Was there anything else from him or another early mentor?

The other guy I'd probably cite is Bill Jack, who was Chairman of the London office and of the firm and my champion for a good period of time. The thing that he exhibited was that if you worked hard enough and tried hard enough you would succeed. He had boundless energy and a hardness actually; he was a robust Scot who had come south and made it his mission to make this a London recognised practice, not an offshoot of a firm that had come from the north. He just had great energy and basically infected people with that energy.

Do you think that level of determination and energy is a rare thing?

It's not a rare thing; I think it's a difficult thing to sustain, or it needs things to sustain it. It needs success to sustain it and I think that is actually one of the key challenges in today's economic climate. You see it generally, a weariness that kind of affects the populace almost because they are just hearing constant bad news and you can sense it. So that what's my point is, it's about how you reenergise, how you recreate that will and that determination and keep sights set high.

To succeed collectively, people need fire in the belly, tenacity and creativity and so on, but that character and the will to succeed, not in a cut-throat way, we've dealt with that, not in a knock everyone else out of the way, but a will and an almost optimism that if you keep going you will succeed, and if you don't succeed then sit back and re-strategise and have another go.

Would you say both you and Roy had that unusual level of will, and out of interest how would you contrast the two of you?

I think Roy is slightly quieter than me and he would take two or three particular things and drive them to a point of completion and sometimes maybe exclude everything else. I'm probably the other way around, I try to do everything and maybe don't complete on some of the things I should have but I'm more reliant on others to see that completion through. So, there is a definite contrast in our styles, but fundamentally we had the same values, same respect for people, same ambition.

You talked about the need to keep energised when the times were tough, how did you cope with that yourself?

This is like a psychotherapy session! Actually, that is a very, very interesting question but I probably didn't, I'm self-reliant on it so I didn't have a coach, I sort of did once or twice, but to be honest I don't have an answer to how you do it, you either do it or you don't.

Did you think about it?

All the time, I thought about it from the moment I woke up, if not before, I was thinking about how to drive myself forward, the people around me, the firm.

How did colleagues help you with that?

I suppose in your working career you do have lots of relationships with people and a few of them, turn round to you and say, "you know what you do, don't you?" and you say no and they tell you.

And you'll listen to them and think maybe they're right. There were only about half a dozen people at BDP that would pull you to one side. Actually there were one or two really good friends outside of BDP, both clients actually, who took you to one side and would say, "this is what you do and you mustn't forget that" and you would think, "I didn't even know I did it, never mind forget it!".

They were talking about the things you did well?

Yes, things like always being approachable, being available, always available to listen and always being positive. They said to me, "You always want to find a way through a problem, and you'll listen and listen and listen until you get there rather than just jump in and say the first thing that comes into your head."

Are you a very patient person?

Yes, very, worryingly so, too patient. But I think that is good because you can make rash decisions that turn out to be wrong.

Do you trust your own judgement?

Yes, I do because I'm prepared to work it out, but there were times when I really didn't know what to do and sometimes I would just say, "I don't know what the answer is and until I know what the answer is, let's just keep working at it." I'm very resistant to jumping in and just taking a pot shot at something. I think that is a strength, but I think that could also be a weakness.

Decisiveness is often seen as an important leadership trait. Some people will say that any decision is better than no decision, even if it's not the perfect decision. Where would you be on that?

I don't think so. Any decision being the right decision… I just don't believe that. There will always be a better decision, I guess. The most interesting thing about being a CEO is that I didn't have a degree in Chief Executive-ism. I'd not been to a business school, most Chief Executives haven't been to a business school. You have learned the business on the job and there is also an awful lot outside of the business you have learned too, i.e. the industry, related businesses, the economy and social society. You try and learn those things as best you can but there are big parts of it that you are asked to deal with where you don't know what the answer is, you go with a gut feeling. There are times when you think, "I don't know the answer to that question" and you know even the 'experts' don't know the answer to that question. So, you jump in. I've got a 50% chance of getting this question right, I would love to make it a 60% chance of getting it right and I think a little bit of time helps that. There can be a macho aspect about being a business leader, I see a lot of that kind of machismo in the property world and some of it works and some of it doesn't.

My observation is that people like to believe that the person at the top knows where they are going, they take comfort from that clarity and decisiveness.

The big picture stuff is absolutely critical and it's important that you do show unwavering certainty about strategic direction and don't signal any wobbles, there are barriers that you erect so that people don't know you're thinking "I don't know" but in other areas you do let it out and I think that is quite valuable actually.

What leaders from other fields do you admire and why?

As you know I am a big Arsenal fan so we could talk about Arsene Wenger. He has an unswerving view that his strategy is right, and he has an unswerving faith in the people he brings to the club, at least until he transfers them! But he gives them an awful long time to succeed. He trusts his own judgement but sometimes he gets it wrong, he doesn't actually say he gets it wrong, but he knows he gets it wrong; but he has this quiet determination that this is the right thing to do, in his overall strategic sense and he'll never blame his team, or himself, just the referee! He is a great leader almost too great a leader because he doesn't have anyone in the bigger club society to push him or suggest a different way of succeeding.

I think he finds it hard to find people that live up to his standard as though he'll say, "I'll do that myself", whereas in David Dean when he was at Arsenal he had someone there who could go out and do a deal on players and who could fulfil the dream of a move to the Emirates stadium and so I think some of those relationships and working relationships happen by accident, you strike upon somebody, they are the ying to your yang or vice versa - Clough and Taylor, Wenger and David Dean.

There was criticism that Wenger was too focussed on not spending money, worrying about the profitably of the club and therefore failing to invest and keep up with competitors. How much time do you spend looking after the numbers versus doing the right thing and assuming the numbers look after themselves?

That varies, when you are on a very positive trajectory then do the right thing and the numbers will look after themselves, when you are battling with economic pressures the numbers become more important. My tenure as CEO was split fifty-fifty. The first five years were, "we're going up, we're going up, we're going international, we're doing this for the right reasons". The second five years were, "we've got to contain some of these dynamics, we've got to look after this cash, we've got to try and improve profitability, change funding arrangements, whatever it might be". So, the numbers became more important.

Do you enjoy the numbers side of things?

No, I don't. Actually, I don't not enjoy the numbers, I liked to see the cash coming in, I loved to see the firm profitable, business profitability was always my thing. The top forty projects in any one office will always constitute a mixed bag, the less mixed it is the better it is. If you can reduce the number of unprofitable projects, you are doing well. The numbers themselves are a necessary evil.

How would you define your success as a leader if you look back now?

I suppose that operates on at least two different levels. The social level - the people you have brought through that you have seen come up from a very young age, the satisfaction I get from seeing a young person develop. But it works the other way, if you see someone with great potential and they get a serious illness and can't develop as they should for some reason, it's distressing all that talent that goes to waste. On the personnel side, seeing people come through is really important. On the bigger picture, it is about the firm being in a better shape - has it achieved a trajectory three notches from when you started and is it well set for the future?

I saw the company go up, as CEO I managed the company through the most successful period in its history in terms of profitability, diversity, quality and scale in a consistent way, to being at the wheel when we were having to downsize back almost to where we were, in the light of the post-2008 downturn. That begs the question, "did I succeed?".

I understand the impact of those post-2008 years in economic terms but conversely I'm sure that the previous five years were not just reflecting a strong economy. I'm sure there is some pride in the amazing growth you achieved in those first five years?

Without a shadow of a doubt, if I could look back to 2008 I would say, "what a good job you have done, Drummond, you're a genius"! But the true test of a business leader is what they do in the most difficult of times, how they behave, their personal qualities are tested in difficult times much more. It's easy to know what to do when you are steering at the helm of a ship when the winds are easy, it's what you do in a storm which is the true test.

Do you think that a successful leader is defined by a small number of big decisions, or building reputation and respect is more of a slow cumulative process?

I'll use another sailing analogy - Your true progression is measured by a series of the moves that you make in that journey, not that one tack, because you can always tack back, it's the progression of the decisions you take every day, every six months, every year, rather than the big strategic move.

How did you choose your leadership group? Apart from technical competence, what were the key characteristics you looked for?

Trust, loyalty, energy, ideas, commitment - all of those things, complementary skills. For a long period of time, Tony and I were entirely complementary. It really did work, we would start at different places and end in the same place, that was really great. [Tony was BDP Chairman]

How did you hold people to account and tackle difficult people decisions?

In BDP consensus was very important, they are a relatively flat organisation, they don't have a pyramid-like hierarchy but are project based, unit based, sector based, so you have to have everyone aligned as best you can to the common cause. There is an unwritten and written common cause which people sign up to and you really notice when people fall off that. The answer to that question is, "what do you do when you see people fall off the side?". Well, you have to bring them to task and confront the situation. You have to do the very difficult thing of saying to a colleague, a peer, a company director, "this is not good enough, what's the problem, what's the blockage? You're not acting in the spirit of the firm, there is something going on?". You have to get to the bottom of it and if you can't get to the bottom of it or if you get to the bottom of it and it still doesn't change, then you have to change it. You have to remove them for the common good of the firm.

How did you approach decision making and balance risk and opportunity? What process did you employ?

Always discuss it - discuss, analyse, think and think again. Try not to just respond to a gut reaction. If I've got an innermost philosophy which is not to be intuitive. My wife is very intuitive, as are a lot of great business leaders. If I feel my intuition telling me something, I want to test it and analyse it. I might come back to it, step back for a moment. Even if it's obvious, I just need to make sure that there isn't a better way.

When I was at University I was taught, "survey, analyse, plan". That was the planner's motto, and I think that's why I did it, because it comes very naturally to me. "Survey, analyse, plan."

Is it a coincidence that two of the firm's most recent CEOs have both been town planners, which is a relatively small practice within BDP?

I don't think it is a coincidence, though I haven't really thought about it. Firstly, an architect cannot be an architect if they are not a practising, designing architect. I think part of the training of the planner takes in a broader spectrum, which you can interpret in many different ways. So, I think it is a fairly natural thing - now I consider it, I think that thought process of "survey, analyse, plan" is a pretty good mantra for a CEO, actually.

Are the qualities necessary to be a good Chairman very different from those required of a CEO? How?

Yes. I think a good Chairman is strategic, spiritual and sanctioned – not sectioned! Spiritual is about making sure the life blood of the firm is fuelled, fed, in order that things can feed off it. That might be about celebrating successes or people and I think that is a really important thing in the company that people are in line with what the company is about, your market position, what you say you do and all those types of things. And that is obviously a lot to do with people, the way you encourage, cajole, lift people's spirits and so on. CEOs find that difficult to do all the time, I do quite a lot of that I think, in fact some people think I am having to do a lot of it. Which comes fairly naturally to me, although I find myself being more impatient these days.

Sanctional, which is a strange word, is basically somebody whose face isn't up against it, up against the detail of a particular issue. Who can land and say to the CEO and Board of Directors, "Just stand back from that for a second. Are you sure you've got that right? Have you noticed things are going really pear shaped here? You've been so close to this, you've missed what's going on." That might be what's happening in the market, with clients. The sanction is to pull people up, make them stop and think and if they are not thinking, make them think. Almost take sanction on them for not thinking. That is a fundamental Chairman quality. It's not about just chairing the odd meeting but about throwing something into the pot and saying, "I think you have forgotten about this".

Do you prioritise your time?

Prioritising is important and I'm probably too soft in that regard, I'd always invite people to come and chat it through rather than tell them to go and sort it out. Quality time is important and making the right decisions on priorities. There is a view that as a business leader you should never be copied on an email. If you have something to say to the CEO, say it, don't just make him pick it up by copying him in on it.

Do you agree with that?

I don't know if I agree, but the ways in which people communicate in business these days with comments flying around the airwaves, it's so easy to just copy someone in and that isn't necessarily a way of tackling an issue, you're just offloading it.

Talking of things flying round, did you find it difficult to clear your mind of all that 'white noise' in the business? Did you consciously try and manage that?

I tried to constantly manage it but I didn't have a strategy to manage it. I think managing that kind of throughput of detail is very much what a CEO does, because that enables them to keep a measure on the business and make adjustments all the time. It was very much my philosophy as CEO of BDP. It was never "let's take these five things and you all go off and do them and let me know when they're done". To me, there is constant tweaking and pulling and adjusting. So, I think there are other things that come within that. When I say I'm taking a chunk of time so that I can prepare another line of argument, another strategy, think around a big business planning issue, that's when you need to be disciplined. That's when you say, "right, I'm going away for five days, tie up the ship and just keep sailing in that direction".

Are you a reader of management books?

Not particularly, I do like the Malcolm Gladwell view of things. I like the way he stands back and looks at things from a different perspective over long time continuums. Asking, "why is this happening to business leaders here, when it's to do with education there?". I like that approach to stand back and connect the dots, rather than just deal with the singular dot.

Do you regularly try to stimulate your mind by exposing yourself to different types of ideas?

No.

Do you see any value in it?

No, not really. I liked to try and switch off which I found difficult. If I didn't switch off I became a bear. If you're Prime Minister or Arsene Wenger, leaders of part of something bigger than what I did at BDP, I wonder how on earth they switch off.

Are you good at switching off?

I used to be good but became worse at it over the last three years of my tenure. It was passion. I hated things not working, I hated things not succeeding, I hated losing projects or people. So, when you are in that very difficult world it got me in the gut. If we lost a project or made someone redundant it would hurt me. I think that is a big weakness of mine (between me and you) because you can only take so much of that.

Did you spend much time with clients? How did you see your role in this respect?

One of the big fears I had when I become CEO and what a former partner said to me was, "do not lose the connection with what you do". As a service industry, BDP works for clients, so I very deliberately tried to have a project interest if I could. So, for the first five years I had Liverpool One. The other thing is you can become too locked in, too insular, and you know when things don't go well the clients are going to come to you and if you're not equipped, not au fait with the world of design, building, contracts, you become useless and I didn't like the thought of becoming useless! So I think it's important to be au fait with what clients are thinking, what's happening in the various marketplaces you work in and I think that actually becomes quite a good selling proposition for the firm. If you are talking to someone who doesn't expect you to know something and you know it, they are quite impressed by the way in which the communication works within the firm.

What about business development, did you retain a hand in that?

I did. For many years I was actually president of BCSC, the shopping centre thing, so I interfaced with clients on that all the time.

From previous conversations I know that you thought about how you could help people who were not naturally business development people tackle that part of their roles, as they developed their careers. Can you talk about that?

BDP have a sector-led organisation and we tried to strengthen the sectors a bit more by giving the sector heads more authority and influence in making the right decisions in terms of the way they approached the market. We tried to push that quite hard to take the temptation away from people to keep an opportunity to themselves and see if they can win it, instead open it out and let someone else take that judgment, and it worked. In fact, in this day and age it's become more critical that there is a specialism, BDP are seriously succeeding in hospitals, education has become difficult because of the schools programme decisions in the UK but the firm are now being engaged as hospital designers all around the world, and we only got back into hospitals ten years ago.

Has the firm's standing as hospital experts come about from a concerted strategy to be that?

Yes, absolutely. BDP grew in the '60s and '70s largely through hospital work, in the '80s we got out, the public sector was in a race to the bottom, consciously or subconsciously the firm got out of it and in the early '00s it was Roy's decision to get back in. Then Roy left and I said we'll continue to try and get back into hospitals, I actually bought a company to try and help us, and we succeeded.

Has making the right acquisitions been an important part of the firm's success?

It is fundamentally important but difficult to get right, certainly for the BDP business the moral has been, "don't pay too much". There are companies that get in a mess, they may be very talented, they have got in a mess through succession planning, work in progress, debts, whatever it might be. The fundamentals might still be good. I would much prefer to take a firm like that and add it to BDP and make it better than to take a successful firm and graft it onto BDP in a country. Because I think that is a much harder thing to do and I think there is much more at stake. Because you've paid serious money and the return that you are wanting to get on that, the valuation of the business then makes it a much harder thing to achieve.

Do you have any particular learning about successfully integrating acquisitions?

If there is any doubt about turning it into a BDP brand or your own brand as quickly as possible because the existing owners don't want it like that or that's not the right thing to do for the market, then don't do it. That immediate shift I think is really important.

Did you have a clear view of the BDP brand? Do you see brand custodianship and development as a key part of the CEO role?

Yes and yes. We had a clear idea of the brand; you have to be part of it and aligned to it otherwise you just get lost and are making decisions for different reasons. You are what you are and need to build on that and act with integrity (as you've always told me!). It's not about a branding exercise it's about the values and so on and I think this is so, so true and I think you have to live and breathe that as a Director of the firm, regardless of whether you are the CEO and the job is to make sure everyone else lives it and breathes it as well. I think they do; you have to keep it simple, there is a danger of over philosophising it, particularly in this world where we love to turn architecture into poetry and vice versa. I think brand is important and you have to be single-minded about it.

Think about your biggest failures, what did you learn from those experiences?

I think I have probably alluded to it, if you are thinking about a big acquisition, think about what could go wrong, don't just get carried away by the business plan and not just what could go right but what might go wrong.

What advice did you give to your successor?

This is more of a procedural thing, but I thought it would be an interesting idea for the handover to be third partied, extracting what I felt about failures or success or whatever, I thought that needed extracting in a different type of way. Just sitting down with my successor John McManus, I don't think I would have given a very good handover. My handover from Roy was, "see ya"! It was extraordinary! I worked with Roy very closely so perhaps he didn't think we needed to do anything more. I think the only thing he said was, "you need to keep people smiling", it wasn't a hand over about lessons learned and I think that would be a big danger.

I don't know if this is a business practice, or a management technique, if you think about the ego of the person who is exiting, and the ego and ambition of the new person coming in and the importance of continuity, the imparting of the deepest thoughts around fragilities, ambitions, it's really, really critical and I bet people don't do that very well.

The person going might have been unseated, he might have been challenged, he might have been just worn out, done, I'm out of here, heading for the golf course. You really need to break down all thoughts and potential influences to say 'well what you have learned is really important' and don't let that go and if you can't pass on at least half of it then you have wasted all the things you have learned and absorbed along the way.

How would you like your tenure as CEO to be remembered?

He made a difference in terms of the big picture; the firm was in a better place than it was when he began.

Since our initial interview you have retired and handed over to John McManus. Before you retired, you also saw through the sale of BDP to the Japanese engineering consultancy Nippon Koei. Tell me a little about the thought process behind the sale and how it has worked?

To be honest, initially there wasn't a thought process as we had never previously looked to sell. However, the inquiry triggered a response to a long term question for BDP, namely "were we serious about becoming an international firm?".

For over 30 years BDP had tried different ways of developing an international presence. But as a privately funded partnership there was always the dividing pull of long term investment against shorter term gains. These shorter term gains were really BDP's historic success - adapting brilliantly to, and succeeding in, its UK market.

After the 2008 crash, but long before it had any real impact on the firm's success, we made a strategic decision that we could not achieve further growth in the UK market. I recall making a speech to a directors conference in 2009 which had a simple theme - that in ten years' time we could not remain the same kind of firm as we had been for the previous 30 years. So we embarked on opening new studios in mainland Europe (the Netherlands), India (Delhi), Abu Dhabi, and China (Shanghai), partly through acquisition and simply setting up shop. This taught us a great deal, developed an internationalism to the BDP brand, and opened our synapses for future opportunity. We also learnt that, even with this platform, there was a continued and exacerbated leadership and investment stretch. We never contemplated a sale to achieve international acceleration, but after a few years of a broader strategic base, opened synapses, and a fair portion of happenstance, when the approach came from NK, the opportunity and the fit became startlingly obvious.

How has it worked? I should point out here that by the time of the sale, I had handed on the Chief Executive baton to John McManus. John drove the process, supported by the Board (which still included me) with a brilliant clarity of purpose. I experienced the first two years of the relationship developing and learning. From the outset, NK were true to their word, hugely respectful of the strengths and personality of the firm, and helped drive the development of the BDP brand to new locations such as Canada and Singapore. They have allowed the BDP leadership almost complete autonomy. How has it worked? Brilliantly.

What is your sense of how well the handover to John went?

John was my intended successor. When I advised him of this, he was initially surprised, or maybe he was being deliberately modest, in a Scotsman kind of way. "How can I do the job from a Glasgow base?" he asked. "John, you are going to spend more time away from your base than in it, so it really doesn't matter" was my reply. I'm pretty sure he would agree that turned out to be the truth. The main handover was a heart to heart chat in a pub in North London; not quite sure why, but it seemed like a good place from which to look at the firm both holistically and in detail, and to consider how the handover should happen. His main question was to ask what was I going to do? "John, you'll be the Chief Exec, mate, you decide." He asked me to return to the leadership of the southern region of BDP, including my beloved London studio, something I was truly delighted to do. So with the groundwork done, John just got on with it, ably supported by a truly wonderful Finance Director, Heather Wells, who had helped me go in the right direction for the previous decade. They have driven the firm to ever greater success, which makes me hugely proud (and with only an occasional and fleeting tinge of envy).

Are you enjoying retirement and do you miss work? I understand you do some mentoring?

I am truly loving the time and space of retirement, and the freedom to do what we chose. Sometimes I miss the buzz, but quickly realise that for me, the other side of buzz was always a pressure to push, and that's what I was happy to give up. I miss some of the people, especially the younger generations, who are developing and emerging as future leaders of the firm.

I have taken on a few roles in the charity trustee world, and mentoring young professionals in the property world – both of which are very rewarding.

Looking back now, what would be the single best piece of advice you would give a young person starting out on their career?

Have a big picture of where you see yourself being in fifteen or more years ahead. Think about it, refine it, state it, but don't overplan it - your talents and sense of direction will be an iterative guide. Find people and business cultures who have integrity and values, and stick with them.

And you're welcome to come and have a chat.

PETER DRUMMOND

"

My drive is linked to my independence of spirit, I think. Also perhaps because of my childhood experiences, I grew up in a community of Hungarian refugees in London who had lost everything, but were so positive. That foundation meant that I was very driven.

"

SOPHIE DARANYI

INTERVIEWED 24TH JUNE 2020

Back in 1997 I recruited Sophie into my marketing team at Seagram from a position in corporate communications. She was keen to learn about brand marketing and proved to be a very quick learner.

After Seagram she joined Haygarth to launch its PR department and quickly rose to become Managing Director of the group and later CEO and Chair. She led Haygarth's sale to marketing services multinational Omnicom Group in 2014 and was then made President of RAPP UK until 2016.

Subsequently, she was appointed Global CEO of the Omnicom Commerce Group. In this role she oversees four agencies (Haygarth, Integer, TracyLocke and TPN), driving and co-ordinating multi-channel commerce and retail strategies at Group level at Omnicom.

Talk to me a little about your current role.

I'm CEO of Omnicom Commerce Group globally, responsible for setting and managing our strategic direction, developing our portfolio offer and our competencies across a collection of agencies which employ 2,500 people across the world.

The thing that's interesting is that I effectively created the role because I felt strongly about the changes in the way people shop and how as a group we could better serve the sector. I pulled together a market review, developed a strategic framework and ultimately ended up creating and leading the Omnicom Commerce Group.

It was initially a challenging role because as I've suggested you have to influence without direct authority and I am used to leading an organisation with its own P+L. I've needed to adapt my management style and reflect on how I work to achieve what I think is right for the business overall. That requires a different mindset and skillset.

What are your views on what's happening in retail today?

What's interesting is that in the old world you had a clear path of influence at consumer level from awareness to consideration and purchase, very clear steps. Today conversion and awareness are completely merged. I can buy a t-shirt on Instagram in a minute. I think either on the client or agency side, to optimise conversion, you need a mixture of multichannel skills. A lot of my work involves thinking about how people buy across physical, digital and social boundaries and how to optimise different areas of marketing more effectively to offer a seamless, rich experience for consumers. I love it because it's changing all the time. There are new tech capabilities emerging every day and a lot of new 'challenger' brands in the retail space. It's a very exciting space to be in at the moment.

I also really enjoy the challenge of getting people to adapt and develop the way they work, challenging the status quo and, as you know, at times that's quite complicated in a big organisation, but we're getting there.

How do you see high streets in five to ten years' time?

I think they will need to be about more than the purchase. It's about the experience, entertainment, a reason to visit and spend time at a retail destination for reasons beyond simply buying stuff. Though it's tough on the high street, people enjoy shopping and we forget that. E-commerce is really growing in some categories more than others; people do need inspiration and they do like shopping, so I think that understanding the mechanics of experience and exploration, sociability and exploring the reasons beyond simply shopping itself will be important drivers of retail over the next few years.

I was talking with a developer recently who said that the UK has 40% excess capacity in retail space. Town centres were once mixed-use communities but now they are very retail focused and that needs rethinking. How can mixed-use communities be created for the modern world?

I agree that it's an important challenge. I think there is a point about community and locality. Covid has seen a lot of people turning back to their local shops which is a good thing in many ways. Tomorrow's retail will operate in communities with new norms and dynamics and that will throw up a whole new array of opportunities.

I'm interested in your comments about the matrix leadership challenge. How do you think people would describe you as a leader?

I think they would say that I'm very open and honest, straightforward, which is a strength and a weakness, especially when working with Americans. I like to work in a direct way and that doesn't always sit well. There's more corporate hierarchy and sometimes there's an expectation that you follow orders. I think sometimes in corporate life it's whether you tell people what you think they want to hear, or whether you tell them what you really think. I say what I think.

I would hope people would say that I listen well. I think they would say I have strong opinions. I'd like to think they would say that I've got integrity and am very professional and I'm sure they would say I'm pretty driven!

Where does that drive come from?

We've spoken about this before, I think it comes from my childhood. My dad was a refugee who left Hungary in 1949 just before the borders shut with the Russians. His family had enjoyed a very privileged life in Hungary but they ended up in Switzerland in more straitened circumstances. His dad died from a heart attack in the late '50s and Dad, along with his mum and his brother, moved to England where they were supported by friends. He couldn't go to university because he didn't have any money so he worked in a variety of low level jobs and ended up at a screen printing company in Fulham called Sericol. He eventually became Marketing Director and then Managing Director and found himself running the business; he oversaw their business in the United States for a while too.

Did you move to the US as a family?

No, I've always been very independent. I left home when I was seventeen, my mum left us when I was fifteen and it was not great. I never thrived at school. I left home because I was unhappy at home and not enjoying school, so I lived with friends. I did my A-Levels and I got a place at Manchester Polytechnic to read History, Art and Design. In the year between I worked and I hit my groove. I got a job as a PA in a PR Agency and found out I was good at it. I could get things done and quite quickly became an Account Executive. I went to university for the first year but for a variety of reasons I thought I'd rather be working. So, I left university. Dad told me to follow my instinct at the time, which turned out to be good advice.

You said you weren't good at school but you're extremely bright. Why do you think that was? Was it because your home-life was a bit troubled, were you just not disposed to the discipline or did you fall in with the wrong crowd?

I don't know, Chris, it's really interesting. My mum tells me I was bad at Primary School apparently, she says that at one point the teacher said I was totally illiterate and innumerate, "we don't know what to do with her"! [Laughs] I don't know what it was, maybe there would be a name for it now but I did find a way to succeed.

Long story short, my drive is linked to my independence of spirit I think. I remember getting overdrawn at university and having a massive argument with my dad, him saying he wanted to pay it off and I wouldn't let him. I was living on about £10 a week. I'm the middle child, I was always the one who 'coped'. When my mum left, I ran the household, I took that on. You know what it's like with families, you create roles for yourself. I think my childhood experiences at the time and growing up in a community of refugees helped shape me. There were a lot of Hungarian refugees in London who had lost everything, but they were so positive and nobody was bitter. Some people had lost their liberty and even as a child that was quite moving. I think that foundation meant that I was very driven, I was a daddy's girl who wanted to be successful at whatever I did and make him proud of me.

Did you want to emulate him?

Not literally. I spoke to someone recently, a really good strategist, and he explained to me that he really wanted to be a CEO. I asked why and he said his dad was a CEO. I thought that was a ridiculous reason and told him so! In my case I certainly wanted to make my dad proud of me and to be a success but didn't set my sights on being a CEO specifically. I just grew into things and stepped into the gap when the gap appeared.

Has it been harder for you to progress as a woman in business?

I think so. I am of a certain generation, I'm very optimistic that it is changing behind me but I've spent much of my career being the only woman in the boardroom and rather sadly I am still in that situation. What strikes me is that, certainly in your mid-twenties as a woman, you have to think about your gravitas and how you come across. I know this sounds wrong but sadly, I think if you're an attractive woman you have to consider how you're taken seriously. I've seen this in agency life, where I have actually sat down with some of my team to say, "think about how you come across in a meeting. Don't wear a jangly bracelet or flick your hair". I don't mean don't be proud of being feminine and being a woman but do be conscious that you don't want your femininity to distract from your gravitas, and that's a hard balance to achieve sometimes.

It's crazy really but it's true, certainly in corporate life and you know I originally worked in PR so the opportunity was to be seen as 'fluffy' and I was conscious of that! It sounds like I was very premeditated, but I think it's natural, it's intuition that you use. You think about how you come over and make sure you're not seen as a flighty person. Later in my career, when I was already at CEO level, I remember someone asking me if I wanted to take on HR or Communications. Why would I want to sit in that corner? I think there are some stereotyped roles that senior women often get put into but I learned that I have very strong commercial capabilities and I have run businesses for a long time now.

Do you still see those sexist pre-conceptions?

Even now, what worries me more with the whole "Me Too" situation is that it has meant that overt sexism in the workplace is gone because it would be called out immediately, but everyday casual sexism is still there, unconscious sexism. I'll give an example. I had a new boss within Omnicon a few years ago, the first time I met him (he didn't know me at all) his second question to me was whether I wanted to work full-time or if I would like to work part-time and spend the rest of my time working for a charity. I asked him why on earth he would think that? He wouldn't have asked that of a man.

I remember sitting on a global Board and looking around the room and thinking I am probably the only person here who doesn't have a stay-at-home wife. The way you work as a woman is different, it just generally is. I am proud to be a senior woman. I now find myself in a major multinational organisation as a senior woman and I'm really thinking about the responsibilities that brings, making sure I promote and encourage other women. How best do I mentor and champion them? Am I leading by example as well as I can?

Interestingly, if I look back on my career, without counting, I've hired lots of people and I'm fairly certain I've hired more women than men.

You're absolutely right and that team you built at Seagram was one of the best teams I've worked in. It actually was very diverse, not just by gender but by character. Many are still very good friends of mine. You brought together a really good mixture of people and we were a great team. I've learned not to just recruit people who are like me. I value people who are very different, who give you a different perspective. I may have learned that from you!

What do you wish you'd understood at the start of your career that you understand now?

You don't have to be perfect all the time. I wasn't so ambitious that I wanted to be a CEO, but I always wanted to be the best that I could be; I think that's the best mentality to have. Sometimes I would push myself to be perfect and I've learned that's not sustainable or realistic. My advice to myself would be do the best you can, which doesn't mean you have to be outstanding all the time. Choose your battles, think about where you're really going to push hard or where you're going to let things go. You do need resilience but saving your energy for the right challenges, the most important ones, is important.

What's the best piece of advice you've ever received?

It's about taking people with you. My current boss is very good at that. I'm naturally very driven, I want to get things done, probably impatient. He's very good at working with people to let them verbalise what their concerns are, allowing them to come with him. I continue to try and learn that.

The second one I learned from you, and I'm not just saying that because I am talking to you. I learned to anticipate the questions that would be asked of me when I presented a specific recommendation. You would always ask the most difficult questions, which made me prepare and be really thorough before I went in to meet you. I still carry that with me and I am very surprised when people come to me without being really well prepared.

When I was CEO at Haygarth I had a Non-Executive Director called Alan McWalter who was ex-board Marks and Spencer Group. He was a fantastic counsellor to me as a CEO. My advice to others would be to find someone who can be your objective counsellor. A lot of people think (especially in leadership) that they need to solve every problem by themselves but we all need someone who is a good foil, especially when you are in that senior leadership role. Having someone to bounce things off was really valuable. I have enjoyed good partnerships like that through my working career and I've always set up structures where people have that kind of support.

Have you ever had a coach or an official mentor in any of your roles?

Yes, once, and it was really interesting. I am ashamed to admit that for years I didn't know why people bothered with it and then I reached a point during a period of tumultuous change two or three years ago when I felt I'd benefit from it. I met someone through Omnicom who was fantastic. What I loved about her was that she understood the industry, she understood our roles. I personally paid for it instead of getting Omnicom to pay for it because I wanted it to be mine. It was great, I really learned from that experience and it helped me overcome a few big challenges at the time. So, yes, I have done it and if I had lots of spare cash I would probably do it again!

If you think back on your career to date, what were the pivotal moments?

Well there was a period of personal evolution and there are moments where you really learn and you come into your own. One of my clichés is that 'the worst of times can be the best of times'.

In 2008, Haygarth had an absolute car crash of a year; we lost a cornerstone client that was worth a third of our revenue. We were about 150 people, £10 million and it was absolute carnage, I was CEO at the time. The business changed a lot and a lot of people who had been in the business for a long time had left including the Founders, so I was pretty much on my own at the top.

There was a period when I would go through the cashflow with my CFO every morning because we were that close to tipping over, and I realised that I was good in a crisis. I remember picking up the marker in the board meeting and saying, "Right, this is what we're going to do!" It was really tough, challenging personally; back to the point where I said you don't have to be invincible personally, in that moment I felt that I did have to be invincible, because everyone was looking to me and you do have to be strong in that situation. I think if I had gone around looking woeful all the time everyone would have probably gone home. There are times where you do need to lead by example. We went through a voluntary redundancy programme, we made a third of the business redundant, we had to reshape the business, renegotiate our rent, it was absolutely full on.

I led from the front and got us through a very tough time. For the first time, I had ultimate authority and leadership and I rose to the challenge. My qualities of energy and optimism came into their own. You certainly need energy in difficult times and you also need to believe that you will come out as a better business, and we did. I learned that if you're doing the right thing and people can see you're trying to do your best they will follow you. I was being very open with the team all the time. That year we won a couple of amazing clients. We also made The Sunday Times's "Best Companies to Work For" list. To achieve that in a year with such challenges is probably the proudest moment in my career so far.

That was a pivotal year for me and a humbling one as well because people can be amazing when you ask big things of them and are prepared to lead from the front. We went into a period of sustained growth which lasted for five years afterwards, I'm proud of that legacy.

Let's talk briefly about strategy. What's your take on strategy?

To have an effective strategy you have to be clear and explicit about what you are trying to achieve. I think one of the reasons I'm relatively good at what I do is that I am able to focus on that. I work back from the outcome I want to achieve and piece together the strategy to achieve it. It's very easy to write a business plan and then put it in a drawer and forget about it, but it's not an academic exercise. Articulating a strategy plan is just the start. Good leadership is about being able to keep focused on your strategy, keep coming back to it like a dog with a bone and then find a way to deliver it. Another thing I am conscious of is also being able to demonstrate tangible progress. However you articulate your strategy, you must make sure you are measuring your business or your team's activity against it, reporting back, holding people's feet to the flame who have accepted responsibility for delivering their part of it, and of course it's very important to learn and adapt as you go.

How do you piece your strategy together?

It's a bit old school but if I'm saying this is the vision for our agency, I want it to grow by x% and we want employee engagement to grow at y%. I would think about the three or four main areas of focus that we need to deliver on to achieve that. You have your swim lanes of activity that support the outcome and you need discipline and clear lines of responsibility to drive progress in each of those.

Do you revisit your strategy every year?

At Omnicom we have a quarterly meeting with the Group CEO. I literally go in and say this is what I told you last time, this is the progress we have made, this is what has worked, this is what hasn't worked and this is our next set of priorities. When I was running agencies directly we would do that on a quarterly basis. I think approaching the year in quarters is an incredibly useful way to make sure that you're maintaining momentum.

Do you think that most CEOs are good strategists?

That's a really interesting question because in very general terms, if you think of a Venn diagram of strategists and CEOs there aren't that many people that sit in the middle. When I think about people who are very good at strategy in my world, they're often individualistic, quite maverick, they've got a very high IQ and a low EQ (this is a huge generalisation by the way). But they're hugely valuable because they can think in a different way. The person that I was talking about before who aspired to be CEO I saw as a fantastic strategist but perhaps not a leader of people.

Did he follow your advice?

Well he's a CEO now, we'll see how it goes! I think that a CEO does need to be an inspiring leader. Some strategists don't have the people skills and some CEOs don't have the strategy skills.

Do you know what your Myer Briggs profile is?

ENTJ. I'm literally 50/50 intuition and logic, I think I'm more people focused, but my logic always brings me back, it's quite interesting. Do you remember at Seagram they held a skills assessment day? The one thing I remember from the report was that they said I was the one person who talked about learning from my mistakes. I obviously had the ability to be open-minded, I'd like to think that's an important part of my skillset.

A good business needs a leadership team which is complementary, it's very rare to find an individual who ticks every box.

I agree. The other thing I've learned is that people don't really change and you shouldn't expect them to. Because of that I try to play to my team's strengths. We all need to be conscious that we have our particular strengths and weaknesses. I have never seen someone totally transform. I think we've all seen people evolve and I certainly hope I've evolved but I think that when people think they can change people's behaviour fundamentally they're wrong. But getting the right team combination is always key.

Do you use your intuitive sense of a person's character and style in recruitment or some more formal way of assessing those things?

Well, the reason that CEO asked me if I wanted to work part-time and work for charity was his perception of me. He obviously thought I was some middle-class, middle aged woman toying around running an agency, so you need to be careful about making superficial judgements, but in interview situations I am a good listener and observer, I ask good questions. I like to think I am good at assessing character and strengths, so to that degree I use my intuition.

What do you think makes people productive and effective at work?

We tend to know, for example, if people are more productive in the morning or the afternoon and you should work around it. Really you need to know yourself and what makes you productive and your boss and your colleagues should understand that too. For me it's about having a deadline, now I create my own deadlines! I know that I will walk around something, I'll percolate it for ages so I create a meeting with a client to make myself do it otherwise I'm not going to do it. I think there's your environment, time, deadlines and then there's the general passion to get things done. We're all going to be pretty good at doing the thing we love doing and then there's stuff we don't want to do that drags behind but we have to do it. You need to get both things done.

Are you an outcome-based manager?

Good question. I used to be such a clock watcher boss and get annoyed at people arriving late for meetings. But it's ironic because, when I went to work at Haygarth, my daughter Bella was six months old and I remember saying to them you don't need to worry about what time I'm in the office, I'll get the work done. Productivity is just about the ability to get the work done in a good way and anyone who thinks it's about time these days (especially at the moment) is simply wrong. I think you're seeing in your business and we're seeing in our business that productivity has gone up during the pandemic, not down. I think it is very much about getting the job done in your way, playing to your strengths and dealing with your circumstances. Getting something done quickly is not necessarily getting something done well, I'd rather it takes a bit longer and is something that I can be proud of versus just getting it off the desk, which often happens as you know. I will give work back to people and say don't give it to me until you're a 100% with it because it annoys me to receive work that's not as good as it could be.

Do you think organisations, not specifically advertising agencies, will be very different in ten years' time? If so, what do you think those differences might be?

That's a great question, I haven't put a huge amount of thought into it. I'm thinking of being on the beach at that point [laughs]. It goes back to something we touched on earlier about hierarchy and organisational structure. There are non-hierarchical organisations in some parts of the world and it's interesting how they function. I'm not convinced they always function well actually. I think collaboration is really important but you do have to have someone at the top ultimately who's prepared to make the tough decisions. You will always need that.

I think expectations around careers are very different from the way we looked at things when we started out. People's paths and their expectations are much less linear. Their aspirations might be different, we see it with our own kids. I admire their ambition to have a much better work life balance, I just wonder whether the give and take will change to allow them to achieve it. I've managed many talented people who I know have great potential say to me that they don't want a senior role because they don't want the pressure. People need to find ways to cope with stress and it's certainly unhealthy to be in high stress situations constantly. On the other hand, adrenaline in business can be a very good thing. I hope that people are able to 'know themselves' and then hopefully build a career which suits them, rather than just do what's expected. Real self-awareness is actually quite rare but I do think people can be coached in it. Like we talked about earlier regarding strategy, start with what you want to achieve (in life), figure out what's important to you, play to your strengths and work back from that. Build that life if you can.

When you look back on your career so far, would you change anything?

No, I wouldn't actually. I'm very lucky I've had a wonderful time and worked in and with some great teams. When I started out, I was learning and soaking it up. Seagram was great for me actually, my corporate communications role before I joined your marketing team was really interesting, you learned how to deal with different stakeholders. Even as a junior person I dealt with very senior people, sitting in on calls at Board level was a fantastic privilege at that early stage of my career. I've made the most of my skills and personality and responded to opportunities as they have opened up. It may not have been a 'textbook' career but I've enjoyed it immensely.

What do you hope your legacy will be?

I can proudly say that at Haygarth I left a good legacy. I left the business in better shape than when I joined and it's run by a really good team who all grew up with me or around me. It's a successful ongoing business, the culture I inherited I also successfully handed on. I definitely feel that I left a really positive legacy there.

As a female CEO, I hope that I have led by example, showing that you can be your own person, have your own style, be a woman and not have to become a macho A-type. We spoke about this at our last lunch together, I think that the profile of leaders has completely changed from what it was when we worked together earlier in our careers. I am or was a quite pioneering woman. I'm proud I've done that in the context of having a very happy family life and I hope that can be some kind of inspiration to others, because it's tough when you are a dad or a mum to hold it all together.

I'm really proud of the fact I've had a good career, but the most important things, my friends and family and the fact I have a good balance I hope is testament to the fact that you can have some success but also take care of the things that are really important. That comes down to family and relationships.

"

I like telling stories. I like trying to get people to see things through our eyes, the logic that can help solve the problem. That's why I was born to work here really, because logic is what I'm good at and I can be a good storyteller.

"

GRANT BROOKER

INTERVIEWED 4TH APRIL 2019

This conversation is with Grant Brooker, a Senior Director at Globally renowned architects firm Foster + Partners, famous for buildings including the Shanghai Bank in Hong Kong, Wembley Stadium, The Gherkin and many more. They have a reputation for technically accomplished and elegant design solutions and are one of the UK service sector's most admired international premium brands.

Grant and I became friends when we were both living in Hong Kong in the early 1990s. I was working as Marketing Director for Diageo (then United Distillers) and he, as a young man, was leading the project to design and construct Hong Kong's new Airport. The project lasted six years. Now that he's one of an influential handful of Directors on the Foster + Partners Board, I was interested to hear about what it's like to work with a famous and famously driven founder and to understand how such a well-known, distinctive and successful organisation was built. As well as, of course, to talk about how Grant's own career has developed and explore his thoughts on success and leadership.

Tell me a little about Foster + Partners and its history?

Norman launched the business in 1967 as Foster Associates shortly after leaving Team 4. Team 4 itself was set up in 1963 – it was Norman, Wendy Cheesman who eventually became his wife, Richard Rogers and Su Brumwell who also eventually Richard married. They all met at Yale as I recall. One of their first projects was a house called Creek Vean, it was commissioned by Marcus Brumwell (Su's father) who was founder of the Design Research Unit. They also designed Skybreak House in Radlett; the interior is featured in the film 'A Clockwork Orange'!

Afterwards in 1977 Richard established Richard Rogers and Partners which, following his passing in 2021, still continues; they have designed buildings like the Lloyds Building and the Millennium Dome. It's quite a different firm from ours today but very well regarded in its own space.

Foster Associates became Foster + Partners in 1999. In 2007 3i took a stake as part of an expansion strategy, but we bought their share back in 2014. The business was then wholly owned by our one-hundred and forty partners and that in turn enabled us to form a new partnership with Hennick and Co., the private investment firm established by the Hennick family. Their investment has allowed us to continue to expand our ownership and accelerate our growth. That's a whistle stop tour for you!

I remember that you joined the firm in 1988. Tell me about what you know of the early years before you joined, how did the firm begin to establish itself?

In the early days they became known for designing very contemporary and technical buildings at a time when that was not common. A notable one was the Willis Faber Building in Ipswich, also the Sainsburys Centre, but it was the Shanghai Bank Building in Hong Kong which really put the firm on the map. It was transformational for the practice and the tallest building in Hong Kong at that time (1985). Foster + Partners went from designing a three-storey office building in Ipswich to a fifty-storey skyscraper for one of the most powerful banking corporations in the world.

Later, when I joined the practice we had won Stansted Airport, but otherwise in London the BBC HQ project had been cancelled and things were a little quiet. A lot of energy in the preceding years had obviously gone into the Hong Kong Bank Project. That's always a challenge for a relatively small architectural practice, you need to carry on winning other work while existing projects consume a huge amount of organisational energy and talent. A lot of businesses get swept away because they can't cope with those dual pressures. We managed that and we have had a philosophy since that we want to keep growing. We take the view that we want to retain and develop people and to do that you need to look at different opportunities to grow as a business all the time.

Other practices scale up and down, perhaps to keep their overhead exposure manageable, but I think to grow a healthy and sustainable, world-class business you need the best people and you have to give them the opportunity to constantly develop. They can't do the same role all the time, that seems to me the flaw of the static office model, you do one building and when that's finished you move onto another one, and that's how people move through the organisation, but it's snail slow. To me that feels very old fashioned, whereas if you have a world view that you will keep taking on more work there are more opportunities for people to grow and the excitement of being a part of that organisation is maintained, but of course you must take on the right work. Our Board of Directors make those decisions directly.

We look with a very hard light on the projects we take on. While we have offices all over the world, they are not commissioning offices, we decide what to take on at board level.

What are the decision-making criteria in that respect?

It's absolutely about quality and interest. Most of us have run offices overseas, I ran Hong Kong for six years and while running a local office you will have fallow periods and you're looking for work to take on to fill the books and keep everybody going. We're much more dispassionate from London and we won't take on the work unless we think it's the right kind of work. If there's not enough, we will close an office and bring everyone back home.

How is the organisation structured today?

It changed after the private equity play in 2007. We had a valuable business with a single shareholder, and we needed to unlock that. Today all partners have equity. Six of us Directors run the studios, two of the founding Directors operate as a design review panel. We have our Financial Director who also serves as our Managing Partner, and Norman, who remains the largest individual shareholder and is of course our Chairman.

Tell me about Norman. What makes him special? What is it that enabled him to build such a major business from these relatively modest beginnings?

He is relentless, tireless, beyond driven.

Does that make him a challenging person to work for?

Can be, I've been doing it for a long time - but we always say, "it doesn't seem to matter how hard you go at something, he'll go at it harder". He has that passion.

What's his motivation?

He cares.

He cares about the business or the buildings?

Always the buildings - design, design, design, always design. Making a building as good as it can possibly be, that's always been the thing for him.

What would you say is the most valuable thing you've learned from him?

His approach to design. He sees it as a problem that needs solving and he conducts a relentless examination of the problem to find the best solution.

In search of perfection?

Yes, that's what I've learned from him. You take a problem and break it down, look at it, look at all of the constituent parts, edit again and again and again, throw away the stuff you don't need. It's a process of ruthless editing and control.

Like a distillation process?

Absolutely it's a distillation process and you must be able to work without fear.

What would you be afraid of?

Designers don't like having their ideas challenged!

Were you afraid early on?

I suppose I was.

Can you explain?

Very early on in my career, we were approached by another developer wanting to design the new Headquarters for the television company ITN. ITN had the site and the developer had bought it from them since ITN were struggling a little to understand how to do the development themselves. I went to the first meeting with the developer and ended up running the project.

I learned a very important early lesson from Norman on that early project. I assumed I think; everyone assumes when you are working in a 'name' office that I'd cracked it. I naturally, and very mistakenly, assumed at that very early age the firm had recognised my talent as a designer, but of course they hadn't, I didn't realise how little I knew but everyone else was very aware. At the outset of the ITN project, I presented what I and the team thought was a brilliant idea. The client hated it and wouldn't be persuaded by my force of personality.

What happened?

I came back and I'm thinking that the end result definitely will be that the partner that I'm working with or Norman himself is going to get on the phone to the client and just pretty much tell them how it is - "don't muck around with us, we're great designers" (this is a common fantasy among young designers). So, I was absolutely delighted to stumble into Norman when I came back, he asked how things were going and I told him straight away that I had endured a very difficult meeting with a client, and he didn't like our idea. He asked me to explain it, so I dragged the work out, put it in front of him and explained it all. He understood, and asked, "Why didn't he like it?" So, I told him, and he said, "Well he's absolutely right, isn't he?" I was confused, I didn't expect the conversation to go like this. So, he said, "Let's get together tomorrow morning" (and this must have been about six or seven o'clock in the evening) "and you can take me through some other approaches to solving the problem."

You came up with something overnight?

Yes, I got the guys together and began to brainstorm different ideas, and of course that's when you start realising that there are obviously other ways. Not just thinking about the things that the client is raising, but actually thinking about the problem from different angles. You have to break away from people's arrogance and test their intuition. The reality is that you're collecting information, balancing the requirements, there's no perfect answer. You will prioritise certain things in any answer, you will put the emphasis on different parts of the sentence and that will change its meaning and that's what you've got to do as a designer, that's design. What it also means is you can't just compromise a design, if it isn't working you have to know and say that it isn't working well and so try something else.

When you said Norman was right what was the thing that he was right about?

He was sending a message, making it very clear – in two words that you can't push something just because you want it or it intuitively appeals to you as a designer, that's not good enough, it's lazy, and that's the essential point he was making.

On the other hand, you can't compromise.

Yes, I think that's the difficulty if you just compromise the design you can bend things and say that it will still work, but it's likely not an elegant answer. When you've finished a building, you don't want someone to say, "did you ever think of doing it that way?" and think "Christ, I wish I had because that would have been brilliant"! There's no going back with a building, the time spent examining, testing and looking at options. That's your moment, that's the design, so you have to keep pushing, don't leave anything behind. If you just do things intuitively you have a spirit in the design and that's great, but you'll leave too much behind.

The qualities in Norman – relentlessness, the drive, etc. Is that what you admired about him?

Yes, but more than that he's also one of the great persuaders.

Through logic or personality?

Both, he is very focused, he hasn't maintained his position in our very competitive world by chance.

Do you think you have similar qualities? How do you think people here perceive you?

Doesn't sleep, decent person (that's important to me), does things in the right way, treats people in the right way. They should think I'm a good designer, but I should imagine they think that everyone here is a good designer, it's pretty much the price of an entrance ticket here.

Doesn't duck responsibility. I don't mind taking the lead and helping people make a decision, but leading the interaction of other designers is the most fun. I'm fairly decisive, and that can be dangerous as it's wrong to close the door too soon in this studio, so I will just make decisions in those hard moments. I suppose I possess a fearlessness, a certain self-confidence, but it's more of a belief in our collective ability to find the right answer. It's a mix, it comes out of your personality.

I don't mind standing in front of people and taking the hit if that's what's required.

You're good at managing teams?

I like the idea that we are totally inter-reliant and we're playing a team game, putting different skills together. The way we built the office is that we have far more skills than the general architectural skills, we look at it like an orchestra. We have incredible fire power around us and an amazing collection of intellect and talent, a very different set of skills that we just have to bring together to focus on the problem. Not just designers, it's everyone here that's involved in bringing something to the table.

What makes a good leader in a business like this?

One who understands the importance of collaboration and someone who's an astute listener.

So, you're a good listener?

You have to be, design is about information gathering.

Explain that a bit more?

Otherwise you're just doing drawings - you've got to understand that you're trying to solve a problem and to do that you need information.

What is the problem that you're solving?

Actually, not all clients understand what they want. Quite a lot of people want designers to solve problems that they have in their organisation and the building simply isn't capable of solving those problems. The one thing that is interesting is that if you execute the project really well it will flush out those problems and the organisation might eventually evolve positively as a result of the discovery.

What else is important as a leader?

You can't lead without motivating people, you have to be able to motivate people, to understand where they are coming from. Also, you need to have the ability to make them go the extra yard, further than they actually thought was possible, and of course they need a sense of purpose, otherwise there is no point in doing anything. Try to leave the world better than you found it – that's not a bad motivation for a builder. That said, one thing you have to be a little careful of is designers that get a little too grand and start thinking that they are social engineers, be very suspicious of that – they have their own world view. If you look at some of the great disasters post-war, a lot of architects thought they were social engineers… turns out not!

How do you divide your time as a leader in the business?

Quite a few units spent travelling, time reviewing design work, I sit in on all the design reviews that I can. Sometimes I'll be directly involved in presentations and I lead some of our relationships but not all.

You're good at presenting I should imagine.

I like telling stories. I like trying to get people to see things through our eyes, the logic that can help solve the problem. That's why I was born to work here really because logic is what I'm good at and I can be a good storyteller.

As a leader in this business how much of your time is spent on the numbers?

Not a lot, but enough. It's not that I don't think it's important. All of the teams are structured to look at resource utilisation very carefully. You've just got to remember that any fool can work for nothing, you need to make sure there is balance and make sure that you are being properly rewarded for the work you are producing. As long as you are, that's fine.

In business terms what's the best piece of advice anyone's given you and who was it?

Very early on and it was my mother. I was talking to her about a client who was an absolute firebrand, very aggressive and she said, "What a ridiculous person, if you treat people like that no one will ever *want* to work for you." She was right, treat people like that and they might work for you, but they won't *want* to work for you. If you want to succeed, people have to want to work for you. If you don't generate that, certainly in our business, then you will definitely fail.

What's the key to that?

Caring about people, seeing it from their perspective, which doesn't mean to say that I don't push people very hard and expect them to treat being here as a privilege.

I'd like to go back and hear about how you came to join the firm and your early experiences.

It was the 1980s. Around that time the firm had won a project to produce a new HQ building for the BBC on what is now the Langham Hotel site. That was to be the next big project after the Hong Kong Shanghai Bank, but then quite suddenly the project was cancelled. The BBC decided that they didn't want to be in central London after all. Ironically, thirty years later that's exactly where they are, on a site directly opposite the one we were going to develop with them. It was a massive blow for the firm at the time.

Following that disappointment, the team were very actively looking for something else and they became engaged with the King's Cross development. I'd finished college, recently qualified and had been working for Lesley Welsh at HLM for a year or so.

The team were already working on the master plan as part of a larger group of designers for King's Cross in a pitch situation. As I understand it the design had become a bit bogged down, so they came up with an alternative idea for the developer they were working with, and he thought it was fantastic.

How did the competition process work?

It was one of those big public competitions. Two developers were in the running and our (I'm saying 'our' now) developer thought that this new idea could win it for them. They said to Foster + Partners, "the design needs to be ready in two to three weeks, can you do it?". The office obviously said yes but actually turning it around in that time was almost technically impossible! What they hadn't realised was that the developer had checked the rules and discovered that whilst everyone was assuming that they could only submit one idea there was actually no limit to the number of ideas that could be submitted. So, they submitted our idea as well as the original group master plan, they effectively had two horses in the race, which changed the odds massively in their favour. We had no idea; we just assumed the developer was putting all of his money and trust in our idea, which put even more pressure on us!

At that point you weren't with the firm yet?

Not quite; while they were developing the design idea, they had to figure out how best to present it and that's when I became involved in rather an unusual way. I'd been working with one of my friends from HLM, we'd been doing schemes ourselves and to make our work look better we were doing these massive airbrush presentations. They were an ambitious exercise, rather overambitious probably, and we were roping in our friends at the weekends to cut masks for airbrushing, everything was really labour intensive. We were making these giant drawings, you know, five to six feet long and trying to look very professional.

I had another friend from college who was already at Foster + Partners, he was interested in the way that we were doing these presentations and the speed we were doing it at. They were floundering around with their two to three weeks, now down probably to two and trying to figure out how to present the work. I came in to see Gordon Graham (the Managing Partner) at my friend's request to show him what we were doing, and he said, "that's fantastic, you're hired!", which wasn't really what the conversation was about because I already had a job, but I said okay.

What happened next?

I came in, we set up a team, took over a separate office and started to produce our giant drawings. What I did was I took a week's holiday from my existing job and we just worked twenty-four hours a day. By the end of it we had most of the office working for us.

We were using unusual techniques like motor spray paints and KZ guns, all kinds of things to make these drawings come together.

Whose was the idea behind the design itself?

It's like always, the design comes from across the team. People say, "wouldn't it be better if we tried this?" and we say, "ok, let's try it". You capture people's imaginations. It was so much fun, we're all in the middle of it, making changes as we go along, seeing how it looked, changing things right up until the eleventh hour which is always the way in competitions. It's like a living thing, the energy was exhilarating, and we won it!

How much would it have cost the firm if you had lost?

Now a competition like that would cost say up to a million pounds, so then perhaps about £250,000 for our part. But remember this is a developer competition and the developer picks up a great deal of the cost, they pay the cost for us to do the presentation and submission that's part of their bid. The rules of engagement vary, in China today for example they pay your costs to develop competition submissions because people simply can't afford to be working on ideas on that kind of scale. So that kind of competition work is not money-making but it's also not a loss-making proposition. What you can't recoup is the energy you put in, you couldn't run an office just doing competitions and not winning, everyone would effectively stop - so you do need success. It also means you need to choose the ones that you compete in very carefully, because it takes a lot out of you.

Your start here came about almost by chance, a chance which you really capitalised on. Today, Foster + Partners is a more mature organisation. How do you approach recruiting people?

We have about 20,000 applications for roles here every year and so it's a big process to get the right people. In design roles it's our practice generally to recruit people with no experience. Which may sound unusual.

Why is that?

It's always been our model and the reason is clear to me now. We have a very different approach or philosophy to design here and it's born of Norman's approach to problem solving which we were talking about before. We need people to buy into that philosophy, for them to be really behind that approach and to become really adept at it. Often more experienced designers come with a different schooling and it's difficult to change it.

Can you expand?

We like our designers not to ignore their intuitive instincts but to be rigorous in testing them and looking at alternatives. That might sound very obvious, but it goes against the grain for a lot of designers. We want our people to have the confidence to really be able to test their ideas.

We obviously hire people who are good intuitive designers, but the point is that's not enough. Today we are looking at people open to that challenging design process, who are adept at using technology and we like to be able to see how they use technology to push their ideas forward. We're always interested in people that are innovating.

How does the interview process work?

It's about really connecting with them and talking about their work. I always have two of my senior partners interview a candidate together and they both have to say yes without any reservations. It's really, really hard to get an interview here and we want it to be a very positive experience for everyone who comes along. Nobody has a difficult interview, that's not our purpose, but they can be quite long and extended.

When people join the firm they tend to stay, and they stay because of the work. We pay a fair salary, but I think everybody here can leave and get more money somewhere else, that's everybody. People who work here come from all over the world because they want to experience the kind of projects that we work on. A lot of people are joining from overseas and they might come to work for us for a period of time and then go back home and take that experience with them.

Do you think the attitudes and aspirations of people joining today are very different from your own when you joined 30 years ago? Are millennials different?

People are changing constantly but I think it's over played. Perhaps they are fully focused on their own experience. Someone explained to me that in the past people worked for companies and then for individuals and now they work for themselves and I don't think that's true. I think people still work for their teams. Relationships between them as a team are very much today as they were when I began all those years ago.

The thing that I do appreciate is that young people have different pressures today. They are more exposed more often - they have social media (not the case in the 1980s) and that brings new pressures and perhaps they feel they have to succeed more quickly. When I first started working the general line was - you look for responsibility, you do the job and eventually the position and title will follow. I try to work to that policy. People have a little less patience today, but that's not something that's happened this year.

Are young people today less loyal to firms than previous generations were?

I don't think so; people are not stupid. If they are doing great work on an interesting project, learning, growing, building their experience and progressing – they tend to stay. Our people stay because they want to develop themselves and we help them do that.

What makes a firm like yours valuable do you think? You have defined your ambition more in terms of growth, the quality of your design and in terms of making an impact on people's lives, but I'm interested in where you think the value lies in Foster + Partners?

I understand, and of course as a partnership we are all interested in that to a degree.

For me it's more than a distinctive brand and a strong order book, it's the scale of the work that we have completed and our potential to grow the business in different areas. Those are the things that people value, I believe.

What's at the heart of your brand?

Our difference essentially; our different way of doing things and the quality of our work as a result.

One of the things that we believe makes a company valuable is the quality of relationships both internal and external, do you agree? You talked earlier about relationship dynamics being a key motivator.

Yes, I do agree. We've tried different models to see what works and what we've discovered is that you can't compete with one another internally at all. The whole way we are structured and our reward system is such that it just doesn't benefit you to compete internally. Our six studios are very, very porous, we 'swap' teams, people and experience all the time. We pass people around and lend people to one another, we share projects and we share talent and experience all the time.

Do you have what you would recognise as a strategic plan?

Yes, really our strategy is to grow the business.

Isn't that more of a goal than a strategy?

Yes, I suppose that's right. In terms of a strategy for growth, that's really about deciding which areas to move into and making the right choices. I think a big part of strategy is being clear on what you want to focus on, be smart at adding to your portfolio. Strategically we are always asking "is this a new opportunity in an area where we should be operating?".

Sometimes growth can be geographic or in terms of type of work and we look at both of those and try to figure out where the opportunities are, how those fit with our strengths and what our priorities should be.

Growth is clearly important to organisations but we touched earlier on a broader concept of how value is created and the impact a firm and its people might have. Do you think about the impact of the buildings you've helped to create, on people's lives?

Definitely, I get a buzz out of a genuinely good building. I think about the people on the street – you have to make sure it works for them as well as those working or living in it. Like the Hong Kong Airport Project. Eighty million people go through that building every year, that's almost two billion passengers since it was completed! I'm constantly meeting people who have experienced it and because I had a part in that project and because it works so well you always have a good conversation. That's tremendously satisfying and rewarding. It's very uplifting to think that the work you've done has had a positive impact on people's lives.

What in your career so far are you most proud of?

I'm proud of the office all together, what we've achieved and where the organisation is now, and I'm certainly proud of a lot of the buildings we've created. It's funny though, it's like your children, you are completely involved with them, totally committed, they can't exist without you, you assume that feeling will never go away, but the building goes on to have a life of its own and you're not involved! I remember turning up at the ITN building just after we'd handed it over to the occupiers. I'd been the lead architect on that project, totally involved in it, every waking hour devoted to it and a complex network of relationships all revolving around it. A couple of months later I was meeting someone there and I couldn't get in the building! Reception thought I was some random guy off the street. Your part is instantly and completely forgotten, you find that that the engagement is incredibly intense but then it's over and everyone has moved on.

You are incredibly passionate about your work; do you think you could have possibly done something different with your life?

I don't know. When I was young, I always wanted to be a writer, if not then an artist and I ended up being an architect! It's funny how life and passions evolve, isn't it?

Your work and career has clearly been incredibly demanding and consuming. How have you achieved balance? Has your wife Trish played an important part? I was interested to learn that Norman and his wife worked in the same practice early on.

She has played a really important role, not in the way that Norman and Wendy worked together but it's absolutely the case that I couldn't have been successful if I didn't have our family. I need to be able to switch off from work completely. Without Trish and our son, the whole mix couldn't work.

Do you use them as a sounding board?

No, actually I don't! Trish is very interested in art, design and literature but not consumed by architecture at all. We have arrived at a good balance in our lives and interests. We've been together for such a long time, I was still at college when we met, she understands that the life and work that I have is quite consuming. In the end though, the truth is that I would probably be the happiest just the two of us just hanging out really, not doing anything in particular, just enjoying each other's company.

You said to me once that architects never retire; Norman's over eighty. What did you mean?

I look at it this way, it takes such a long time to achieve things like buildings and you don't feel as you've got enough buildings in your life! Buildings take so many years to come to anything and people like me feel that it's a shame that that creative process has to stop. We still like to think we can help shape things; we find it very difficult not to help doing that or contributing on some level.

We've both been working around forty years, it sounds like you might be working for another twenty! How much has the world of work changed since the 1980s when we started out? I'm interested to understand how you think tomorrow's successful organisations might look; do you think will they be different from today's?

I think they'll be more like ours, more organic, less structured.

That's interesting. From what you've said you seem to hover between intense structure in terms of the critical processes you describe and a certain fluidity within the organisation.

Yes, I think you have to be fluid. One of our advantages organisationally is that we do things that are interesting, just interesting, which is where we are all happiest. Creative businesses are driven by people that think like that, and I think they will be the future because everything else is replaceable. So many things that people do are programable and predictable and creative businesses are less predictable. We're playing constantly with people's imaginations, switching between the virtual and the actual.

We don't even know what kind of businesses there will be tomorrow, we have no idea, they will work and develop in different ways and the people behind them I guarantee will be different versions of people like you and me, but I believe they will be creative people and they'll go off on different paths and find different things to engage with, and they will work in structures that allow them to do that in the best possible way.

If you had one piece of advice for people starting out in their careers what would it be?

Find what you love, commit to it, work hard at it, don't hesitate. Be brave, treat people well and try to make a difference.

GRANT BROOKER

“

I think I see dots on a good day. I see dots to be joined-up and I see a way to join them up and I'm impatient about it.

”

JEREMY HOCKING

INTERVIEWED 5TH JULY 2019

Jeremy was President International of the US-based furniture business Herman Miller. He retired in 2021 after 37 years with the firm. Originally established in West Michigan in 1905, Herman Miller has long been associated with famous designers like Charles and Ray Eames and more recently Bill Stumpf who designed the iconic Aeron chair. Herman Miller has net sales of around $4 billion and is now led by its first female CEO Andi Owen who was previously President of Banana Republic.

In 2011, whilst President of their business in Asia Pacific, Jeremy oversaw the purchase of Chinese company POSH – a designer, manufacturer and distributor of furniture - which has led to a significant period of growth in China and across Asia. In the US, Herman Miller diversified into retail with the purchase of DWR (Design Within Reach) which sells designer furniture through over thirty retail studio outlets. Most recently, they bought the Danish company HAY to strengthen their contemporary home furnishings capability.

I have known Jeremy since the early 2000s when he was Herman Miller UK's Managing Director. He moved from that role to Asia Pacific where he led the business for eight years before moving to the firm's US headquarters to become Head of Strategy and Acquisitions. He took over the International role in 2018, replacing his former boss when he retired.

Jeremy possesses an unusual balance of warmth, humour and hard-edged commercial nous. In this interview I was keen to uncover what drives him, his views on leadership, thoughts on how business is evolving and how his and other organisations might evolve in the future.

When did you join Herman Miller and what was the appeal?

I joined in 1984 having spent two years following my degree with an IT company in a sales role. I was 24 and I joined because their workplace was drop-dead gorgeous! Not because I particularly wanted to work in the furniture industry, I really didn't, but the office was gorgeous, I'd never been in an office like that. It was luxurious and honestly I thought, "wow, this would reflect on me" if I could work for a company like this. Most companies have boring offices, even today, and don't quite understand the emotional impact that a beautiful workplace can have on perceptions of their firm. Anyway, that's my story and I'm still here thirty-five years later, so something's working!

How did your career with Herman Miller start?

The company was in the process of hiring graduates to develop into sales and marketing roles in the UK. I was cycled through every aspect of both disciplines so benefited from a great breadth of experience. By the late '80s I had my first management job running the UK division which built relationships with the Architects and Designers who specified furniture - A&D.

You enjoyed sales?

I did, yes, and I still do. It's the lifeblood of any organisation. I still make sure I spend as much time as I can out in the field in any market I visit with customers and dealers. I hugely admire the risks our dealers take to invest and set up a business in Timbuktu to sell our products. I go to as many showroom openings around the world as I can because I have a lot of respect for them. They're investing their money, not mine, so I try and be there for them. I am, to be honest, embarrassed now that I don't spend enough time with customers in this role. When I was in Asia I did very intentionally because we were trying to build a network, but right now I don't spend anywhere near enough time with end customers and I need to get that right.

Going right back to those early days, what did you learn about the science of selling?

That it's essentially a numbers game, you need to undertake a lot of activity to create a funnel of opportunities and then slim those down into the best ones, from which you might win one in four. So you need to be relentless about opening up conversations. You need to be skilled in communication and get your timing right – look for the moment when the customer is bought in or willing to be persuaded to be bought in. I think that those are quite rare skills, reading that moment when you can say, "can we get this done then?".

You enjoy that challenge?

I do and I get a real kick out of winning and growing a business, not only for myself but as part of a team. Probably the most fun I had early in my career in London was leading a team called the SBG (Strategic Business Group). It was formed in the nineties and I was a founding member. I went on to lead it for some time. We sold as a team, someone covered the architects, someone else the end clients and one of us worked internally to make sure we were aligning resources in support of the opportunities we unearthed. They were large opportunities, I mean $10million+ deals often. We had a real purple patch with government clients during the PFI era, we had great success actually.

You mentioned a desire to win, was that always there?

I think though I wouldn't have used the word at the time, I was always ambitious - I would have been too cool to admit it then. But I had a certain drive and I still have that - a desire to achieve and ultimately to win.

What do you think is the source of that inner drive?

I was financially driven and I was never ashamed to admit that I wanted a bigger bonus next year than I had earned the year before. I understood that to progress in your career you needed to outperform in order to get the next great opportunity.

I probably have always had a healthy (rather than unhealthy) fear of failure, one doesn't want to be unemployed! That said I was always very confident in my ability, and very determined.

What kept you at one firm for so long? What's special for you about Herman Miller?

Our heritage. We're over a hundred years old for goodness sake, there aren't many one-hundred-year-old companies. Part of the reason for that is financial prudence, you know we don't do stupid things.

So there's a relentlessness, and you can call it on the one hand financial prudence which sounds boring, but also a deep held survival instinct in Herman Miller. After 9/11, we were staring down the barrel of a gun and the company did the toughest stuff it's ever done. Facilities were closed, people were cut and this was a very humanist company, conservative and paternalistic because of the strong Christian culture in West Michigan. People were shocked because you don't get fired from the church, right? So letting people go was really painful, but there was an instinct to survive and thrive.

Tell me more about the culture at Herman Miller.

People think of us as design-driven, a design-led company and we are and we want to innovate. We want to change the world for the better and be admired for solving problems in new ways and for being good at business. Though with our new CEO we are looking quite fundamentally at how we work, Andi brings a fresh new perspective. In truth we have actually been too slow, in danger of being an organisation that's not agile. We need to read the tea leaves in terms of how the world is changing and adapt and innovate in that way.

My sense is that amongst those that have been with Herman Miller a long time, you are seen as something of a change agent. Is that true?

I believe that towards the end of my time running Asia I'd been identified as a lead candidate to be the next person to run international and the CEO at the time insisted that I go to the US and spend some time working in strategy and business development, including M&A. I did that for two years. I was contentious, putting challenges on the table, painful things sometimes, and trying to speak reality. Culturally the company was not comfortable with that kind of challenge but the CEO loved it. He used to say to me on the side, "I love what you're doing," but I could definitely feel the reaction from more conservative parts of the company.

You worked closely with that CEO, what did you learn from him?

He came up through the Finance route. He had huge drive; he would drive very deeply into every detail. He would say something like, "I've got to understand lean manufacturing," which was a big part of our focus in the '90s. He wasn't an Operations specialist at all, but he came to know as much about it as our people running Operations, and that's what made him a formidable CEO. You had to be very well prepared to deal with him. He was a leader who worked out what he thought iteratively. He liked to discuss an issue and argue, he was argumentative and quite fierce. A lot of people were daunted by his style and frankly by his brain's bandwidth, but actually he liked being challenged. One of the reasons why my predecessor did so well was that from day one, when the CEO earlier in his career spent a period in Europe, my boss used to banter with him all the time. He was never afraid to challenge. I did the same with that CEO and I found that he reached a point of view by talking with colleagues. I'm a little like that, I think. I'm not the smartest person in the room so I like to discuss things and throw them around to arrive at a developed point of view.

Your old boss and Head of International had an important impact on your career too. Tell me about him.

He was just outstanding with people, incredibly articulate, a man of very few words and what you came to learn was, they had been exceptionally well chosen well before he came into the room. It seemed like a remark or a question off the top of his head, but it never was. He had a great gift of getting to a point, getting under the skin of the issue. I formed a very trusting relationship with him as a boss, he was very much on the human side of the issue - we would talk about people all the time. Another thing that I really benefited from with him was him telling me early on perhaps for the first time in my career how highly valued I was by him and by the organisation.

What can you remember about that conversation?

I can remember it very clearly. He said it one evening over a few drinks. What he said was, "you've got it all!" and what he meant was that I surprised him. I was across everything - manufacturing, in particular finance - I understood the numbers and then I really had a lot of fun with marketing. I used to make sure I spent our budget every year and I was pretty good at sales and very good with people. I seemed to be able to deal with difficult problems and make difficult decisions. I probably already thought I was okay at what I did, but him saying it made a real impact on me. Because before that, nobody had told me, so what I learnt from that is that it's really important to say to people, "well done" and "we recognise your gifts and talents".

To raise their confidence?

Exactly, because confidence is actually very important in business and in life. I tell you, my confidence rose 40-50% after that conversation. Later I became a confidante for him – he would literally come and download after leadership meetings. Interestingly, I had a gin and tonic with him just the other night, although he is retired now. We keep in touch and he asked me, "who is your go-to person?" because you need one in this role.

Is there?

Yes, inside the firm there is one, and you occasionally! [Laughs]

Was he a visionary person?

I think he was visionary about the drive for Herman Miller to contribute to a better world. He used to say that what he loved about Herman Miller most was that you could help really pull people up around the world. He personally did one-week and two-week business schools in India. That was what was very visionary and inspiring about him. He was a very generous person, very generous with people less fortunate than us and I think that is inspiring in a leader.

Let's talk a little about strategy and M&A. I know M&A was a big part of your strategy in Asia and of course you had that time in the US as Strategy Lead a few years ago. How do you approach strategy?

I think I see dots on a good day. I see dots to be joined-up and I see a way to join them up and I'm impatient about it. What I'm probably not good at is the detail then around execution. But I definitely love seeing the picture, the implications of that picture and figuring out what needs to be done.

In some ways I used to find strategy a bit intimidating. In that role initially I wasn't a confident presenter in front of our Board of Directors. I'm getting better at it but I was very nervous when I started and the Chairman was really surprised. He took me for lunch and said, "Jeremy, this isn't the guy I know. Where's your humour? Let me tell you about how Boards work." He wrote out an A4 page of points for me about how Boards operate, and at the end he said, "You need to remember fundamentally that as an experienced business leader you know much more about the business than they do!"

Was it just performance anxiety or something else?

A bit of that, you know it was a new brief for me. I was very new in the role. There were probably people on the Board I assumed who knew a lot more about strategy than I thought I did.

What makes for a good strategy in your experience?

A clear plan to achieve a clear goal. How you are going to win the battle or the war. It's joining dots. There are some excellent strategies around but of course the hardest part is execution and that's why most of them fail. That's why boards lose confidence. You know, they might buy a strategy, but if it doesn't happen they say, "was the strategy bad?". Well, I don't know but the strategy might have been right, we just didn't execute it well enough.

In your thirty-odd years, have you seen different approaches to developing a strategy? Can you discern the things which indicate a good one?

I think the exercise we've just been through was the best. I think we did a great job of understanding what's going on around us. So, the context in which we're operating, and we've been brutally honest about what is working and what isn't working, and that's taken a lot of honesty and it's been painful, we've not always been great at being willing to do that.

Why?

Perhaps a conservative culture - but in 2018 we had a new CEO Andi and there's kind of a freedom in having a new CEO. And maybe two or three of the team have changed as well, they're no longer in the room. There are new, bright, interesting, bushy-tailed people in the room! You can and do have a very different dynamic very quickly and that's what we've just experienced at Herman Miller. It's been really positive.

Can we talk about M&A and the lessons you learned in that area?

I learned that there are lots of companies for sale and most of them are terrible! And you learn that your acquisition strategy must be driven by your overall strategy, only buy things that are consistent with it. We've probably in the past bought businesses that were outside of that. It sounds obvious but they should reinforce the strategy. The second is you need to be really good at harnessing and then enhancing the value. Why do you buy this company? Well, because it's best of breed. It's a great brand that adds to the family, so be sure to identify and keep a hold of the great people and avoid actions which will destroy the value you're buying.

What did you learn about that, getting that part right or wrong?

Integrating too fast - for example premature and risky IT integrations.

Driven by a desire to get costs out quickly?

Yes but more generally in pursuit of immediate 'synergies'. Clearly synergies are there to be realised otherwise any deal would never have happened in the first place, but executing them perfectly requires a tip-top team of highly engaged folks from both "sides" with their eyes on the (same) prize.

People were lost, customers were disrupted?

Yes, that's one example. I think IT integration done too quickly or poorly can turn things upside down. I think the leadership who built the company into the one that you wanted to buy - what's their role post-acquisition? Do you keep them in the business with some skin in the game or do you buy it and wave goodbye to them and then think "oh dear, there's nothing here!"; or, you get in there and you realise actually they were the thing. There's nothing left. You know they were the brand. There are lots of ways to screw acquisitions up!

What we try to do is to really focus on integration. I'll give you an example. You know we made an investment in HAY which is like the coolest furniture brand around right now in Europe. The husband and wife owners are the creative directors and we've invested in that company with a minority stake before moving to majority. That's our intention, but only on the basis that they have said they want to be around for ten years. I mean it says their name over the door.

There was another transaction done at the same time in our industry of a similar kind of company. The two founders who were really creative people went as part of the transaction and you might think, well, how was that a good idea? Maybe it will be a more successful one but for us and having the essence of the brand, you know maintaining and developing that, is a big piece of successful acquisitions.

Acquisitions are a great way of creating growth but can be a huge drain on internal resources as well. On the other hand, you're bringing in really interesting new groups of people. Both parties can get a huge amount from that. So, I think this sensitive integration planning focused around people is absolutely critical to success.

It's interesting to think about the value related directly to the key talent in a business. That's partly ideas, creativity, entrepreneurship, but also the value of leadership. What do you think makes a good business leader?

Great communication skills with multiple audiences. And I say that advisedly after our earlier conversation. I think you've got to be able to engage in a compelling way, you've got to be able to talk to investors and your Board in a convincing way.

What's key to being convincing in that?

I think its clarity, you know I look at our strategy now, we're unveiling a strategy which I think is simple and clear and makes people think "Yeah, I get that. Clear, logical and well thought through".

I think as well that great leaders are leaders that people want to follow. They're inspired by them, they trust them, they feel supported by them. They have integrity. You take it for granted, don't you? But I think straightforwardness and I'm coming back to the importance of trust.

Things happen under great leaders, good things happen. They grow the business. Growth creates opportunity for everybody. So if we're not growing we will get stuck with the same people doing the same old thing. Whereas if you're growing, good people get promoted, we can add graduate programmes and we can move people over to Singapore on assignment.

Any other insights around leadership?

I was on a course recently run by the 'Higher Ambition Leadership Institution'. I'm not always a big fan of courses but this was great. The speaker was Doug Conant, he had been the CEO of Campbell Soup. They went into a deep recession in the '80s, and they lost almost everything. Doug came in when they were on their knees and turned them round. Here's the thing he said, I wrote it down and I used this with my team just this week. He said he's had sixteen bosses in his life – eleven of them he can't really remember at all, three of them were really bad and destructive people and two of them helped change his life, and he wants to be a leader that changes people's lives for the better. That really stuck with me. It resonated with me then and it still does. You don't want to be an average leader, you don't just want to be another leader, you want to make an impact on people's lives.

A great leader also has passion, I think. I read something else recently which resonated with me. It was in The Sunday Times about an entrepreneur whose name I can't remember. It was talking about the key ingredients in his success and he said, "You have to be really passionate to the point where the energy is bleeding over the table when you talk to people." I think on a good day that's what I am. If I'm talking to small groups, I'm able to really enthuse them, I get just like that, blood everywhere.

Great leaders can create a positive, energised environment. What's important in that?

A pace, an energy. Let's talk about meetings, for example. They can be a real problem if you don't get them right! They're usually an hour when they need to be twenty minutes!

Some meetings can be pivotal in a team's evolution I believe, and I think big strategic meetings are better done offsite. I like to take people to a different kind of setting. To your point, you know around productivity, is it better to go to the large conference room on the second floor to have our brainstorming about where we go next in our strategy, or is it better to go to an old rundown chateau in Champagne and have a tour and have someone come in and talk about Champagne, drink a bit of it and keep meeting. I did it last week.

That's about creating excitement and energy?

Yes, because people are inspired by their surroundings and they appreciate that the company is making this investment, and this seems like a luxury, but it doesn't really cost that much. And you get better work and you build tremendous relationships back to the point you always make about social capital, how internal relationships create value. Herman Miller is unbeatable in the market if we can build fantastic internal relationships, because most companies can't, most companies are all stuck with internecine warfare. And that group this week felt to me so pumped actually that it gave me great hope. It really was quite moving.

What would you think, perhaps hope even, people would say about you as a leader?

I think they'd say he's quite tough and demanding, but that he's warm, he's focused on developing the team. But that he doesn't have enough time for me because he's always flying everywhere! Sometimes he's a bit rushed and I don't get enough quality time with him one-on-one.

How do you divide your time as a leader?

Three weeks in four, I'm generally out of the UK. When I'm in-market, I like walking around. It's not all in set pieces. If we go to an office, I generally have a town hall of some sort, some food in the office and take the leaders out to dinner. I call that breaking bread with the team. Not just the senior leadership but the second tier, their direct reports, and that gives me an opportunity to listen and for them to get to know me. And therefore, what might be important to me and translate for them a little of what the company is thinking about, our priorities and why they're important.

Are you quite disciplined about managing your time?

No. I think you know the answer. And you know I'm not proud of it. If I'm over-running, it's because I'm with someone, I have soft boundaries about time with people.

Are you good at switching off and conserving your mental and emotional energy with such a time-consuming job?

I'm not great at that. I'm still battling with it. The way that this particular role has been constructed, I probably don't switch off as much as I'd like to. When I do it's generally family stuff but I also make time for some fun. For example, tomorrow I'm going to Goodwood Festival of Speed and that's one of my favourite things in the world, and I'm going to the Lord's Test match for two days later in the month, in August - you're coming!

We were talking about leaders I admire and I'd say, for most, a successful home life is really helpful. I mean in my case it's essential and it's increasingly rare, so many people don't have that. And it's not to say that you can't go on to have success. Maybe it's because they want their individual focus and they're not really good at sharing their lives. But for me having a great wife and family is an absolutely fundamental part of my success, my life balance.

How does it work with you and your wife? Do you share lots of things?

Yes, we talk a lot. She's actually a very wise consultant.

What are you most proud about in life?

I think most proud would be family first. Honestly without a doubt. And keeping all that together somehow, because I think that's foundational for success, at least in my career.

What do you think you'll miss about work when you retire?

The social side of work. You know the interactions with really interesting people in really interesting places. I've had the great privilege these last ten years of travelling all over the world and I still get a huge kick out of that, it'll be hard to stop.

We'll both be moving on in a few years' time and of course things will continue to evolve. Do you think organisations will look and work very differently in ten years' time from now? And if so, how might they be different?

I think they might be nicer places. By which I mean that corporations will have had to get in touch with their societal impact much more.

Last question. If you were to be talking to a group of young people at the outset of their careers, what advice would you give them?

Pick a strong brand to work for and a company that is going to invest in you and your development. Good companies take care of their people, they have great induction programmes, they train them, they develop them and if they're really bad they'll even get rid of them! Find your passion, bleed over the table sometimes, fall in love with a good partner who loves you and have fun!

JEREMY HOCKING

“

As a leader you have to navigate change with your hands on the tiller, always keeping your attention fixed on the destination. I'll see risks and opportunities open all the time as we move along, things pull at you and you've got to work out what's a distraction and what really might need fixing.

”

PAUL BUTTIGIEG

INTERVIEWED 7TH JUNE 2019

Paul is Director of Operations for Unibail-Rodemco-Westfield in Europe, the Paris-based company which acquired Westfield in 2018 for an estimated 25 billion AUD. Paul opened Westfield's landmark centre, Westfield London in 2008 and later oversaw the launch of Westfield Stratford when he became General Manager for the UK. Westfield London has attracted 270million visitors since its opening, generating an estimated £9billion in sales. It is a major tourist attraction with 17million tourists flocking to Westfield London in 2017. The two centres situated in White City and Stratford in East London are also credited with making a significant contribution to the socio-economic regeneration of both areas.

Clearly a central figure in Westfield Europe's UK success, Paul is keen to downplay his own role. Instead, he prefers to talk about the dynamics of the mould-breaking team put together to mastermind and deliver two major assets and the development of Westfield as a brand in the UK synonymous with innovation and quality. In our interview I was interested to understand the thinking behind Westfield's strategy and Paul's take on how value in this highly competitive market is created. I wanted to explore his own influences and learning, and his thoughts on how the business of retail and leisure is evolving in the digital age.

Paul, take me back to the beginning of your career, how did it all start?

I took my first job in 1984 straight out of school in Australia. It was in the back office of a local bank and I really started at the bottom doing all the usual back-office stuff, it was good experience. I learned the basics and eventually found myself in a role in the Head Office of the State Bank of Australia.

Tell me about what you did there.

Well, in those days in banking everything was a manual ledger – before computers! It took you from 8am in the morning until 3pm in the afternoon to balance the whole bank's balance sheet and that's what I did, it was a great foundation. At the time I also began a part-time degree in Finance working mostly at night, it took me six years to complete it.

From there you moved into Industry. What made you make that change?

I decided that I wanted to be involved in running a real business rather than just counting the money. I joined a storage and logistics company in the Finance department and it proved to be a good grounding. My boss there and myself got on really well and eventually when he moved he asked me whether I'd like to follow him to his new company, and I did. That business was a well-established British company called Jardine Matheson. I began there as an Assistant Accountant and stayed for five years, the firm grew fast and I grew with them. When I left I was Finance Manager reporting directly to the Managing Director of one of the chains.

Tell me about how the firm grew.

When I joined that chain had one restaurant, and when I left there were forty. It was a great experience for me, I learned a huge amount from those around me about the fundamentals of how a business works. Our CEO at the time interestingly was a Brit called Clive Schlee who later went on to become CEO of Pret a Manger. After five years I had wanderlust and was keen to take a break and explore Europe – you know, the way us Aussies like to do! Clive tried to persuade me to stay and take the trip as a sabbatical but I wanted a clean break and a new adventure. I set off for Europe and had a brilliant time. Afterwards I headed back to Australia with lots of ideas and I joined a leisure firm that was part of Westfield, they were operating indoor leisure technology spaces within shopping centres. After a while I moved into Westfield itself and from Melbourne to Sydney.

What took you there?

It was an exciting opportunity. Westfield was an official partner in the 2000 Olympics and in the build-up to that event they wanted an accountant to be responsible for finances across the entire Olympic partnership operation, a big role. In the course of my work there I came across a guy called Denis Carruthers who was to play an important role in my life. Denis persuaded me to move into General Management and that put my career on a different trajectory.

How did it start?

Around 1998 I became a centre manager in Australia. I ended up running a few, the last one was a struggling centre in Melbourne. We managed to turn it around and by then I was beginning to really enjoy building and managing teams, learning about brands, marketing, people dynamics - everything. I found and still find commercial management a tremendous challenge with so many component parts to bring together.

I remember, you're a finance guy that loves marketing!

Yes but actually a finance guy that really likes managing people - which is perhaps even more unusual! That's where you can really make your mark - developing and coaching people, watching them grow, understanding and managing the dynamics of a group.

So what eventually brought you to London?

I was looking for the next challenge. Denis had been posted here and he rang me and said, "I've got a big development, a really big one called Westfield London. Would you like to come here and help me open it?" I couldn't resist.

Was it built by then?

No, God no, it was still being built when we opened it! [Laughs] We took over the construction ourselves from Multiplex who'd begun it, I think by then it was January 2007, and as I remember we committed to opening it in October 2008, which was a hell of a challenge, but we did it.

It sounds as if Denis had great trust in you. Tell me about your relationship with him.

Yes, he has been my mentor definitely and his advice has been important to me over the years. He is very genuine, which I admire, and massively motivated. People are very loyal to him and he's fantastic at making time for people. He keeps in contact with me even now from Australia, though he's retired he'll call and ask how things are going and he acts as a sounding board for me both in whatever role I'm in and my career development more widely. When I was offered this current job he said, "You'd have to be mad not to give it a crack, it's a wonderful opportunity to expand your skills." He's almost like a father figure to me in many ways. I trust him. I hope that I'm viewed a bit that way myself by some of my people. I try to follow his lead and think about what I might have needed at a particular time in my career, when I perhaps lacked a bit of confidence or was unsure about taking something on.

Is there any advice in particular that he's given you that's made a real impact?

Yes, surround yourself with great people. He'd say, "Your challenge is, no matter how good you think your team is, always try to hire more talent. Look as hard as you can, keep raising the bar. Get the best person you can for every role." So today when I look at people, I'm thinking about how they are going to develop the role, what different values and different ways of thinking might they bring to our party?

He offered another bit of advice too in a different area. A long time ago, he said "don't ever assume people know what you do and in particular your boss". What he meant was that we all need to promote ourselves a bit, and it's true. You've got to be your own PR manager to some extent. I'm not naturally a great self-promoter but I'm conscious of it and now when I sit down in a review with someone I'll ask, "What have you done about developing your own brand?" It's important that people think about that in building a career, not in a selfish, self-promoting kind of way but they should really understand their unique strengths, seek ways to build on them and be aware of the impression they create, how they are perceived and to a degree have a strategy for that.

Let's go back to when you answered that call from Denis to help launch Westfield London, was the model based on Australian centres you had run?

No not really. We wanted to create the finest, most innovative, stylish shopping centres in the world. Actually as a team we coined the phrase "Better than Bondi" to spur us on at every turn. How could we push the envelope, raise standards, move beyond the expected?

As the construction project completed, were you the main driver of decisions?

No, in our model the developer leads on construction definitively, they're the experts absolutely. They are the ones at the hub of the wheel as you approach completion but then the baton is handed over to the Operations team, my team. The important thing is that the developer and the team that are going to run the centre are working to the same vision. When I've seen projects fail it's because there hasn't been a clear vision for the project articulated, something that the whole team is working towards.

Ten years or so on, what do you think it is that made Westfield London such a success?

People. A great team of amazing people. Hugely experienced many of them and with very strong opinions, strong people survive well in Westfield. Our culture was key, almost a fear of failure actually, we were desperate to create something special and we absorbed and reflected a lot of what London had to offer and mixed it with what some of us had learned back in Australia.

What was the strategy?

We set out to break boundaries and do the unexpected, like put Louis Vuitton into Shepherd's Bush. Everyone thought we were mad, Louis Vuitton belonged in Bond Street! But when people say that, you want to achieve it even more.

We aspired to create new standards in terms of the range and quality of the food offer. Shopping centres had previously tended to rely on the big chains. We looked to develop a segmented offer with a focus on quality and freshness. This was ten years ago, remember.

We wanted to lead on technology and service too. Everything had to be better than we had seen done anywhere before. So essentially the strategy was to break new ground and build the reputation of Westfield London as a quality brand with innovation at its heart.

What does strategy mean to you?

I think people mix up strategy with vision. A clear vision is actually surprisingly rare but once you are clear and agreed on that, strategy is about putting plans together to achieve that vision. So for Westfield London we had a clear vision for what we aspired to create. I won't share the exact phrase but it was succinct and inspiring. Our strategy was then really about setting out a series of goals, milestones, to get there. The team created clear plans in each area of our business mix which put together would create a distinctive brand. A centre like Westfield London is a sophisticated physical asset, it's in the right place, service delivery is top notch but it's more than that, it's a brand and that multiplies the tangible asset value. We've created a brand and we work hard to enhance it, we're looking to polish it all the time. We worked on our marketing activity relentlessly to keep it front of mind and ahead of the curve.

So to execute an effective strategy I think you need clarity of vision, you need talent, you must introduce an element of 'stretch' and have a real drive to achieve, a palpable energy and commitment to compete.

What's the key to creating something with real long-term value?

Well I can tell you that if you just go chasing money in the first place, you won't do it, you'll just end up selling things – it's more than that. You've got to create a unique customer experience and put huge energy into that. It's not a formula, there's a certain magic about it.

For us that started again with the people, the team we created for Westfield London, many of them had never worked in a shopping centre before. They brought completely different perspectives; I didn't want traditional thinking.

Looking back, that combination has begun to pay off and the results are actually quite tangible. That centre cost about £1.6billion to build and now it's worth probably £3billion, that's £1.4billion of value created in ten years and it's primarily driven by the intangible things, it's not the bricks and mortar, that's just the start point, after that you get creative!

In the ten years since Westfield London opened, things have moved on. How are retail and leisure changing in the digital age?

Clearly retailers are needing to rethink the way they build and manage relationships with their customers. It's no longer the traditional over the counter relationship, that's still important of course but it's really a whole new way of creating and maintaining relationships – it's about creating 'relationship capital' to use that phrase you use and to do that you must engage a multitude of channels and techniques. It's about creating 'experiences' – Instagram-able moments which get your brand talked about. Now that's at the forefront of our thinking when we're meeting with retailers and brands. In our centres we are looking at working with brands to create truly immersive experiences and two-way conversations. In the old days, the experience was about great parking, all of those great shops in one place, then more recently using mobile phones enabled with 'push' technology – you walk into a centre and get a prompt text on your phone, a call to action. Today it's about an ongoing conversation and it has to be as real as possible.

You're using your imagination to create experiences which attract and intrigue your audience. Look at Amazon, they started off as an online bookstore and everyone thought it was the end of bricks and mortar. Recently they opened up a pop-up bookstore in Soho based on a Victorian bookstore, an immersive experience, book-related movie sets, drama and characters. That kind of initiative is happening more and more, retailers and brands creating unique events and curating conversations around them to keep their audiences engaged. It's exciting because the media for building great brands and delivering unique experiences are multi-dimensional now, everything is in-play.

It's clear that you have been successful in helping to create a valuable brand and that the tools at your disposal are evolving all the time. At the heart of it from what you've said is a clear vision and the ability to lead a team to deliver on that vision. So what makes a great leader in your experience?

I think, knowing your own strengths and weaknesses, building a team which complements those and knowing how to get the best out of that team as a collective. I'm an accountant so I surrounded myself with lots of very creative people. They think differently and it's important to be able to build empathy and trust in a diverse group like ours. A lot of good managers in my experience are not necessarily good at that.

So how do they succeed?

Well I think they succeed up to a point, every team needs good managers, needs detail and discipline, but a leader needs vision, a spirit almost of adventure and absolutely the ability to inspire and develop others. You need to understand that everyone is different, unique actually, and know how to engage and motivate them as an individual.

As a leader you have to navigate change, your hands on the tiller, always keeping your attention fixed on the destination. I'll see risks and opportunities open all the time as we move along, things pull at you and you've got to work out what's a distraction and what really might need fixing. That's my role directing the course we are taking towards that end goal.

You started off as a bookkeeper, a manager of sorts, and along the way you've picked up a huge amount about what can make a business great, beyond just efficient and well run. Talk to me a little more about what you've learned and what perhaps you know now that you didn't know at the start of your career.

That there is a world beyond finance! [Laughs] No, really I think the importance of people and the complications and challenges which that brings. We are all complex creatures with different behaviours you know, even in my daughters I see behaviour traits from me and some from my wife - are they going to be like us? No, because we are very different individuals. So the challenge is to work out what motivates every individual, what makes them tick?

You have to look at that. How do you grow people? I'm still learning that at 53. How do you grow someone of my own age? It's easier to grow someone in their 20s, but how do I grow a person at 52 when their own ways are quite set in many respects? Where do we find the gap, create the energy to develop again and enjoy the experience? So I hadn't understood when I was young how interesting that is and how building a team of people is really what creates success in business.

When I think back to my younger years I think, "oh my word, how immature was that?"; you know, how I behaved when I didn't get exactly what I wanted. Now I know how I would have negotiated some of those situations more effectively.

How do you think people you work with see you?

The best person I've ever worked with! [Laughs]

Actually one person called me a brain, I don't regard myself like that whatsoever. I've got an average IQ but perhaps I dig into things a bit more than most. I want to understand everything. I hope they'd say I give good direction and that I support them, that I've got time for them, I think they'd say that.

What makes people productive?

Feeling valued and it's not about money. If they feel like they're making a real contribution and growing they will be committed. Think how good people feel when they're in front of senior Board members and these Board members are listening attentively to what they have to say. How good do you think that makes them feel? Let's face it, I've never yet met a person who doesn't respond well to recognition.

What are you most proud about as a businessperson?

The teams that I've helped build, the brands we've helped create between us, and the positive impact, even if it's in a small way, on the areas we've worked in. Helping to create a feeling of energy and vibrancy in some of the places where our centres operate.

In terms of colleagues, it's great to meet up after a year or two with people who've worked with you on a project. There's a real connection about what you achieved together, you reminisce, bring out the old war stories - you've created memories together.

I remember a team from very early on in my career back in Australia. In that business, every six months you had to have nil debt on your books. Even if you smashed your revenue targets you had to clear off your debt every six months, it was a cultural thing. Now at the time as I remember we had twenty-seven vacant shops and some poorly performing tenants - how were we ever going to do that? Well it took us two years, but we did it. In the lead up, I took a Nil Debtors certificate that the Directors used to present and superimposed our centre's name on it and stuck it above the photocopier, everyone looked at it every time they made a copy. We kept it front of mind, every day we'd have a team meeting in the morning and then another in the evening. We'd say, "How did we go today, did we get that money in overnight?" We were managing a very complex business but that was our absolute focus and we nailed it! The euphoria of the team at the time we did it was fantastic and when we met up years later people still remember the sign above the photocopier.

Does work matter?

Of course it matters. Not only do you spend a lot of your life doing it but for most of us it's front and centre in our lives.

I can tell that you're very determined when you are tilting at something. Do you manage to achieve a healthy balance or is it full on all the time for you?

To be honest, I used to be not good at it but it's getting better. Having a four-year-old and seven-year-old helps. I do recognise that we need variety in our lives and that we all need to manage our energy and think as well about the impact that we have on those around us – our families and our colleagues.

How important is your family to your success?

Hugely.

Do you bounce things off your wife at home?

No, actually, I'm not sure she wants to listen! She'll tell me I bottle things up but I'm sure she doesn't want me to share all of my frustrations or preoccupations when she's had a busy day herself. I do tend to think about things very deeply and keep them to myself.

There is a lot of talk today about work life balance. There's an idea – true or not – that millennials are taking a different perspective on their careers and the need for balance and organisations will need to work differently in the future to get the best out of them. Do you see that?

I do think organisations are becoming less of a 'command and control' environment. Leaders need to earn respect, demonstrate humility and be responsive to the changing way that young people think and want to lead their lives. It comes right back to what we were talking about earlier. Organisations will no doubt evolve structurally, the tools of the trade will change and different factors will come into play, but essentially it will be a team of people having a tilt at something.

When you retire, what do you think you'll miss most about work?

The mental challenge, a very clear sense of purpose and of course the interaction with people. I might miss the drive to achieve something, so I'll need to find some new challenges. I love restoring motorcycles, I've got some specific ambitions there. I'd like to work in some capacity with teenagers, help them as they start out in life. It will be a different type of fulfilment, no numbers involved! I'll be doing it solely for the purpose of feeling that I'm achieving something more broadly with my life while I'm here on this planet. My wife is a Director of a charity for young disabled children, it's important to her. She's got a hell of a busy lifestyle but still wants to do it and I'll do whatever I can to accommodate that because I understand it. People have asked me to perhaps do some mentoring work at schools, especially in Stratford. I'd like to but haven't made time yet, I will though.

Last question. If you could give one piece of advice to someone starting out in their career, what would it be?

The first thing that comes to mind is – find someone to take advice from, a mentor. Someone in your career to coach you, help you along, take you under their wing. You need a bit of luck with that as well, to find the right person. And get involved in projects which excite you, which offer the chance for you to leave a mark. Work with good people, be loyal and leave no stone unturned if you want to achieve something special.

“

As a young man, I used to wing it like mad. I think I was a nightmare to manage, I used to do my own thing. If I thought something was right and somebody thought it was wrong I'd still do it and negotiate my way around it afterwards.

”

PETER MANTLE

INTERVIEWED 22ND DECEMBER 2020

Peter began his career in the Property industry almost by accident, persuaded by his cousin who worked in Property at the GLC and had a nice car and good suits. He joined Jones Lang Wootton straight from university and remembers being terrified on his first day. He retired thirty-five years later as Managing Partner. He attributes his success to an inner drive, the desire to assume responsibility and the learned ability to 'know himself' and play to his strengths.

Peter, you spent your entire career with one firm, Jones Lang LaSalle. How did it begin?

I joined JLL, or as it was then called Jones Lang Wootton, in 1969. I didn't suppose I would stay so long but I found I enjoyed it and opportunities kept opening up, opportunities I managed to take and actually to capitalise upon.

I assume you were trained as a surveyor?

I was a surveyor, exactly right, a chartered surveyor. I went to what was then called the Brixton School of Building, it's now called the University of Southbank, and I took a three-year degree there.

Interestingly, nearly everyone else I speak to in property seemed to study at Reading!

We always thought that Reading was the snootier end of the market!

Was it your plan to build a career in Property?

No, it was totally, absolutely by chance. I took arts A-Levels at school and then disappeared off for a couple of months to travel around Europe. I had secured a place at university to read sociology, which would have presumably made me into some sort of social worker, but when I got back, I discovered I hadn't achieved the grades I needed. So I no longer had the place and had to think again.

My parents weren't very well off. I went to a minor public school and they said "Well, you could go back and try and improve your A-Levels?" Through gritted teeth I said, "absolutely not, I'm not doing that," so I desperately needed a plan B. My cousin worked for the GLC in the Estates department. I thought, "he's got quite a nice car and his suits look very smart so perhaps I'll do that," but first I needed a qualification.

I should add that when I left Brixton I went to the US for six months and became an ice-cream salesman! We made tons of money doing that and then roamed around the US in 1968. I don't know whether you've seen a film called the Chicago Seven, but I was in Chicago at the time of those disturbances and watched the film when it came out with interest to see if there were any pictures of me in it, unfortunately there weren't!

Let's go back, tell me about your time at the Brixton School of Building.

I should be honest; it wasn't a degree, it was a diploma which we were told was going to be converted into a degree during our course but it never actually was. It was a diploma in Estate Management. I didn't find it very interesting, but I enjoyed that it was 1968 in the middle of Brixton, which was a really hip place to be! I had an absolute ball. The studying was something of a side show.

After graduating and my time in the US, which I remember was very much the time of hippy ideas, I suddenly thought, "Hang on, I haven't got a penny to my name, I've got to survive!" I wrote to eight firms and it just shows you the difference in the times, because I got six interviews, three job offers and chose one. Today I know that young people can write five-hundred applications and might not even get a single interview.

I chose the firm, Jones Lang Wootton, and turned up in my duffle coat, I had to shave my beard off, bought a suit and cut my hair. I was terrified. The first day I remember clearly being frightened of answering the phone, every time the phone went I nearly jumped out of my chair.

What was your job role?

I was a junior negotiator in the industrial department, which was one notch above the post room. I mean, photocopying would have been just slightly below that, but it really was the bottom of the pile, ignored by everybody. Actually the firm turned out to be a great one with lots of good people, it had the cream of the crop really, probably the best firm in its field in the UK at that time, and with a high quality client base.

Who was your first boss?

He was a guy called Kenneth, a very, very technical man indeed, so I learned a lot from him about how to value property, how to measure it up properly and all those sorts of things. It took a lot of getting used to working in an office, understanding what you were supposed to do and how you were supposed to behave.

Did you actually do any negotiating as a junior negotiator?

As a junior negotiator, no. I must have been the worst negotiator imaginable, I had no idea what I was supposed to do. The other experienced negotiators decided that I was a bit of a waste of time. The Partner who headed up the team was much more of a valuer, so he took me on as a sort of assistant valuer, but said, "forget all this negotiating rubbish, I don't know anything about that either. Come and value properties with me and hold my bags". So that's what I did. We toured the country valuing all sorts of portfolios and factories – Rolls-Royce when it went broke if you remember in 1972. We were appointed so I went round all the engine factories in the UK which was all very instructive. I learned quite a lot during that period.

What did you learn from your boss at the time?

To be honest with you he was a very, very good technician, but the partners of JLL, when they took him on a few years before I had joined, they wanted a salesman because that's where the big money in property comes from buying, selling, leasing and funding, and he wasn't really a salesman, he didn't cultivate his relationships with the partners very well either. The valuing side of the business is important, but never really made very much money. So I suppose what I learned from him were positive things for me, but he didn't get on very well with his partners. He was a bit socially difficult and that was a pointer for me.

How so?

He was shy I think and therefore a bit aggressive, not very user friendly. I thought that this wasn't the right way to behave, it's much better if you get on with people, you motivate them, you're friendly and you smile, whereas he always seemed to be irritable. So I learned that.

The second thing was that, as much as I enjoyed belting around the country, this wouldn't be the route forward for me. I used to get in my car and drive up to Leeds and then across to Manchester and then down to Bristol and all the way back all in one day, photographing properties and looking at them. I'd set off at six o'clock in the morning and get back about midnight.

However, despite enjoying being out and about, I came to realise that valuing was a bit dull for me. I'm a bit hyperactive, even now. I certainly was then. Clients kept asking us to value things, we'd value them and the client would ask, "can you recommend somebody to sell it to?". I'd say, yes, we've got agents, but in truth I thought that many of them were pretty useless. I'd go along with my Rolls-Royce instruction to sell something and they'd say, "I don't know, come back and see me next week." It didn't look very good. So I started doing it myself. Actually, I really enjoyed doing it. I used to take out advertisements in the paper, all in the firm's name, not personally, and started selling things. People would say, "What are you doing, you're supposed to be a valuer?" And I would answer, "Well, I don't really like being a valuer!"

So, you didn't apply for a job as a salesman, you just assumed the position?

Yes, exactly. Well, all within the firm. I said to my agency department, "If you don't want to do it, I'll do it!"

Why on earth wouldn't they be keen to win the sale themselves?

Well, because they weren't very good at it, remember they were led by the boss who was a very academic, technical guy. He wasn't a salesman at all, so he didn't pick good salesmen.

How would you sum up the culture of the firm at that time?

The culture of the entire firm was fantastic. Really top-class people. But the bit that I was in wasn't up to that standard; nice people but some of them not very good. Luckily, the guy who ran the agency side underneath the partner, who was a very nice guy and I still see him, left and the partners took on a guy from Peterborough Development Corporation as manager of the agency department. He and I got on very well. A few months went by and we went out for lunch. He said, "You know what? I really hate this job. I'm not cut out to be a salesman at all. I hate it. I'd like to do what you do." And I said, "Well, I'd like to do what you do!" He said, "Why don't we swap?" So, we went up to the partner and told him, "We have agreed to swap." He thought for a few seconds and answered, "Alright, if you're happy then off you go." So we swapped jobs, I ended up as manager of the agency department and through luck and hard work, built it up.

How did you start that process?

When I first got in there, I realised that it really needed organising. I split it up into areas and said to everybody, "what do you think of this? You have this area, you have that one," and started organising it, really not with any official backing, but just because I thought that if we were organised that way we'd be much more efficient.

With hindsight it was pretty extraordinary really because I didn't have any authority to do that at all. I just did it. Everybody seemed to think that was fine. It wasn't an aggressive thing. We started making reasonable amounts of money and in time I did gravitate to become the manager, but I really seized it rather than being given it to be honest.

Looking back, were you very ambitious or did you just think it needed doing?

I was incredibly ambitious, absolutely, it was a passion to get on. I came from a fairly modest background, with lovely parents, but not hugely successful financially.

What did your father do for a job?

He was a Clerk in the County Court, not a Solicitor, Chief Clerk of Gravesend County Court. Lovely guy, but never earned any money. He sent me and my sister to private schools with a little bit of a legacy they got from somewhere.

Part of that legacy was shares in a barge company on the Thames, which paid for the school fees, and it went broke when I was about 15 or 16. We didn't have any money, we were completely bust and I thought, you know what, I never want to be in this situation again.

Was your sister similarly ambitious to achieve?

Not at all, she was very much smarter than I am but not in any way ambitious. She became a special needs teacher, spent time in France and speaks fluent French and German.

Going back to that time when you had assumed control of the department, did you feel confident in yourself?

To be honest with you I used to wing it like mad. It fills me full of horror when I think back. I think I was a nightmare to manage. I used to do my own thing. If I thought something's right and somebody thought it was wrong, I'd still do it, and I'd negotiate my way around it afterwards.

You must have been very charming.

I was and I never really made any enemies, a lot of the guys are still my mates, I still see them occasionally.

If you could distil down the attributes that enabled you to be successful at that time, how would you sum them up?

Well, it's funny you should say this because we're in the middle of moving at the moment and I've been sorting the house out. I found in our attic all my old business papers including a pile of Saville & Holdsworth assessments, I don't know whether they still exist but they were an organisation who did psychological tests. They analysed you and gave you a complete picture of what you were like. I just read them a couple of days ago.

Things that I think looked a little unusual might be that I was characterised as extraordinarily energetic. They said, "he goes off the scale on energy," which is true, no doubt about that. Not so much now, but definitely then.

Another was that I was very tough minded but also very fair. I'm always giving praise where it's due, giving people the right recognition. Thinking back, I was really tough-minded in the sense that if I thought somebody was really good and they proved themselves I would push them and promote them, but if I thought somebody was a fool I'd chuck them out! I would do it nicely, but they wouldn't be hanging around, they'd be gone.

That said, it does sound as if you invested in building relationships?

Yes, I did invest a lot in that, but then the psychological tests also said, "he's not really interested in personal attributes, he's very interested in business performance but not very good at finding out how many children they've got, which school they go to". I had to develop that,

I had to work at that. These tests were when I was about thirty. I found them very useful.

At about this time in my career I went on a NatWest Bank senior managers course. They were big clients of ours and they phoned up my boss and said, "we're running a course at Oxford University for two weeks, can you send somebody along because we want a bit of cross-fertilisation," they asked contacts at the army as well so there was a good cross-section of people and backgrounds. My boss said, "Peter, we've decided to send you on a senior managers course." I thought, you must be joking, I haven't got time to do that, I'm so busy! I didn't want to go, but it turned out to be one of the best experiences of my life.

Why?

I got to work in an Oxford college for two weeks, with thirty other guys from different backgrounds. We weren't allowed out at all, personality tests for everything under the sun. I came back from that so much more aware of myself. That probably did me the most good to be honest with you. I had been a bit of a rough diamond, a bit like a bull in a china shop, but with a smile. In fact, my mates these days, we play a lot of poker together, they call me the smiling assassin!

Did you find you had a good commercial sense, a head for numbers?

Well, that's interesting. No, my numbers weren't great, or at least my appreciation of numbers. In these tests I came out totally average, verbally higher, but certainly on the numbers not so great.

Did you develop an interest in the P&L though?

My passion to create a profit and produce surpluses was huge. The reason for that was because I was highly competitive, I wanted to beat everybody else and I wanted to end up top of the pile.

Were you like that in school? Could you always see that in yourself?

Not really. In fact at school I always had a bit of an inferiority complex because of course we didn't have any money and everybody else did. So whenever you went into the tuck shop I could never afford to buy a bloody ice lolly or whatever, which was embarrassing!

I did play a lot of squash. I played individual sports. I wasn't great. This is going to sound funny, after talking of building teams and things like that, but I was much better at individual sports than I was at team sports because I always felt myself to be the weak link. Whenever the rugby ball came in my direction, I missed it.

At work it sounds like you were good at reading and influencing people. What other strengths did you have?

I think reading people was a strength and finding out what they really wanted, why they did what they did. Also having very thick skin, somebody would have to bash me over the head with an insult for me to feel aggrieved. I was never upset by other people's behaviour, obviously unless it was extreme, which was very rare. I always viewed people as being good people first if they performed, if you chose the right people with the right skills and you put them in the right job, that was the important thing. I was always drawing charts, aware what the role was and defining the role.

Would you say you're more of a detail person or a big picture person?

Both actually, I see the big picture but I'm also detail oriented.

The way you were describing your organisational plans sounded like you did pay attention to the detail.

Yes I did, and I used to keep records of how much we earned and what the fees were. I was much more of a detailed person than I was prepared to admit. I'd say "no, I'm good, don't give me the details, I'm not interested in that". But actually when you examine what I actually did, there was a lot more detailed stuff. What I wanted other people to do there was to do the job, I never wanted to do it for them. There were people around who were really good - they weren't called just salesmen - you have really good chartered surveyors if you like, but they were on their own and they did very well inside our firm, they made a lot of money. Well, the way I reasoned it was that if people could motivate five people, ten people, thirty people, fifty people, we'd multiply the amount we could make enormously, so it would be much better for me to spend my time organizing and motivating other people, and that way we could win and be much better. Obviously it would reflect well on me as well, because I always put myself at the top of the pile on all the charts. There wasn't much modesty, I'm afraid!

At this stage of your career you're thirty-ish, you've become the head of the agency side. How did it progress from there?

That would have been in the mid to late seventies when we went through quite a recession. Actually, we went through two or three recessions during that period, and I remember many of my colleagues were being called up to the boardroom for a meeting and I wasn't called. I said, "What the bloody hell is going on? Why am I being missed out?" They all came back with their pink slips, they'd all been sacked. We went through several periods like that and I seemed to manage to survive each time.

When did your career take off?

The firm was going through lots of changes. They decided to bring in an Associate level. We had partners and staff, but there was a big jump between a partner and a member of staff. I was one of the first Associates.

Then we hit the early eighties with tremendous changes going on in the property world. Back then there wasn't such a thing as an out-of-town superstore or out-of-town retail parks or out-of-town offices. Jones Lang was divided into town centre offices, suburban offices, retail and industrial. I was lucky in that running the industrial department, anything that came through the door that was a bit abnormal, they'd say, "oh, Mantle will deal with all that crap, that's for him," so we got all these massive sites which we converted into retail sites for stores and instead of earning a fee of like, twenty grand, we might earn two-hundred grand, and then business parks came along and everybody said, "well, nobody will ever move out from the town centres into a business park".

Clients of ours developed Stockley Park, which is a great big park right by Heathrow; it hit the news and improved my reputation in the property world enormously because I was seen as the guy at the head of marketing that development. I played that like mad and used that to my advantage. I ran a trip for all the other agents to California to see all the American business parks. My partners said, "What are you doing that for? You're giving away all your secrets to all the other guys!" I said, "well, they're going to learn it anyway, so why don't they learn it from me? They'll feel good about me and the firm, and they'll also be my friends, so I'll get tons of business from them and they'll bring us in," and that's exactly what happened.

You're still in the commercial division at this stage?

Yes, I always was in the commercial division. To cut a long story short I was then made a partner. I was probably thirty-two or thirty-three and a salaried partner, so a partner in name only. You're given a percentage of the profits, but you never know what the profits are!

The department started making a lot of money because of the boom in business parks and out-of-town retail. We became a market leader in the sector and that really began to grab the attention of the owning partners of Jones Lang Wootton as it was then. Basically, I was made a partner and then I was made an 'owning' partner at the age of about thirty-seven.

Were you the 'owning' partner in the commercial department?

We decided to merge the suburban office department with the industrial department and call it the business department. The guy who ran suburban offices was quite a tough guy, a mate of mine but quite a tough bloke. We decided to run it jointly and everyone was betting on how long it would be before there was a nuclear explosion, but there never was. Actually, we ran it and worked very well together. He then went off and did something else and I took over the whole thing. In parallel I'd take on additional roles. I became Marketing Partner, I headed the marketing committee and was responsible for the marketing department and anything I could get my fingers into, I would do.

Were you working very long hours?

Yes, I used to get in the office about half-past seven. I lived in London so I used to drive in, so I wasn't leaving at five o'clock in the morning or anything like that, but I was in the office by seven thirty; by the time everybody else arrived at say half past eight to nine, I'd done half a day's work. I was miles ahead of them.

Was it a culture where you needed to wine and dine in the evenings?

Yes, lots of that, which I must admit I thoroughly enjoyed!

Did you cope well with the workload? Did you ever get stressed?

I'm not highly stressed and I'm not laid back either, I'm in the middle. Occasionally things got really fraught, you can imagine some of our clients were like Trump, really tough guys out to make as much money for themselves as they could, but generally I took it in my stride.

How did you manage your work life balance?

I did get stressed occasionally, but I always went on fantastic holidays. By this time I was happily married with three kids, so we always went on terrific holidays. We went skiing, we went sailing, I had a boat and we used to go sailing every weekend. That was like a week's holiday. We used to go down on Friday night and spend the weekend on a boat and come back Sunday night. I used to get back on a Sunday night and head off to the squash club and play two hours of squash. My wife who had her own teaching career was very understanding.

Did you find it possible to switch off quite easily?

Yes, not too difficult at all really. I would always think about things, but I was decisive. On the NatWest senior management course we had an exercise to run a company and they said, "You took more decisions in this exercise than anybody has ever taken before." And I said, "Well that's good isn't it!" And they said, "Well, we're not sure…" [LAUGHS] But I'm very decisive, once I decided to do something I did it.

What's the best piece of advice that anyone has given you?

I can't name an individual but as a learning exercise that course at Oxford University was the best thing that ever happened to me. Before that I had never thought about myself at all, I was never thinking, "Am I good at this? Am I bad at this?". That taught me a huge amount. The advice I give other people now is to know yourself. If you know yourself well it's a massive advantage and you can play to your strengths and feel at ease. Know what you're good at and what you're not good at and fill the gaps with people who are good at those things. If you're not honest with yourself you've had it. I've also learned to take advice from people highly knowledgeable in an area before making decisions, not assuming I know everything about the subject myself.

I do remember a piece of business advice from one of our senior partners who was a guru in the property world. He said, "Always follow the money." We had a very diverse portfolio of activities, all related to property, but the ones that made the biggest return were anything that was associated with the financing, with the banks, with the investing institutions. That taught me a lot. The people who spoke the most loudly and who grabbed your attention were the developers who were probably the least important. I always stuck close to the clients with money, the investing institutions and banks.

Were there any colleagues that you particularly admired?

Yes, there were people who became, I think we used to call them supreme specialists, they were like investment partners, surveyors if you like, who could ratchet up massive amounts of fees. I always, in a funny sort of way, wished I could have been like that, because I was running around all over the place! These guys had a laser focus, they'd get an instruction to sell a central London office block as an investment, do it and move onto the next one. They became sort of gurus. Whereas I spent my time running around the place getting involved in absolutely everything. I admired them but I recognised that I could never really do that. It just wouldn't fit my personality. If you gave me a bloody great office box to sell and one assistant to help me with that, I'd be bored in five minutes and I'd be off somewhere else.

What I haven't added was that after I became a proprietor, I became an international partner, we then owned the entire worldwide network. We had offices all over the US, Europe and the Far East. I spent a lot of time flying backwards and forwards. I set up an international business division, trying to tie together initially Japanese investors with investors in Europe and the Americans. At about this time our partner left the West End offices, which was a very profitable and high-profile group, I took that over and then became Managing Partner. That was my official job but I had all these other jobs on the side as well.

You enjoyed that period?

That's why I stayed there for the whole of my thirty-five year working life! Every five years I changed role, which kept me hugely motivated. There were many things to do, to get involved with. I certainly liked knitting people together, that's what we did internationally. This is spanning a few years, but we put the whole of the international operation together under one partnership, it had been fragmented so there was a lot of selling to get everybody to agree, to form an operating holding company. We were then very weak in the US and we ultimately merged with a company LaSalle Partners, a US company. Then we floated the combined operation and I became lead partner of the agency division in the UK. I formed that into a European agency division because I reasoned that if, for example,

IBM were looking for an office in Paris and we didn't know IBM in London, we should be crossing that information over.

The client management matrix become quite significant then so I instigated a comprehensive client survey. We asked our clients to fill in questionnaires on what they thought of us. I got all the partners to fill in what they thought the clients would say about us. We matched the two together. We found there was a complete mismatch as to what the clients valued in us and what we thought they valued!

The Property world is a world of deal-making, perhaps with less of a focus on customer understanding than in some other sectors. Is that fair to say?

Yes, and perhaps that knowledge helped me become Managing Partner because I went to a management consultant, I can't remember his name actually, but he did a lot of work in Professional Services firms and he said, "What you've got to do is understand your clients, understand the people that are providing your living and make sure that you treat them as very special people, give them what they really want." And of course we probably had become a little complacent in that we were top of the pile, best firm internationally. Somebody would say, "I work for a big investment firm," and I'd say, "well, that's good," and he'd say "I've done this. I bought this office building and I did this and this," and I'd say, "how much business do we do with them?" and he'd say "I don't know." [Laughs] I'd say, "Well, hang on a minute, where do they fit in the pecking order?" "I don't know!".

Inspired by the chat with a consultant we began for the first time really to analyse all the clients by fee income. Then we analysed who knew them and who they thought were their partners, who they were close to, and tried to make it a little bit more scientific. In fact, I tried to get a database together so that for every client you knew whether he played golf or whether he liked sailing and what his children's names were and all that. In the early days of computers, I tried to pull together a database so you could get that up on a screen in front of you and you could seem to be so smart. "Oh, hello Brian! How's Paul, that son of yours?" But of course we could never do it. This was thirty years ago. For a professional services firm understanding your clients is absolutely key, they're much better at it now.

That was a telling learning. Any others of that ilk?

Yes, make yourself a very desirable place to work. If you do that you will always attract the best people. That's why I've never understood people like Maxwell and Murdoch who beat their people up. I had Developer clients like that who used to beat the hell out of their people, I'm assuming they had to pay them double, which of course meant they took it, but a normal person wouldn't. I never understood how those organization managed to survive and of course many of them didn't.

The secret is to have an organization where everybody believes in what it's about, what it's doing, feels part of it and an important part of it. Not everybody can be an important part of it, but a lot of people can be made to feel valuable because of the role that they play. If you create an environment like that, you will always attract the best people, you won't necessarily attract the best people by paying them the most money, it doesn't work that way. Again, I've never quite understood the investment banks who rely on money to attract people. The minute they start falling off on performance, they chuck them out.

And I assume the moment someone else pays them more money, they leave?

Yes that's true. In our case we had very loyal staff. During the purges in the recessions, we always looked after people. If we had to let them go, we paid them a year's salary. Some of them became fantastic clients when they left and afterwards employed us. Very rarely did we create enemies in the property world.

When you were a Managing Partner, did you have a strategic plan of some kind?

Yes. I mean, again, I mentioned to you that I was good at drawing boxes and things like that. Early on I undertook a strategic review of the entire firm. I divided up the firm into three big units, it had been something like twenty before. That seemed to work. We had all the commercial people in one box, all the professional valuers in the other box, because they were very different people, as I mentioned to you.

Did you have a very clear view on where your growth would come from?

We did. I formed a management committee, which the firm didn't have before. I knew that we had to keep our clients happy, I knew where the money was coming from, which clients were paying us the most, but in a funny way being the largest firm in the world there's only one way from that position, which is down. What I tried to do was to bind everybody together so they weren't just in silos. There were lots of crossing points, a lot of cross-selling. Cross-selling was the word in my time. Some of those things worked well and others less so. Some people were so silo orientated that they couldn't bring themselves to work with one of the other silos. Either it was a competitive thing or they didn't value them or they just couldn't see the point.

How long were you Managing Partner for?

For five years.

Can you remember how the numbers went in that time?

Pretty well. I mean, as some colleagues would say, "Timing is everything, you hit the end of the nineties recession and you picked the up slope and up we went!"

What was the scale of the business at the end of your period as Managing Partner?

I think at the time when I finished the firm had a fee income of £150 million or something like that and about £20 - £30 million in profit. These are old figures, they wouldn't have any relevance today.

When I retired, we employed 7,000 people around the world and had a market capitalization of something like a billion. I haven't checked it in the last year, but about a year ago we employed 85,000 people with a market capitalization of five billion. That's quite something, isn't it?

In my time what we did was merge everything under one partnership. We then formed a limited company because we were all taking too much personal risk. There were only twenty of us who owned it at the time so we created the limited liability company partnership, and then because we were so weak in the US we merged with LaSalle and floated on the New York Stock Exchange.

Was that after your time?

No that was in my time, That's how I was able to retire so early because we all had golden handcuffs and had a lot of shares!

At what age did you retire?

Fifty-five. And then I went sailing around the world.

Can you talk a little more about how you pulled the international operation together?

I must make absolutely clear that all this was very much a team effort. I suppose of the owning partners, probably about five, of which I was one, were heavily active in drawing everything together.

We owned Europe 100% and we needed to bind the Far East in, which we did through strenuous negotiations.

The way we did it was by selling the big picture, getting people to buy into the big picture and the people who worked for us largely were big picture people. They didn't want to be part of a small firm otherwise they'd have joined one! They joined a big international firm because they valued what a big international firm gave them.

There was a strenuous negotiation about who got what, how many shares went to who, but we got there by painting the big picture. The issue was that we felt that unless we bound everybody together, we might fragment. One of our big competitors at the time was Richard Ellis and they did fragment. Their overseas operation went one way, and the UK another, New York went somewhere else. They were greatly weakened at the time, we didn't want that at all. We wanted to remain top of the pile, very much a force in the property world. I think we largely achieved that, today we are the number one or number two, depending on which way you look at it.

When you think back to your time as a Managing Partner, a very responsible position, did you consciously think about how you managed your work / life balance?

I never worked at weekends. I don't mean if we went abroad for an office visit, then of course I did, but when I was working solely in London I made it a rule that I never worked a weekend. When I left the office on Friday night, which might be the very late on Friday night, I didn't work again until Monday morning. That was a very strict rule. Second rule was to always have fabulous holidays. I never worked on holidays.

I suppose when you asked me if I learned anything later which I wish I'd understood earlier in my career, one would be the power to delegate. You acquire that ability over time, the ability to trust people comes with time. If I had really understood that you can trust people and they'll do a good job if you chose the right ones, I wouldn't have to go through all that pain of doing so much of it myself!

I think as Managing Partner I should have split the role earlier. It was split at the end into a management role, which I had, and a COO, because I was getting very bogged down in all the detail, which a COO should do.

Did you stand down as Managing Partner when you went public?

Yes and my big problem was, what the hell do I do now? What do you do after that? I didn't want to leave and go somewhere else. This was the time of the dot com boom. I was having lunch with Morgan Stanley and they said, "You've got so much knowledge property-wise, why don't you set up an international electronic trading base? We'll lend you anything you want, £50 million, and we'll float for £500 million. How about that?" I said, "I like the sound of that," and we did it.

You created a company with Morgan Stanley's backing?

Yes, It was called Pathway. It was the Rightmove of the commercial world, but it collapsed in a heap at the end of the dot com boom, and we pulled out of it. Was it ever going to work? Was it ever going to make any money? I don't know, but Rightmove makes money.

What's your view now on the impact of digitization on your industry?

Everybody says it's much more efficient but far less fun. We used to have tremendous fun, my working life was enormously good fun. I made really good mates and we had a really good time, we did business together, we worked hard and made a lot of money. It was enjoyable, there were down times, but overall I can say that it was really enjoyable.

Now I'm told it's much more of a churn. Everything is much more regimented. I can't really believe that because people like dealing with people they like and know.

We are all locked down at the moment and working from home. What's the impact going to be long-term for the commercial property market?

As a property man it's a bad thing. Property prices are going to go down. If you don't need so much office space, if you don't need to live in a city, you can live outside. There's a massive amount of change going on at the moment which looks very much more negative. I said in the early eighties there was massive change going on in a positive sense, at the moment all the change seems to be negative, but positive things will come out of it. Who knows what, the guys that can latch on to what we can positively take out of this will make a lot of money. Everybody's very depressed at the moment and all the prices are depressed. But I think working at home from a work-life balance point of view is probably a good thing.

I think what triggered my question was you would lose some of that fun you were talking about of 'colliding' with colleagues.

For me, I would hate it because I need people around me. I'm not happy on my own. I need lots of people to talk to and if I'm doing any sort of task, people to organize, I like organizing people. If you asked me to work at home, I'd be busy organizing everybody on the internet!

Do you think it will make it much more difficult to build a cohesive team culture, a feeling of joint identity?

I would think it need not necessarily lead to that. You could, if you worked hard, you've got people who understand these issues and you would then have to have frequent events or think-tank seminars. Let's say you worked at home three days a week, went into an office two days a week, which presumably is hot desked so you move around, you've got no allegiance to a floor, then you would need to work hard at getting people together and get to know each other.

Some people don't like these Zoom calls, I think they're fine. You can interface. I feel I'm interfacing with you. We could be sitting opposite each other.

There are always changes afoot in Property, but for those who are on the front foot like in your own career with the business park boom there will be opportunities?

Yes, the people that saw those changes early did very well. Me and a few others capitalised by building reputations, becoming experts in those new areas. I must admit, I can't think what they are at the moment, but there will be opportunities to come out of this tremendous change, because at times of change, opportunities emerge.

In your long career what are the things you are proudest of?

I was thinking about this the other day. I'm actually proud of everything I did! I'm now seventy-four, so I'm contemplating things perhaps a little more and looking back at whether I'm happy with everything I did. And the answer is yes I am. Maybe that's just a personality type and there's plenty of things not to be happy about, but in my head I was very proud to have been part of the total reorganization at Jones Lang LaSalle, although some people would not think that was a great idea. They said, "We liked the old Jones Lang, we don't like this public company with shareholders."

What do you think people would say about you as a business leader?

I think they would say he was cheerful, single-minded, tough-minded, fair, energetic, humorous – I sound like that bloke from The Office – I suppose strategic might well be in that description as well, or at least I hope so!

Did you see yourself as more strategic than some of your colleagues?

Yes, I was always trying to think five steps ahead. Why don't we do this? Why don't we do that? And then talking about it a lot. The idea of forming the international company I kept on and on and on, mentioning it and talking about it because I could see that that was the way to build a stronger position in our market. Some people recognised that, some people didn't, but I would count myself as strategic, yes.

Do you think that tomorrow's successful organisations will be very different from the one that you were working in during the eighties and the nineties? Will they work in a different way?

I think they will. I was very lucky in that there just seemed to be a lot of opportunities at every turn. I never thought, "I'm bored with this, there's nothing to do." There was always another avenue to go down, a thing to do here, a client to get there, a new business opportunity to open. Is that likely to change? I suspect not, actually. Surely as we've just said, times of change are opportunities, they'll just be very different ones. I think you've got to be very digitized. It's very difficult for somebody of my age, and possibly even yours, to visualize a world that our twenty-five year olds and thirty year olds will live in.

I suspect to be successful, firms will be able to or need to own less, which is interesting for a property person, whether it's property or whether it's plant, they may be much less likely to make things themselves. There'll be smaller overheads, they'll be more nimble and more about collaboration.

I think that's possible. You see your staff and think if they can work from Leatherhead then they can work from Singapore or Thailand. That's something that hasn't bottomed out at the moment. There's all these finance guys working from home. Why not hire a finance guy at half the price in Singapore? There's a lot of that which could come, but then that might be frustrated by political protectionism. Populists are trying to pull themselves into smaller groups. I think the virtual organization, is that really going to fly? It could do, could do, absolutely it could. My daughter does very much that sort of stuff, she coaches Executives on how to cope with the modern digital world. She's thirty-five and they're all fifty-five, and she seems to make quite a lot of money out of it!

Last question, if you were sitting in a room of eager-faced twenty-two, twenty-three year olds keen to make their mark on the world and you were asked to give them some advice, what would you say?

Know yourself really well, learn about yourself, don't kid yourself, learn what you're good at and what you're not good at, be proud of what you're good at and invest in doing it better and better.

Whatever you do, enjoy what you do. Don't do it if you don't enjoy it. People are good at what they enjoy and they're terrible at what they don't enjoy. You'll be successful if you find something that you really enjoy.

I think energy is important. I don't think you lie in bed all day or sit around, you've got to be energetic to beat your competition. Energy creates opportunities.

Always have a sense of humour, see the funny side of life. Don't let stress get you. I used to do a lot of physical exercise. I used to go running around the block every morning and on the exercise bike. If you stay physically fit, you'll be mentally fit. Also always take advice from experts in their field. You don't always need to take it but do garner as wide a range of views as possible before you make a decision. Then move quickly to implement it.

Always learn, keep learning, learn all the time, never stopped learning! I'm still learning, I'm currently doing an MA in Philosophy. I didn't even know what philosophy was five years ago! [LAUGHS] So I think those are the things I would say. Also, don't be vindictive, don't harbour grudges, get on with people, look for the good in people rather than the bad, we all tend to look for the bad. Lastly, have fun. We're only here for a visit, so make everything you can out of the hand you've been dealt, embrace the opportunities which open up for you and have fun doing it.

“

I've noticed that, once a decision is made, good leaders articulate the 'why' and the 'how' very clearly and somehow connect with people on a human level to carry them along and create a certain energy.

”

MARTIN LEWIS

INTERVIEWED 7TH FEBRUARY 2020

Martin is the combined CFO and COO at the law firm Taylor Wessing and previously UK COO for the global property giant CBRE and a senior director at top law firm Linklaters. His career has taken in spells in accounting, property and law; a career spent almost entirely in the world of professional services.

In this interview, he gives his unique insights into the challenges and opportunities involved in working in a professional service firm as a non-fee earner at a very senior level. He also shares his personal insights into human dynamics and how to be successful in complex, sometimes political organisations.

Perhaps we can talk about the start of your career.

I went to The University of Canterbury and I had no clue what I wanted to do in terms of my career when the milk round came around. I studied computer science and accounting. Utterly needlessly as it turned out, because of the accounting technique we were taught. When I went on to be an accountant, they told us to ignore it all because it was the wrong technique for commercial business. The computing was a bit of a waste too. Within six months of leaving, the programming language I had studied had been superseded by a better one! So, there you go. When the milk round came around, a friend of mine signed up very early on and joined Ernest & Whinny (that's what it was called back then). He was set and I was slow, but I didn't really know what I wanted to do. Then Arthur Young turned up, they probably gave a bottle of wine and had a nice party. I didn't really understand the world of big firm accountancy, but I thought they would be good career choice. My mother played her part because her brother had been an accountant and she said he didn't do badly. That was probably the extent of the analysis!

Did you join as a graduate trainee?

I joined as a graduate trainee accountant and funny thing was my girlfriend at the time was based in Manchester, so instead of joining in London, where most of my friends went, I kicked off in Manchester – where I had no roots and, having gone travelling for nine months, by that time no girlfriend!

How long did you stay with them and what are your early memories of your first experience of work?

I was a trainee auditor reviewing lots of businesses, but it was the manufacturing companies that I was fascinated by because we went out and saw people actually make things – paints, cookers, windows. It was just great to watch products I recognised in the shops being made – I was quite fascinated by that.

I thought the role of the auditing accountant was pretty dull. In fact, I found it very dull. I quite liked checking the fixed assets, going to the warehouse and seeing the kit in operation, but I didn't really like auditing, it was checking other people's work, there was little room for creativity. I saw an opportunity to work my way out by getting involved in the then embryonic world of computer audits. The first PCs had arrived; the floppy disks were nine inches wide back then!

What year was this?

I joined in 1985 so this was '86 or '87. Companies were using big computers by then; the skill of the time was to be able to extract samples of data from them for audit testing. I got quite good at it which saved me from doing the regular auditing work. At that time, my other goal was to get back to London. I saw my opportunity when an opening came up in the firm's Audit Automation department – which was based on Fetter Lane near Fleet St – they were developing auditing software and simplifying the process of auditing, building it all on Apple technology. I got in with the team there and I thought that was fabulous. Experimenting with application development, engaging with software developers, working out what the business really wanted. I was a business analyst I suppose. I couldn't do anything with the coding, but I worked out what the business wanted and went between the suppliers and developers. We built some quite impressive technology; it was very exciting. I also finished my exams whist with that London team qualifying as a chartered accountant.

Unfortunately, after I had been in London for a couple of years Arthur Young was involved in an international merger and became Ernst & Young (EY). Like all big mergers, a call had to be made on which technology was going to be the standard across the new unified firm.

Ernst & Whinny seemed to be the more dominant partner and so their technology won. They were using IBM Compaq machines and we were using Apple and everything that we did was shutdown. They tried to merge us as IT teams, but it didn't really work. I felt gutted at the time because I had helped develop all this technology and it had gone.

A big quoted real estate company called MEPC were looking for somebody to join them to assist a major systems implementation. They paid very well and provided great cars and I wanted to get away from E&Y, so I joined them on an internal auditing ticket but largely to do a big systems replacement.

You were about 25 when you joined MEPC?

I think I was 26. It was unfortunate that the wider economic condition of the country started to fail badly and there was a major downturn. The ambition the company had to do large scale change in their IT was put on the back burner, so I became involved in the running of the business. I managed to get myself involved in some of the business strategy for the firm – just in a small way working with some of the more senior people – I really enjoyed it.

Were you working in the finance department?

I was technically in the internal auditing department, there were two of us. We were in a lovely office for a while on the top floor of a Park Lane des res overlooking Hyde Park – before we all moved to St James's Square. The lady who was head of the Audit Practice was also in charge of treasury – securing credit lines for development projects. She worked closely with the Finance Director and it was through that arrangement that I got my first exposure to corporate strategy work.

I worked for three years with MEPC and from there joined the big international law firm Linklaters. The context for my joining Links was that, elsewhere in the world, Steve Jobs had by then fallen out with Apple and left them hooking up with another business developing an object-orientated technology called NeXT Step. At the time, this was ground-breaking and was seen as the future for desktop computing. It inspired the recruitment of an IT guru by Linklaters to help them deploy a strategy for the adoption of a different kind of distributed networked system. They had been using a long-established technology called Wang. It was an old character-based system which had a relatively limited server capability – the firm was expanding internationally and wanted much easier documents sharing between its offices and teams.

Andrew Taylor was the guru / visionary behind how that change was to be made and so he went looking for a team to support him and I was lucky enough to be picked. So, the truth is I joined Linklaters not because it was a famous law firm but because I was excited by its technology ambition! They were experimenting and I was excited to experiment too. So, I took a role once again with a solution-finding responsibility sourcing software from around the world that would fit the solution. There were quite a few trips to the American west coast and a lot of Europe in search of word processing, spreadsheet management and presentation software – we were definitely on the leading edge and quite often it felt like the 'bleeding edge' it was so new… but I loved every minute of it.

So, with MEPC in between you found yourself at a big law firm after your experience at a giant accounting practice. How did those two cultures / industries compare?

I came to realise they were quite different but at the time it was harder to tell. I was a young junior accountant - it was all about projects and getting them done – I don't know if I really understood the wider firm culture. I did get my first exposure to a merger and the impact of two big entities coming together, the challenge of uniting cultures is very great – it's a rough tough journey, I found it very instructive.

Did you distil any learnings from the experience?

Well those were the times when the big four were created. There were ten or eleven big names in accounting and they rapidly merged down to the four we have today. There was a lot of crude management to get people to work together. It was attritional, big ticket decisions that tended to flood over the foot soldiers on the ground like me. Whereas today I think people are much more cautious and clever about how teams are brought together – it will always be difficult but the science and the learning behind how it's done is so much more sophisticated.

They still say that most acquisitions don't create value, don't they?

That's a commercial assessment that is probably true but the big four have dominated the market ever since so who's to say they were wrong.

My first-hand experience since then has been that for mergers to work at firm or team level the match of personality and talent level are both critical for success. When I was at Linklaters, if you didn't get the match between the individuals right then you didn't get a win. I remember being on a team that explored a possibility of a tie up with a Japanese firm. At the conclusion of our 2 day offsite shared with their leadership team we came away convinced the marriage was on – they came away promising never to meet again!

That was my point, actually. Can you talk a little more about your observations?

In the late '80s and early '90s, I don't think that the understanding of the way teams can be encouraged and supported to work together had been thought through well enough; it certainly wasn't handled with any subtlety! In the end, if two groups don't like each other they won't come together well. There are ways that you can make the situation better and try to ensure that the foot soldiers have the best chance of uniting. The sophistication of management processes feels so much more advanced today. Back then many law firms were run by people with a limited amount of management experience; they were the best practitioners but not necessarily great managers. I think I've lived through the period of transition from expert practitioners who also tried to run the business to one where the leadership teams are proper business managers who surround themselves with senior experts in the full range of management disciplines.

Your first experience was as a small cog in a big machine, then the coming together of two companies, then property, then law. Tell me a little more about your first time in real estate, let's go back to that for a moment.

Do you mean when I was at MEPC? For sure – the real estate people were different to the accountants. The latter were generally professional advisors, the former were deal doers – interested in property development and investment transactions which was where the major money was made, clearly. At the beginning of the 90s the markets had crashed, it was a tough time; no sector was feeling particularly strong. So it was a cautious period, the air hung heavy, the blame game was greater, everyone's focus was on getting through – weathering the storm. It was a difficult time. People were on the back foot; the real estate industry generally needs a rising market to do well. When I crossed over to the law world, they seemed in a better place; it was still a difficult market but nevertheless there was still a lot of work being done – it was a more optimistic environment.

The James's Square MEPC offices were magnificent in their fit-out but quite dated in their culture – old-fashioned ivory tower stuff; all of the main board directors were together on the top floor in massive palace sized offices – they even had a red carpet when you emerged from the lift!

Different toilets, different carpets [laughs].

I remember it being quite different to the professional services world I'd occupied with EY - sure they had Partners, but they weren't as clearly differentiated from their teams as the Board Directors were. I guess the firm's success was all about the long-term real estate bets the Directors made - there was a lot of tension - it was my first exposure to share price accountability and reassuring the City investors. I was seeing politics at the top of an organisation for the first time (literally, given that lift).

I imagine that law firms are very much like that too.

I think most commercial institutions are political and hierarchical; I was growing comfortable with all of that. What I experienced for the first time at Linklaters was the divide between the direct fee earners and everyone else, which was a culture challenge for sure.

Has the power balance in a law firm between the lawyers and the 'others' changed since then, given your more recent experiences back in the legal sector?

Thankfully it has moved on massively. At the time I think that recognition for non-lawyers was hard to land but we did have something to bring to the party and it was recognised. There was the realisation for me back at Linklaters, that here was a profession of people (lawyers) that had a view on the competence of people in other roles, not a very well informed view obviously, and it was harder, much harder, to be a non-lawyer in a substantial law firm and have your value recognised. I guess there was a common belief across a lot of the lawyers that they could do everything if only they had the time to spare.

Non-fee earners were looked at differently. I seem to remember when they brought in the system for the catering you got given cards, and one said 'lawyer' and the other 'non-lawyer'. We were non-lawyers. I knew how to work in the space and I built relationships quite strongly with a lot of partners. I liked those partners a lot, but it was very tough for people to have their expertise recognised.

Tell me more about your role at Linklaters as it developed.

Soon I was running the operations. I was put in charge of all sorts of functions and I didn't even know what some of them did, but I was trusted. I think people thought, "He's a good guy, he understands the way we see the world, let's see what he can do." We looked at how the operations were run, there were some excellent professionals. I learned a lot about service delivery and how to make everything tick. For the first time I was managing a large number of people as well.

Who were you reporting into?

Ultimately the Managing Partner, but there were a group of directors in what was called back then 'practice support'. I was lucky that a guy called Tony Angel, who had been a successful Tax Partner, was elected to head the firm. He was in some respects a little scary with his sharp brain and laser focused business mind, and he was definitely slightly counterculture to the history of the firm and what had gone before. I was attracted to the way that he worked and ended up in a function that started to look at the performance of the business quite forensically. It led, for the first time, to business planning being introduced to the firm in a serious way.

What was it about the way he worked that you liked?

He wanted to find the true drivers of success, to understand why some parts of the business were working well and why some were not working so well. He started to deal with the issue areas and properly addressing under-performance. There had been some wider concerns in the firm that performance was dipping versus competitor firms and there was some tension in the ranks. When running a professional services firm, you need to stay competitive and profitable and there was a dip – they'd dropped too far down the profit table rankings for the comfort of many. It needed sorting, which was probably why he was elected. I've seen this quite a few times.

What was his countercultural style?

It was the management, his principles of applying management techniques to the running of a successful law firm. Prior to then, my sense was the leaders were fabulous lawyers with stand-out market reputations but not necessarily a great deal of commercial nous. We developed some sophisticated models that enabled professional service firms to operate more effectively. It felt to me that I was on the wave of something new.

As part of an international firm, how much scope did you have in the UK to do your own thing?

At that time lawyers from across the world came together more and more to collaborate on solutions, it was the time when the 'one stop shop' idea was starting to land for law firms. We could offer comprehensive international coverage under one roof rather than recommending good firms or people in other jurisdictions. To some degree, I think our firm had been a little behind the curve in this respect. Clients needed an international network but with the credibility of respected English brand name at its core. English Law was a world success story - a trusted code for contracts and agreements. The powerhouse inside the firm was really the UK, it made the most profit and was the most renowned. We went on a sort of acquisition trail but all through mergers bringing jurisdictions that were obvious gaps into the firm, some of the tie-ups were naturally matching ones, others were more stretched. It was a time of great learning for me.

The whole need for international coverage was driven by the clients. If you were going to be an international supplier of law to the biggest companies or banks you needed global coverage. The American firms were the big global competitors but for most of my time they tended to stay stateside; it was the English law centric firms that competed in the other parts of the world. In the end I think the US firms made much better progress establishing themselves globally than the English firms did building US presence.

Anyway, this was a time where internationalisation was a big strategic play. The second imperative was profitability. Firms wanted to make sure their partners got matching returns to those they could expect in competing law firms, in order to hold on to their talent. You had to be canny enough to coordinate your actions and deliver a return that meant you stayed competitive in the market. That needed real management rather than a "try harder" approach. It was the joint imperative of achieving international reach and maintaining profitability which allowed you to reward your top talent. That is what drove the need for a more sophisticated management approach in law firms. I think I was lucky that I was where I was when the opportunities unfolded for non-lawyer talent (!) to play a more important role in firms like Linklaters.

How long were you there?

Seven years.

What role did you have at the end of your time there?

When I left, I was in charge of business planning and finance. I left to make my dot com fortune because that was the time when the World Wide Web really exploded. It was in full flower and someone made me a big offer to go and join them. It was an embryonic business with only a basic plan, a little start up fund but with the promise of big backing to come. They had big ambitions but not a real strategy of how to get there. That is when I learned that cash is king. Ambition isn't worth much – if you don't have cash, you don't have a business. I was doing everything operational for the business night and day including managing all the financial spreadsheets – I could see what was playing out.

A bit hand to mouth?

It was hand to mouth but not much in the mouth, a desperate descent actually. The big money that was supposed to come in to help the business didn't show up because people got worried about dot coms. The business as it was went down and down and got very ugly by the end. When there's no money left, I learnt the hard way that promises are worth nothing – if it's not written down in the contract, when the going gets tough it counts for nothing and loyalty dies under pressure. Businesspeople are friendly and warm when there's wealth, but when there isn't it's time to don your tin hat!

You went back to the law firm. Were they welcoming?

I was very lucky given the state of the economy at that time – it was opportune timing because somebody left Linklaters at short notice and they had a hole to fill. I only went back for six months on a contract basis and ended up staying six or seven years. I was lucky twice over, I got into the firm at a time when they were on a massive expansion curve. I worked closely with a powerful corporate Partner called David Cheyne – he was a big voice in the firm at that time.

Had Tony Angel gone by then?

No, Angel was in charge of the firm. I'll come back to him, but I re-joined the firm to support David and his Corporate Division of the firm. David was on the firm's Board then - later he became the firm's Senior Partner.

You did well. What was your secret?

I think I was smart, I understood how the business worked but I think the thing I did best was explain the key performance drivers to them in their language [the lawyers]. I could translate accounting speak to legal speak I guess.

Lawyer language?

I could 'translate' lawyer language to business language. I could explain what needed to get done and had the credibility to be listened to which meant change could happen. Being my own voice, talking straight about what I saw, not in a political way but calling it as I saw it. I think people liked that.

What is the key to doing that successfully? It sounds necessary but risky. Is it your tone of voice?

I think it's something I probably developed; I've used it a lot. I've often described it as punching with a smile! I think my style is communicative, it's open, it's friendly but it carries a serious message and people seem to like being told the truth in a nice manner. It's people skills, really. A combination of people skills and being able to tell the truth, then you have that anchor of trust, it helps you because people know how they can relate to you. If your wife asks, "do I look good in this?" I'm probably the one that says, "there might be better combinations"!

Which is a brave thing to say! At least I call it out and so people know where they stand. I think it's an honesty but also a friendly tone. I think I'm good at it. If you meet people that have had a similar journey, we have similar skills dealing with incredible people who are outstanding players in their sport of the law, have played in the largest deals, gifted with incredible brains but they can certainly use help in other areas of the business and that is increasingly understood.

You talked about knowing others in similar roles with the same tone of voice, people skills and perhaps an equally solid finance foundation. What helped you get to the top? Do you think you had another level of drive to move up?

It was often said in the group that I was in that I had very strong ambition. It's true, back then I was impatient to make my way.

You didn't start out in your career with a master plan, you figured it out along the way and had an innate drive to progress?

When I was younger, I was given advice from time to time which was helpful, but frankly I think I went up a few cul-de-sacs with my career along the way. It was much later on that someone gave me proper, skilful, and focussed mentoring and that was an eye opener to me, they taught me about influencing people. Then in terms of career progression I seemed to simply fall into the next thing, there was always something about going forward but I wasn't always sure where exactly I was headed! Eventually at Linklaters I was made a Director, you couldn't be a Partner unless you were qualified in law. I often characterise my career like a set of cricket stumps. A cricket wicket has three stumps, first for me was Ernst & Young, the second was Linklaters and the third was CBRE. The two gaps in between were my attempts at start-up businesses.

Tell me about your time at CBRE where you were COO when I first met you. How long were you there?

Eight years.

What were the most important things you learned from your days with that firm?

Well the first thing is very fundamental – if you don't make good profit and you're not growing, it saps the soul of the organisation. As soon as you stop making money it drags the tone down. People like to be in successful businesses. Life is a game and money keeps the score. Whenever the money wasn't right it was always difficult.

The second thing I learned is if you want to bring about a fundamental change in infrastructure or services or whatever, it's easier to do it in a good market than a tough one. Make your material changes when the running is good because you know it's going to get quieter, so move quickly in the peaks.

I also learned that there were three character types under the same roof: the brokers, there to do trades, buying and selling of significant real estate, people who give professional advice (like valuations) and people who focus on real estate service provision. That's three different types of wired minds and so the way that you communicate with each has to be different.

Three types of roles, but you think the human beings in those roles are similar too?

Well, my observation is that in life, people succeed best when they find a role that suits who they are rather than arrive at a role and try and fit it to them. That's why when you get to the senior level you find people who are really excellent at what they do, because they have worked out what suits them and invested in the skills and experience to excel at it.

When you are communicating with the first group, they are very self-centric, so you have to be punchy and play to their self-interest. To be blunt, everything else is a distraction for them.

The second group responds more to an intelligent collective rationale and the people in the third group respond well to communication which is rooted in process and good order. Which means you have to communicate the same thing in three different voices, in three different ways? You can't put out a single message. Of course, that's a very broad generalisation, but I've found understanding your audience, how they think and what drives them is important in internal communication, as it is for that matter in external communication.

You developed an understanding of how to communicate successfully with different audiences. What are your other strengths?

My strength, I think, is being able to understand the full breadth of the business front and back office and so see how everything relates. You know the phrase, "jack of all trades, master of none". I tend to understand the whole business and how it connects and where things fit. People are usually obsessed with their own roles and projects. In a professional services firm, it's rare for someone to focus on maintaining the broader perspective.

As I remember, you have a relatively unusual Myers Briggs profile, don't you?

[Laughs] I believe I am either an INFP or INTP. Which means, although I have an ability to engage with lots of different people, I'm also a bit of a detached thinker.

Remind me what those letters stand for?

Well I don't profess mastery of this but my interpretation is that 'I' is for introvert, the preference to reach self-conclusion. 'N' is for being drawn to the big picture more so than the specific detail. 'F' is for feeling your way to a decision; 'T' is relying more on logic. The last is 'P' for perceiving options and paths. The alternate is 'J' which seeks to narrow down options quickly.

Do you think you would be a good CEO?

I've never wanted to be one, even though some people have said I could do it. I lead a lot but I'm never right at the top. I've come to feel that the ENTJ profile is what tends to make a brilliant leader. They're straight – you know where you stand, they hold the big picture, they are very logical and they make decisions quickly. INFP is different. I think I learned that piece that I said earlier, it's much better to take a role that suits who you are than to take a role and try and make yourself fit it.

What do you wish you'd understood at the beginning of your career that you know now?

Trust and believe in yourself. I always thought I knew some of the answers but I didn't always push my thoughts through, I was wary of being shut down or challenged; I rarely was but I carried a nervousness that I might be. I didn't take all the big career jumps that were on offer given that cautiousness, there was a chance to have moved faster if I had been more confident a little younger. But of course, confidence comes with experience.

More than half of the people I have interviewed have said the same thing.

That's interesting. Also, I've absolutely learned that how you behave as a leader affects how your team feels.

Did you learn that from observing other leaders or from your own experience?

Both, absolutely both. All of the clichés you have about the difference leaders make is absolutely true. How a group is led makes an enormous difference.

Good leaders can grab the attention and become the human face of the firm. They obviously think about strategy and they make the right calls on the big ticket moves. They are people that have a good grasp of logic and are strong communicators. People know where they stand and even if they don't like it, they'll accept the rationale. That's in contrast with those who procrastinate forever, you never get a landing – they fuel uncertainty. Or those who are too closed off in the office and you don't see them, too obsessed with detail.

Are good leaders born or made?

The lucky ones are born – but it's still all about how the leadership is applied that differentiates.

My leadership career has been built around getting people to believe they can perform. I encourage people to deliver their best. I guess the most skillful leaders are like football mangers, they know exactly when to kick and when to stroke.

That bridges to my next question. If you think of your career to date, what colleague have you most admired and why?

There are two I come back to a lot. The first is Tony Angel who I worked closely with at Linklaters because he had so much courage, intellectual strength, and a certain dogmatic resilience. The way he explained things honestly and clearly, the amount of integrity and conviction he displayed, even if it caused a lot of upset. He listened to the counsel of others, drew conclusions on what he felt was best for the organisation and then pushed it through, often in the face of resistance – which takes a lot of courage.

The difficulty with leadership is that so often you don't know all the answers, so you are analysing the situation, using your best judgement, but in the end you need to make a decision – that can be a lonely place right at the top. I've noticed that once the decision is made, good leaders articulate the 'why' and the 'how' clearly and somehow connect with people on a human level to carry them along and create a certain energy.

Do you have some of those qualities?

I think so when it comes to seeing things through and holding my convictions. But Tony was phenomenal – a great brain. He could assimilate so much on a broader canvas than I could, and he had that courage and tenacity. I mean, he was a difficult man, not easy, but he was definitely effective.

He wasn't difficult with you though?

No, not difficult but he didn't always have the time for the pleasantries though, never offending, he cared for people and would defend his team but didn't always have the time to show it – but I was fine with that. We worked well together; I think my communication skills were a benefit to him.

And who was the second?

The second is a guy called Martin Samworth who was MD for CBRE. He had similar conviction and courage but brought about change by influencing a lot through one to one engagement with the key players. He was very difficult to know yet he was someone who earned loyalty and respect from those he worked with. You could go to him with a big issue – you could trust being open with him and invariably he would help you solve the problem. He wasn't so good at the set piece large audience events, but he still got things done.

What do you mean about the big event?

He didn't prepare well. He did try, but he wasn't a natural. I don't think that mattered as he was able to make change happen. The two of them, Tony and Martin, stand out for me in my career.

What's the best piece of business-related advice you've been given and who gave it to you?

That mentoring I mentioned earlier helped a lot. You and I have had some very useful exchanges too. My mentor taught me the importance of understanding how your beliefs shape your actions and how they derive from our experiences. If you want to change the way you do things you have to reframe your beliefs, which means you have to revaluate your experiences. Sounds simple doesn't it but it's hard to do in a way that sustains in all circumstances. Mastering how to do that made a massive change, I think it was a phenomenal piece of learning.

Let's talk about strategy a bit. You said you became responsible for strategy and became interested in it to some degree later on in your career.

I've always been interested in strategy.

What do you understand by strategy and how do you differentiate it from tactics? What is key to developing and implementing a good strategy?

I think it's all about the big directional decisions a business makes. Where you place your bets, which types of markets are you going to go for with which people? What are your real strengths? How can you invest in them to make them even stronger?

Be really clear about your point of difference, if you can work it out – it's not easy to do, but if you can identify it and then obsess on it, that's the basis for a good strategy. It's important to work out what the business is really strong at, don't worry too much about the weaknesses. Be clear on your strengths and invest in them, make sure you play to your strengths. That's absolutely the key to good strategy I think.

Is your current firm clear on that?

In strategic terms, yes we are. I was told once that all professional service people share three common objectives: do interesting work, be well regarded for doing it, and make a commensurate reward. It's simple isn't it but it's always held resonance all through my career.

That's an observation rather than advice, how have you used it?

Always focus on what you are unusually good at, that will attract interesting work and the rest flows from there.

Do you think that applies to the broader professional services world?

I don't know but I've worked in accounting, architecture, real estate advisory, law and it seems to be true across all of them.

What other factors are key to making people productive?

In the Wall Street - Gordon Gekko film - the Michael Douglas character says, "Only two things motivate - fear and greed". I quite like that one [laughs]. Over my career I've observed it carries a lot of truth.

You just said the motivation is about doing interesting work!

If you want to make people change, you have to agitate them! If you want more interesting work but you seem to be falling backwards then you have to adapt your strategy, but you also have to commit to it big time - apply a little aggression. Too often professionals are intelligent enough to see what needs to be done but won't drive through the change that's necessary. It's the ones that do that have always won my admiration.

As a leader, how do you divide your time and energy? Strategising, coaching, networking - do you think about that?

Yes, I do. I tend to notice when one wing is out of sorts. You do need to be with your people enough, you do need to be involved with the strategy and the detail enough to keep your hand in and know where the business is at. You need to be networking. I think we all know when things aren't right the trick is to adapt your focus quickly enough - the old thing about keeping all the plates spinning is true. Getting the balance right between outside of work and inside of work is key too. Everything in moderation. I find that if I make a mental note to shift the balance I can, it's quite achievable, you just have to recognise it - playing off a mentor helps too.

What would your colleagues say about you?

I'd like to think they'd say he's genuine, in fact someone said today, "you always have credibility in your story telling, people will follow you".

I think they would say that I was able to see the bigger picture, have a sense of purpose and sometimes call it as it is. I'm quite balanced really, I'm a balanced bloke.

What are you proudest of in your career so far?

In attainment, becoming a full Director at Linklaters was a massive arrival. That was a kite mark award for me.

Does your partner at home play a big part in your success?

When I was at Linklaters I worked so hard, the culture is so strong it sort of owns you, you give so much of your time to it, I was away from my family a lot because I was around the world. That puts a big strain on family life. I learnt some lessons about fair balance between home and work life.

Great relationships matter more than great work. I try very hard now to create a fair balance between work and time with my wife. I take it seriously, put all the socials in my diary and defend the time for them.

What does digital transformation mean to you and do you think successful organisations will be different from the ones that we grew up in?

It's a good question. I've worked mainly in the professional services sector so that might be too narrow an exposure to have a fair view. I do know that everyone in professional services talks about the digital revolution, but they've actually struggled to deliver on it because it's hard to give advice digitally. I suspect it's one of the weaker sectors for digital application. Clearly some other industries have been wiped out from its inability to adapt. A new market entrant 'disrupted' them, to use that phrase. The digital play seems to be more difficult to land in professional services.

A number of commentators are saying that, in time, professional services firms will be gone, everything will be digitised, maybe they are right and I'm in the flat earth club but I think it will take a very long time to get there if ever. The only area where it's really making in-roads is document vetting and analysis but even that isn't real AI. A friend of mine in one of the accounting firms says they are doing some interesting automated audit work but it's still not really AI, but let's see what plays out.

In terms of digital strategy, you can focus on doing things more efficiently or you can solve your customers' need better or perhaps both. Where's the right focus?

In my experience the latter is the more valuable, the former the easier to achieve. Professional services advice at the complex end of the scale, at least, seems thankfully hard to automate - people seek out the reassurance of experts they trust - the more complicated or significant the decision the more prepared people are to pay for the advice.

If you want to go on a holiday to Crete say, you will happily self-book an easyJet flight but if you're going to take six months and tour across Asia say, you'll probably get an advisor to plan the tour and pay them to do so. We like people we trust to advise us when the stakes are high. I think professional advice is a haven in terms of being able to hold off the threat of digitisation, but perhaps I'll be proved horribly wrong!

Will organisations in twenty years' time be different from the ones we grew up in? Are millennials different?

The life goals and success measures my generation tend to reference don't seem to matter so much to today's twenty-year olds. If that holds then the goals and value systems of organisations will naturally evolve.

You really see that?

I was at a meal recently and there were two people I chatted with who were twenty-one or twenty-two. They were both smart graduates. Their interest was so focused on the destruction of the planet being brought about by irresponsible shop window illumination at night! I was taken aback by the intensity of their anger and commitment to do something about it. They didn't have even a fraction of the same passion to developing their career. They might be more extreme than many but I can feel a change in value priorities which might change the way business is organised and focused.

In a good way?

I don't think it matters, it's just that it's going to be different. We all know that our parents' view of the world was different from that of their parents and so on and so on. The things our generation has focussed on investing in may be less relevant to future generations, it will be their priorities that shape the businesses of tomorrow.

My guess is that those core life goals I talked about earlier - wanting to do interesting work, be respected for doing it, and receive a commensurate reward will bridge the generation gap but the way they are realised will be different.

My kids right now want to do interesting things and see the world they're focused on building out their experiences, but I expect they'll come round to thinking about building their careers when they're ready.

When you eventually retire, what will you miss most about work?

Being in the thick of it! I know that's true - I had a year out recently and hated it.

“

I believe the strength of our company was in our personalities. We were young, late 20s, in a very formal industry. The young kids. We knew that and played to our strengths.

We didn't try to be, 'We're very, very clever and we can tell you how to run your business.' We were just skirting on the side-lines. Over time, they started to realise that we knew everything.

”

RALPH THAWLEY

INTERVIEWED 4TH FEBRUARY 2021

Ralph enjoyed a rollercoaster career building a global specialist publishing business with three friends which eventually sold for a handsome price. He attributes his grammar school as a driving force in his later success, giving him the confidence to leave the small Barnsley town where he grew up to compete successfully in a fast developing, international business. A business in which he found he was able to capitalise on his personality and convictions in an area he undoubtably would not have foreseen as a young man.

Tell me a little about your background and influences.

I was born in a pit village called Blacker Hill near Barnsley. My dad was a coal miner and outside of work was a singer in the local working-men's clubs. I had a sister, older sister. Before we were born my parents lost their first son, who was unfortunately killed, knocked down by a motorbike when he was four, so I suppose I was a replacement. There were two of us children with Mum and Dad in a two-up, two-down terraced house. Both parents were one of six siblings, and so there were always lots of aunties, uncles and cousins who lived close by. I was very happy in a very social working-class extended family. Looking back it was a hard community, but back then the pits were booming and Barnsley people by their very nature are sociable, upbeat with a great sense of humour. The men worked hard and drank hard. Barnsley was effectively nothing other than pits.

Can you sing like your dad?

No but we had a piano in the best room of the house and both my sister and I had lessons. I stopped fairly early but typically in my teens got into popular music and now enjoy playing jazz and blues on piano. The first thing I bought when we sold the company was a Steinway, my personal treat.

Did your parents have aspirations for you to break out of the community?

My mum wanted me to go to university so I needed to go to grammar school. To begin with it was passing the 11+. There were two kids, one girl and one boy, from our junior school who went. She passed her 11+ to go to high school and I passed my exam to go to the grammar school. We were the only two, everybody else went to the local comprehensive. I got the bus from our village every day to go to Barnsley to the grammar school.

Did you enjoy your school days?

Yes, it was a very traditional, classic school with some teachers in cloaks. A lot of them had been to Oxbridge, all first-class quality teachers and they had a big impact on my life, I think.

Everybody who went there, on reflection, realised what a first-class education we got from that school. They gave us determination, ambition, confidence, all the traits you associate with that kind of education. I loved it. We were also good at sport, the idea that if you were academic the local schools around you were going to beat you - no, we beat everybody at football and rugby! We held our own, big time. To tell you the truth, that helped me survive in everyday life getting from my pit village, where the local comprehensive lurked. I had to get on a bus with a blazer every day. You had to be streetwise. I kept on side with the local guys by playing football with them. I played for the local village team and I was left alone.

My grammar school pals are still my best friends today. In fact, I actually set up my business with one of them. We all had the same mentality drilled into us – don't stand for any nonsense, you're as good as anybody out there, just as bright, you can do anything you want. You can leave Barnsley, you don't have to go down the pit. That was the big driving thing at our school.

Afterwards you went on to attend Nottingham University to read Economics?

Yes, I did well with A-levels. I had a year off for the Oxbridge exams, I got to an interview at Fitzwilliam in Cambridge. Even before the interview I thought, I'm not so sure I like this set up, it's a bit academic for me. I went for the interview to do law, but didn't get in. So instead I had a year off and messed around, then started looking at where to go the following year. I basically looked at where the biggest female to male ratio was!

I had a lovely time at Nottingham, even met my wife, and it was only an hour from Barnsley.

At university, did you have any clear idea about what you wanted to do afterwards?

Not at all, not a clue. I had another year off at the end of the course because my girlfriend, now wife, did a teaching degree, so she had an extra year to do. I worked in various jobs. I actually got myself my first graduate job at Hawker Siddeley in Stamford and I stayed there two weeks, it was dreadful.

Why so?

It was in the buying department. They said, "In four years' time, you'll be at that desk over there." I could see this awful, almost civil service like bureaucracy going on. I didn't like that, so I left, came back to Nottingham where my girlfriend was and I did various jobs. I was a bomb detector at John Player cigarette factory, a lift operator, various things.

As my girlfriend was coming to the end of her degree, I started applying for proper jobs. I got one by answering an advert in 'The Graduate'. I don't know if you remember 'The Graduate'? I went for interviews with various companies in Nottingham, in Sheffield. I wanted to stay north. Nothing happened and then I saw an advert for a job as an assistant editor based in Victoria, London. I applied, sent my CV and got an interview.

What was the job?

It was a trade publishing house with various reports and magazines on import, export statistics, analysing company reports specialising in the agricultural chemical industry. The ingredients of chemical fertilisers. I didn't have any background in chemicals, but it didn't matter because it was more about trade and commodities.

I got the job as assistant editor, which basically meant reading data, writing them up so you could show that, for example, in the last six months imports of phosphates into the UK from Morocco had risen by 20%, that sort of thing. Pretty boring stuff. You had to contact everybody by letter of course back then, so we were waiting for letters to come back and annual reports to come in. The industry was very formal but very international, which was interesting. All of our customers and information sources were from overseas.

Who was your boss?

Funnily enough, he was only three or four years older than me, Barry. He was from Liverpool, a proper Scouser. We got on well, he was more forward thinking and wanted to change things a little.

Did you have any formal training?

No, in at the deep end. Writing up reports didn't stretch you that much. I was there for five years and during that time the industry was moving, it was getting much, much stronger and expanding all over the world. Communications were getting easier, we could make more phone calls because phone costs were coming down. We started making a little bit more direct contact with industry customers and information sources.

One thing as part of this formal industry was that nobody spoke or published anything about prices. Of course, everybody was as keen as mustard to know what was going on price-wise, but it was a no-no. As communications started to improve, we started asking about prices. They'd say, "We'll tell you roughly what that deal was done at, but not for publication."

Then we started to get an idea of price levels, general prices as opposed to government statistics, which produced official trade prices per tonne. As things progressed even more the industry really did explode. This was the chemical fertiliser business feeding the world, very in vogue. Technology prices were coming down. Fax machines changed an awful lot for us.

Were you beginning to enjoy the industry?

Yes, and I was promoted to editor. I specialised in the sulphur market, looking at sulphur as a commodity. Trade movements, the players in the game, prices. I became a so-called specialist in sulphur.

We started pushing the information sources and the contacts, buyers and sellers. We wanted to start putting price ranges into the report, which didn't give anything away, but gave people an idea. Over time, they agreed to that and it proved very popular.

At the same time, we were getting closer to customer information sources. We got pally with them and started exchanging information - "What have you heard from them?" We'd take them out for lunch and for dinner. These commodity brokers were pretty hard-nosed, hard drinking individuals and they enjoyed and appreciated the position we were in. They couldn't ask their competitors what was going on. We were in the middle, we could ask anybody.

We did very well. The ones who did well after leaving the company were the ones who decided, "To hell with this, we don't need to work for these guys. We're closer to the industry than they are."

There was unrest. People started leaving because you could only go so far. We made the decision that we'd leave too, four of us. We'd leave and start producing a weekly report called the 'Fertiliser Market Bulletin', would you believe, not very catchy!

Were the other three specialists in different commodities?

Yes, including my old pal Kevin from school. He had also come down to London for his first graduate job working for a shipping consultancy. When a vacancy came up at our company I said come over and join us. Kevin became a specialist in phosphate. I was sulphur. Two other guys, Bruce was potash and Clive was nitrogen. Combined they were the fourth or fifth largest seaborn traded commodity in the world behind iron ore, coal and grain. It's a huge industry.

You set up your own firm, the four of you?

Yes, I was 27.

Did you all put money in?

We didn't have any money. We went to Barclays and got a £20,000 loan, went in and explained we were writing this weekly report about fertilisers. He said, "You can't be serious." We took him through the whole thing, the potential subscriber list and what we could initially charge. Again, it was 99% overseas, so everything had to be done by letter because we couldn't afford to do anything else.

Did you have a business plan to take them through?

Yes, we did. It was all conjecture really, but he accepted it. Bruce, who was older than us and posher, he had a house and a mortgage on it. There was a charge put on his mortgage to cover the loan. As soon as we could, we took it off. We set up with our first rented office on Hill Rise in Richmond.

So what was the plan?

To produce a weekly report. We'd get on the phones, talked to our contacts and produced a comprehensive report on as many deals as we could find.

Did you all work independently in your product areas and then meld the whole thing together?

Yes, it was quite a comprehensive report and it took a lot of time to pull together. We sold it at £325 a year, quite decent back then. It's probably worth something like £1,200 today.

Who were the market?

Everybody. First of all, you had all the chemical industry who were buying in raw materials. Some to produce agricultural chemicals like fertilisers, other things like sulphur for sulphuric acid, which is used in everything. All the chemical industry, buyers, sellers. Then there was the shipping industry because all of it is shipped.

Who was doing the selling?

All of us. We'd all got the gift of the gab. We had to, to get on with these guys. You had to be sharp and fast. They accepted us. They wouldn't listen to some guy who didn't know what he was talking about. If you displayed total confidence and knowledge they'd be more convinced about buying the publication.

How long before you could start paying yourselves from the business?

We were using the loan, clearly. We never went skint, ever. The thing is, we only really dipped into the loan. The key thing with a subscription-based business is you get twelve months' money up front. It didn't take long.

Of course, the first couple of weeks the pals in the industry you know, they'd take the subscription. That kept us going for about a month. You'd phone up as many people as you could and they'd say, "Yes, we'll take it." For four weeks it went like that and then we had a month and it just flattened out.

Taking 12 months' worth of money up front, you had to produce 12 editions and six months in you might be struggling?

In practice, no. If it didn't work, we'd have walked away. Nobody would have asked for that sort of money back, not in our business. It was small fry compared to the stuff they did. They spent more on a meal than an annual subscription those guys. That's the other thing, money was in the business. There was money there.

Six months in as a group, what were you thinking?

We thought we're having a very nice time here, a nice lifestyle. We had no bosses. International travel, which if we could afford, we'd do. We realised that the more face-to-face and direct contact you had, the more business you won. If you made friends with these people, they'd recommend you to some of their friends.

We had a little bit of a squeeze when we decided instead of paying rent that property prices were going up and we'd buy an office. We took a big mortgage out. We steadily grew. Then we launched a glossy trade magazine. Once we'd established our name, 'FMB', we decided another revenue stream would be advertising. It was a glossy magazine, so we could sell advertising space in it. Our idea back then was quite new, it was a glossy magazine for free, guaranteed circulation, as opposed to a subscription. Our first glossy was called 'Fertiliser Focus'.

I can see the alliteration there, very catchy.

It was monthly, full colour. That's when we employed an advertising sales guy – he was a good talker.

Did you outsource design and production?

To begin with, we outsourced the design to the printers. We brought in an editor, who'd also worked at our first employers, and an assistant for the editing. We started to grow.

It worked because we said to every advertiser, "This is worldwide circulation. As opposed to this magazine, which had only got so many subscriptions. We can guarantee you that because we all used to work on those magazines in our previous jobs." It worked. Soon we were getting big thick glossies. They were coffee table quality, full of adverts about sulphuric acid plants and god knows what. That worked, so then we had a second revenue stream.

Meanwhile, what was really going in our favour was information technology and communication. A big, big factor. You could call anybody now, the costs were so cheap. We'd got email coming in, which was again massive.

What started out as a weekly report by mail suddenly turned it into a fax report, which could be subscribed by fax so people received it a lot quicker, that made a big difference. Of course, when email came in, even more so. The speed of receiving the report was crucial.

As things evolved, did the four of you assume specialisms in the business?

We all shared various things. As well as covering our specialist products we all had other responsibilities which we shared out. Latest computer and software advances, recruiting new staff, negotiating with printing companies and booking conference hotels. We all fronted-up when it came to selling our services. Clive was the one who left, he left and set up his own business, he'd not got the same style or thinking as the other three of us, these things happen. Until I retired, we still saw him at conferences.

I believe the strength of our company was in our personalities, the way we changed the industry from being very, very formal to more and more casual. More informal, from a very stuffy Second World War style business.

Later you moved into conferences I understand?

Yes, this idea of taking people out for lunch, having jokes, exchanging ideas. We got so close with them we realised there was an opportunity. So we thought, let's do a conference. We set up exhibition-style networking conferences, not information gathering presentation conferences. We wanted this slick, people talking about what's going on in the business type events, rather than sitting down and looking at slides. We announced our first one in London at the Hilton Hotel.

Did you organise it all yourselves?

Yes, we did it all. About 350 people attended. It was informal with cocktail parties and wine at lunch. For the first one we booked 'Talk of the Town' for the evening show. We got buses and bussed them all from the Hilton to the show in Leicester Square.

We had the Bootleg Beatles. As it's in England we thought it's going to be a British theme. That was the other thing, everybody loves to come to London. They came away saying, "That was fantastic." They loved it.

It doesn't all have to be talking about statistics and being formal. It was relaxed, but at the same time they knew that we knew what we were talking about. We could have a conversation about the business. They were comfortable with that.

Were you and your colleagues doing the presentations?

No, not at all. We brought in outside speakers, top people. It was very successful and we carried on year two, year three, year four. We did the first three in London because people like to come to London. We had magicians running around at the cocktail parties, which back then was something new.

One classic thing we did, we had a Margaret Thatcher lookalike. She stood with her handbag and welcomed everybody coming into the cocktail party, "Hello," then mingled. I'm telling you, there were two Koreans who really did think it was her! We had a lot of fun with that.

Were no other countries offering conferences at the time?

It's funny you say that because now there are probably five companies offering the same services as we did then and all of them are in the UK. We've been asked this many, many times. It's because if you want independent information from a reliable source, the Koreans, the Japanese, Kenyans, anywhere, they trust the UK, London. Everybody is comfortable with the UK, it's amazing. The Americans produced something called Green Markets, an agricultural chemical report. Although well respected for their coverage of the domestic industry in the USA, their international coverage was poor. Back then Americans couldn't relate to different nationalities as well as we Brits. It may have changed now but back then they talked 'at' them too much.

No, the conference side of it really rocketed. We finished up doing five conferences a year, one in each continent. They were begging us, "Bring your roadshow." If we had a conference in say Beijing, all the Western companies would go to Beijing, which is exactly what the Chinese wanted.

Then we started getting big money in for, "Do you want to sponsor our conference? Do you want to be the local sponsor?" We finished up getting $100,000 just for somebody to put their name everywhere because we'd be bringing everybody to their location.

We did Beijing for 20 years, every year.

By that time, how many people would you be employing?

When we were bought, they couldn't believe how few people we had, 14. We had people, 'stringers' here and there who were self-employed and sent us invoices if we used them, things like that for the conference work. We had a couple of stringers who'd sent me information, but they worked for themselves. We were tight and in control. Everybody knew everything that was going on, we were on top of it.

When did you sell?

We started in 1981 and we sold it in 2011.

Did you enjoy it most of the time?

I absolutely loved it. There were such great characters in the business. One big boost for us was when communism collapsed in 1989.

Suddenly Russia, which had been one state Moscow subscription, suddenly there were hundreds of subscriptions flooding in. They wanted us to bring the conference to Moscow, so we did Russia every year.

How much of your time were you spending travelling?

Quite a lot actually. We'd do five of our own and then there'd be at least three association conferences, which we'd attend as well.

Were you working long hours? How was your work / life balance?

It depends what part of the 30 years you're talking about. We worked a lot harder in the earlier years and then it became easier, especially when mobile phones came along.

Was the value in the people and the brand?

I'll tell you one thing, we never actually thought we were valuable. We thought, this business is here because of the people in it, because we were all well-known characters. We thought if we weren't doing it, the business would collapse because if it's sulphur, they want me, or if it's phosphates, Kevin, or potash, Bruce. We were all stupid enough to think that. It turned out in practice the brand had been building to such an extent that a lot of people didn't know who we were individually.

Did you decide amongst you that you wanted to sell?

I think we were late 50s and one of us said, "We should start thinking about selling, I think I'm ready now to play golf." Two others were reluctant.

Had you been developing people below you to take over?

No. Not handing on to kids or other people in the business, no. Certain people in the business who were very strong with their own ambitions tended to leave. They'd got so much experience they were offered jobs all over the place. Eventually, we thought we'd have to sell it.

We thought, "let's find out. Let's put a toe in the water and find out if we're worth anything." We engaged with a professional broker. He had a quiet word with some of the publishing giants who buy smaller companies and came back and told us the interest was very strong, we're talking eight figure numbers.

We were thinking, when we want to sell might not be when they want to buy, so we've got to look at this seriously. That's what we did. There was a buyout, so we had a three-year earn-out.

How did you find that time? Was it painful to have a boss again?

It was awful. It was the very reason why we set up in the first place. It's like walking through mud. We realised, that's why we'd had 30 years of fun and happiness, being so ridiculously efficient even though it was effortless. Once we were acquired it was awful.

During that time we had to groom a replacement. I had a young Hong Kong colleague who was very sharp, very smart and is still in the business.

When they took over, they then had their lawyers come in. These price ranges we were publishing every week, a lot of companies started using our price range as part of a formula price during the purchase of millions of tonnes of product. Suddenly, the lawyers from the company that bought us were worried that the clients might sue us. Suddenly, every week you had to justify to the lawyers why you've adjusted the price by $2.

Had it ever crossed your mind in the 30 years there was that risk?

If they'd sued us, we thought we were worth nothing, so it didn't matter. Some things we put in the report we got heavy letters. We'd just say, "Okay, we'll publish an apology. We're so sorry." That would be it. Of course, big corporations have got to think of litigation. The nature of the job changed.

Suddenly some of the traders didn't want to talk about price on the phone. It would be, "Just send me questions that are on email." Of course, you start losing everything. You're not talking to people just about business. You lose all the interesting stuff and it became very antiseptic. All answers to questions.

In 1997 we realised that our industry, bulk chemical fertiliser raw materials, even though it was feeding the world, there was an environmental problem with it. Nitrates in the soil. There was a move to bring in a new industry of agricultural chemicals and agricultural practices.

We got talking to a French businessman we had known in the industry for many years and ended up setting up a new magazine and a new conference under a new company because one of the directors didn't want to join it. It was called New Ag International, covering the more sophisticated end, not the bulk chemical fertilisers but things like biostimulants and biopesticides.

The people who acquired you didn't buy this new company too?

No. Our role in the new company was to help with our experience in publishing and conference organization, with our new French partner providing the product expertise in this specialist area.

Who acquired the original business?

Argus Media. They had many brands of magazines and conferences, similar companies in coal, grain and other chemicals. We fitted in nicely.

Did it cause you pain?

They trebled revenues in the first two years, and a little later they sold out to General Atlantic.

While you were still there?

Yes. Do you know how? They basically doubled or trebled subscription prices, simple as that. We were under-pricing ourselves. Nobody cancelled.

Sounds like everything worked out well?

Well yes and no. In the fourth year of the sell out in 2015 I had a major heart attack. In 1995 I had already undergone a quadruple heart bypass.

Was there a history of heart attacks in your family or do you think your lifestyle led to it?

My dad died when he was 67 of a heart attack. I've always been fit, healthy and sporty. It seems I can't handle cholesterol. That's still the case, so now I have to have an injection every month for cholesterol, statins and cholesterol lowering drugs. I wasn't invalided, I was back at work after a month.

I had the second heart attack in 2015, twenty years after the first. I joked at the time it was brought on by all the red tape at the new company! When it happened, the boss phoned me and said, "Are you thinking of coming back after this?" I said, "Frankly I think we'll leave it now." And he said, "I understand." With respect to the new company which we sold in 2017, I still attended occasional conferences prior to Covid but on an ambassadorial level only and do not have a working role in it.

Prior to the takeover you were travelling a lot but otherwise would you say that your work life balance worked out pretty well?

We had to travel and we enjoyed the travel. But we set up our office local to our homes, so no commuting, which was a great help. My wife Elaine was a teacher, also working locally. We had four kids and so we were able to work together with maximum flexibility such as dropping off and picking up the kids from school. That worked really well.

The other person who set up the business with you, is he the guy from school?

Yes.

You kept a great working relationship and friendship, did you ever have any falling outs?

No, it was a McCartney and Lennon type of thing. I've known him since he was 12. We were in the same first graduate jobs. Not only that, but we joined the same football team in Chiswick. I was working with him Monday to Friday and playing football with him on Saturday. He was always there and he still is.

Do you miss work?

Yes, I miss the characters in the business. Fantastic characters, there are no boring people in it. All smart, sharp, funny and generous. Every place we went to you'd be taken to the best restaurant. We never had meetings in boardrooms, it was always for a lunch or for a dinner.

I think that was always there between the big companies. If the Turkish wanted to do a deal with the French, they wouldn't do it in an office, not then. They'd take them to the finest restaurant in Istanbul. We were part of that and it was fantastic.

As you look back, are you happy with the way your career turned out? Would you have changed anything?

Nothing. We were blessed, fortunate to be in the right place at the right time in an industry that was about to boom. Everything seemed to go in our favour.

What do you think were the key attributes or skills that helped you achieve what you achieved?

I think we brought in personality. You can have a good time and be serious and sharp at the same time. We were young, late 20s by the time we started the new company. It was a very formal industry, so we were these young kids. We knew that and we played to our strengths. We didn't try to be, "We're very, very clever and we can tell you how to run your business." We were just skirting on the side-lines. Over time, they started to realise that we knew everything.

What would you say you are particularly good at?

I can assess other people very well. I knew whether to be serious or whether to crack a joke. Everyone is different. Sometimes I had meetings at the conferences with the Japanese, and I remember on one occasion one guy said, "Where will the price be in September?" This was in May. "I think it will be at this level." Because he wanted a low price. I said, "No, it will be at this level." I said, "I'll tell you what, if it's at your level in September, the September conference will be in San Francisco, I'll buy you dinner. If it's at my level, you buy me dinner." He loved the idea. Suddenly, that became a regular bet and we started doing things like that.

Were you good with numbers?

I could do them, I did economics. None of us were dummies.

The world has digitalised significantly since you and I began our careers. Do you think those same personal qualities will allow someone who's 24 to be successful in a digital age or do you think that's changed fundamentally?

Even without Covid, there's less chance today to have the private conversations I've talked about because everybody is now so conscious of litigation and compliance. The level of compliance in publishing commercial information, like price deals, is tremendous. I feel so sorry for reporters doing our jobs now. They're still doing it, but it's so much more difficult. We were very lucky. Our years in it, we timed it perfectly. We were all cheeky chappies who knew how to get information out of people.

Are you a very driven ambitious person, do you think, or were you?

Yes, I think so.

Where did the drive come from, do you think?

My mother always told me, "You try your hardest and you'll get what you deserve. If you try hard, you'll get there." To tell you the truth, it was probably the same for everybody in that grammar school. The advice from the grammar school was you don't have to stay in a pit village in Barnsley. You're bright enough to get out there and to fight with the best.

If you had to boil down the most important things you learned about building a business, what would you say?

Treat your staff very, very well. Treat them respectfully. In our business, we created a very tight team. We took on two 18-year-old girls to do admin and we still had them when we sold in 2011. They worked with us for 30 years and they were in tears when it ended. Respecting staff gave great stability. Looking back, I think that was very important.

Also, if you've got a good idea, don't be too cautious. That might just depend on your personality but I would say go for it, be confident if you think there's an opportunity there.

Management teams often have a mix of types. It seems you were all very similar, is that right?

Well no. Bruce was Oxford educated, BBC English, in contrast to the two Yorkshire accents, the Barnsley boys. Bruce had done psychology at university. Kevin and I came from the same northern grammar school backgrounds and were often enthusiastic about the same things. Bruce's opinion would be 'hold on a minute, let's think about this', adding balance to the process, and we always finished up working in the same direction.

It sounds like your business life was a big adventure, that you rode your luck, trusted your instincts, got the timing right and played to your strengths. Thinking about what you learned along the way, what advice have you given your children, or would you give to any young person about to embark on their working lives?

Well I try not to put pressure on them but I'd say – find an area that interests you and plays to your strengths, be committed, trust your instincts and above all have fun.

"

I always remember a particular client saying to me, "I have to deal with accountants, banking people, lawyers, insurers, insurance brokers, and actually everybody kind of looks identical and behaves in an identical way. Could you please try and be different? Because if you're different and you pitch to me, I'm going to remember what was different about you." And that stuck with me.

"

AILSA KING

INTERVIEWED 2ND FEBRUARY 2018

Ailsa is one of the most senior women in the UK insurance industry, one of the more traditional and male dominated business sectors. She has an outstanding record in customer relationship development and work winning. Now Chief Client Officer at the world's largest insurance broker Marsh, here she talks about her career, her understanding of customer relationship dynamics and her advice for those like her who aspire to a long and fulfilling career.

What led you to choose a career in insurance?

I had not considered a City career until I learned about Insurance Broking on the Milk round at University. What appealed to me about this line of work was the combination of needing to get under the skin of a client's business, working at a senior level and the thrill of the deal. Unlike consulting which seemed to me could be a little dry and "at a distance", insurance broking felt more like you were in the mix of it - and of course it's a very people-oriented business, which I like.

Where did you start?

In a firm called Sedgewick (acquired by Marsh & McLennan in 1998), what now seems a very long time ago. Much about the industry has changed since then but interestingly a lot of things are exactly the same, much of it is "good" tradition but not all of it. I believe that the level of science in risk assessment can be taken to another level, and the increasing quality and transparency of data is helping with that. This has always been and will always be a relationship driven business but the quality of those relationships and of a client's risk management solution can get better still if we harness the "science" in the right way.

I've heard you talk before about the "science" of broking, what do you mean?

I mean the way in which you can analyse risk areas in a data-driven way and use the analysis to create a more scientific approach to risk management. Combining this hard-nosed approach to analysis with the "soft skills" required to build relationships and establish a position of trust are what makes our industry unique. Not everyone as an individual is lucky enough to be blessed with skills in both areas.

You joined Marsh after many years at Willis (now Willis Towers Watson), what was your brief and what was it that attracted you to the opportunity?

Marsh is a fantastic business with an outstanding reputation, a brand name of genuine value, associated with the international reputation of the London markets. I'd worked in competition with Marsh for most of my career so learned from hard experience about the firm's strengths. I do think the insurance industry, which has perhaps been one of the most conservative in the City, has the opportunity to evolve over the next few years and Marsh is in a good position to help forge a new way forward.

How does a firm like Marsh help create value for a client?

The value of any client's business lies in the combination of its assets. Physical assets, risks to which are the traditional preserve of the insurance industry but also of increasing importance are its intangible assets - human capital, relationship capital and brand capital. These are more complex and fluid assets to understand. They take time to build but can be destroyed overnight. Unlike physical assets on the balance sheet which depreciate over time, intangible assets can appreciate and in part our job is to help clients to achieve that appreciation. In a supporting role we can help them to protect and enhance the value of their brand and their IP for example. As a broker working with a client you need to develop together a deep understanding of the dynamics behind the creating of asset value in those areas and develop risk strategies which can not only protect that asset value but over time enhance it.

Do you see the opportunity for a broker to add value to a client beyond the insurance deal, to become more of a trusted partner / advisor?

I do think we can and do add value to a client's business at a strategic level but we need to be careful about how we go about it. Ultimately we are a broker but we are well placed to help clients to protect and grow the value of their assets and that's a big opportunity.

Does that opportunity make broking a more exciting place to work because the scope of the challenge, of the impact you can have, is a broader one?

I think it does. Honestly I think our world will become an increasingly attractive place to work for bright young people looking to build a career in the City. We offer intellectual challenge, a chance to work at the heart of a client's business model and enjoy the thrill of the "broke".

And on top of that, at our best there is a "quality" about the long-term relationships in our industry, a lack of the frenetic, money is everything culture often attributed to Banks or Strategy Houses - both of which we compete with in terms of attracting the best talent out there. That integrity and desire to invest in long term relationships, take a long-term value driven perspective - is attractive.

How important do you think brand reputation is in your world?

It's always important. From the Marsh perspective and in a broader competitive context where we are playing in a more strategic space, we are less well known in brand terms but in our home territory of insurance broking we are well known and have a wonderful brand reputation. If you're a well-known brand and of a certain scale it gets you through the door and onto a tender shortlist. We can and should be able to attract the best talent in our industry because we have a certain reputation, a great client list and complex intellectual problems to solve. It is our ability to attract and retain the best talent which should be at the heart of our competitive advantage.

How do you build a brand in your industry?

I think it's by being consistent in the way you approach things. The way we communicate our "brand" is by being consistently different from our competitors in the way we approach things, the service we provide. If you are not doing that then you are likely to end up relying on price or individual relationships - and that's a weakness potentially. There needs to be an enduring basis for competitive advantage.

How do you build a brand? I would say by being clear about what you stand for, your brand promise, and then investing in your organisation such that you can deliver on that promise with consistency, style and quality.

How do you think the Marsh brand is perceived at a more detailed level?

I think we are probably viewed as having a real depth and breadth of knowledge and talent but perhaps a little arrogant and inflexible at times - that was my perception. Possibly somewhat staid and traditional as well, like the industry itself.

Having competed against Marsh for most of my career I've been aware of the "arrogant" label but now I'm here I absolutely don't see that. I think the reputation may be partly because there are lots of parts of the business who believe their solutions really are the best, we've probably got more technicians than anyone else - there's a lot more that goes into our R&D than anybody else puts into it. When we go and see a client we sometimes can be too keen to say, "and this is what's going to do the job for you, because we know it's the right solution". We haven't perhaps listened to what the client thinks are their issues closely enough.

Actually having joined the organisation, I find it much warmer than other places I have worked. I find a lack of arrogance and certainly a lack of politics, which is really refreshing.

Why do you think that is?

I think that there is a confidence born both of experience and breadth of talent, but also an inquisitiveness, a desire to push the envelope. Not arrogance at all.

What are the founding principles of your "philosophy", if I could call it that, for client service?

In my experience five things are most important. First, focus on listening to your client rather than setting out to sell them something. Second, be different in your approach and clear about the value you add, otherwise you end up competing on price or simply relying on individual relationships. Third is combining "science" and psychology, creating empathy and understanding with a client is important but needs to be backed up with the "science". Fourth is valuing all the talents. Making sure you build diverse teams in order to provide a diversity of talent and expertise, as well as personality. I think it's a fair comment to say that over the years brokers have been fairly stereotypical in their approach and I think we can add value and "match" a client better by drawing on different kinds of experiences, different perspectives. Finally, "bringing the firm", exposing your clients to the full range of the firm's expertise.

I would be interested to understand the journey that has helped shape your philosophy. In your early career were there people or experiences which were particularly important?

Many people have impacted that experience and my perspective. One in particular was my very first boss who taught me a lot, more by example than anything else. He was head of client management in my first firm which had a very client centric ethos. I chose the client-facing side of the business which I have been in ever since, partly because he described the role and the way of approaching the role in a very attractive way. I thought - that's me. He's informally remained my mentor throughout my career. He was always quietly encouraging me to be ambitious despite the fact that in those days insurance was a very male dominated business.

Can you remember some of the most important things you learned from him?

Yes, funnily enough it was as much behaviour as it was methodology. I would watch how he was with clients, he had great authority in the room but was incredibly respectful of what the client had to say. That sounds obvious but in the broking world there are plenty of people who talk at clients about their chosen area of expertise. He was an expert listener.

He listened more than he sold?

Yes, he was always keen to understand a client's personal drivers as well as the intricacies of their business. I have always kept that in mind, my approach is to consider the individual first, then their business then the wider sector issues they're facing.

Were you similar personalities?

No, I'm quite extroverted but he was much more measured. I tend to work for people who are not like me.

Is balance important for you when building your own teams?

Yes, I certainly don't surround myself with people who are like me. I was once told I did and then I looked around at the team, and thought "no, nobody's like me, we were all different". The fact that we were all different meant that we all got on extraordinarily well. We all had different things to offer which intuitively meant we played to each other's strengths.

Going back to your early career, how did you begin interacting with clients?

I worked in sales quite early on. I was put into sales, supporting a very pushy individual and I guess that's where my hunger to win probably started. I worked in a very successful team who absolutely got under the skin of a client in every aspect to win their business.

Can you talk a little around that experience, that approach?

The approach was to listen, consider and develop a risk strategy tailored specifically to the client's needs. I think this is still a very product-led industry and so people, particularly brokers, readily jump to the solution because they are comfortable with their solution. They are proud of their solution, they know it's a good solution, but unless it relates to the client's specific needs then it's not going to be optimal.

How did you learn the skills which you've come to rely on?

I was given a lot of exposure to clients early on, that sales leader didn't focus on the Head Office relationship but on understanding a client's business from the bottom up. We would go around the country visiting a client's subsidiaries, we were pitching to clients who were learning about their own organisations during the pitch, so we would spend a lot more time talking about what we saw in their business, what that meant for their risk profile and where we thought that would lead to in the future. That was a much more interesting conversation for a client to have than, "This is us, here's what we can do for you." I haven't really thought about it until now, but actually that was a great grounding and it influenced the way I approach the job and how I have coached and developed teams.

Looking at yourself for a moment, what do you think has been key to your own success in client facing roles?

You have to start with the individual, and my personal success has been founded on building relationships with individual clients and understanding what really makes them tick. To achieve that you have to spend time with them. I don't think people always allow that time, even if they have secured a face-to-face meeting they tend to have an agenda with a long list of areas to cover which may not leave sufficient time to really get to know the person, what makes them tick, how their business works at a strategic and a practical level too. How things might be changing, what their new business opportunities and priorities are, how that might affect their risk profile? It's that deep understanding combined with a level of trust and understanding between you as people which makes for a valuable and rewarding business relationship – for both parties. But more and more today I recognise that a firm like Marsh is strong not just on the back of a myriad strong individual relationships but on the collective strengths of relationships across the two teams.

What do you think is the most valuable quality a client-facing person can possess?

It's empathy, because you have to get the client to a level where trust both ways is absolute. You do learn though that you're not going to be everybody's cup of tea, and I'm certainly not. I have always put teams together with a good blend of characters and experience and I think I can work out who's going to best suit a particular client.

What has been the best client relationship that you've had, and what was special about it?

So far probably a retail client, who I think you know.

What was the lead client like as a person?

They were a bit of an extrovert and very sociable so it was relatively easy getting to know them. They were very open and relationship driven and still, whenever that client is in this country we meet up.

Did they, and other good clients, share a lot with you about their business beyond the things directly related to the insurance transaction?

Yes, very much so.

Did you find that they treated you almost as a sounding board?

Absolutely. I think senior people often with very small direct support teams inside their organisations and often reporting directly to their Executive team value an objective sounding board. Someone who understands their business, who is not their boss or a peer internally who they can bounce ideas around with. Someone who might offer challenging or objective advice within the context of a well-established and trusting relationship. If you think about it they are exposed to risk on a personal level, the risk that their advice around risk, their plan to manage it might be flawed and so their personal credibility is at risk. In that respect they value support from someone, a team who can help reduce that personal risk exposure.

Thinking back to when you first won that favourite client, did you learn why they went with your firm?

It was definitely the team fit; we had put together a really good team, in combination with the depth of understanding we were able to demonstrate in terms of the drivers of their business model we were a competitive proposition. There were specifics that we uncovered that they weren't getting from their existing broker but the reason why we could spot that and our team was compelling to them was because we understood them so well. We'd actually nearly won that same client several years before, after the loss I invested three years into really getting to know that business and their people, so that the next time I had the best offering and the best relationship, and then they had to move!

Can recovering from a loss make you stronger?

An early loss in a pitch situation can make you more determined I think. Some of the best wins come the second time around. You learn from the loss and then it's almost guaranteed that you'll win it the next time. In many cases there's not a chasm between brokers in terms of solution or price, it's normally the small but important things that drive decisions one way or another. It could be changing the team slightly, or just the way that you put the proposal together. Second time around on one of my big wins for instance I'd realised that the Company Secretary who I was dealing with was a lawyer, and as such was so into the detail. Our next pitch was all about detail, contract, analysis, and he loved it. He literally appointed us there and then.

In your experience, what is key to a successful pitch presentation?

Being clear about your message and that comes back to clarity on your points of difference, getting buy-in to that acknowledged throughout the pitch, and then supporting the key message with evidence. Keep the message very clear and memorable. It has to be memorable and it can be memorable if it's really clear and concise. The whole presentation should revolve around supporting those key central messages.

Normally you're memorable because you're talking about something the prospect wants to talk about, and that's normally them, their business, the risks to it and how you can help them to manage their risks and so in time build the value of their business. So when we won a leisure park company for instance the whole presentation was based on a park map and various parts of the company's offering, how that worked, where the risks to the customer experience were and how those could be managed.

Can you give me another example of a great pitch?

If I think about some of the pitches I've made where we've been really successful - we went to a retailer many years ago and were required to pitch without knowing a great deal about them - I wouldn't normally agree that we should do this but we knew the retailer used a procurement approach so we knew nobody had a "relationship" with them in the UK. Because we didn't know them that well we had data, we could do all the analysis with the data, but without building that relationship it's quite difficult to make an impact so we designed something that took them on their customer's journey. We designed it around a yellow line that you walk along in their stores and so we had a yellow line running through the presentation. I took them through what it's like to be one of their customers, and each step of the customer journey, which might have been to do with an online, or an instore experience, we then tabled the risks relating to that experience from start to finish. If you're talking to a retailer they want to talk about their brand, they want to talk about their customer experience – I can bet your bottom dollar we were the only broker that talked about it in terms of how their customer thinks about the experience of shopping with them – and how that perception could be damaged or enhanced. That worked even in a pure procurement environment because even the procurement guy gets that!

You attach great importance to memorability.

I do – be clear, be different and stand out on both counts. One of the best pitches I ever did in that respect was for a fashion retailer. The secretary on our team, because I didn't have a big creative team, said "I think we should do the presentation in a cardboard handbag, their new line of handbags" and she got design to do something that was a cardboard handbag, and all the pull-outs were in this handbag – so everyone came in and had a handbag in front of them and it was their latest handbag. So of course that breaks the ice because everyone's talking about it saying "ooh, that doesn't look like an insurance report"! Clearly there is a fine line between being memorable and relying on a gimmick but sometimes be brave, back your instincts, in my experience more often than not that works.

I've heard you talk many times about the value of uniqueness. What do you mean more broadly?

Well of course the driver of value for any client lies primarily in the distinctive experience their own brand offers. As a business they need to be standing for something which is unique. It is our job to understand that important part of their DNA and work with it in developing risk solutions aligned to it. For our part we need to be unique in our approach, our brand as well, if not why is a client choosing us over another broker?

Bringing those two things together is the exciting alchemy of our business. Understanding what's special about a client's business, the uniqueness of their risks and using our own distinctive skills and experiences to succeed in working with them to develop superior risk solutions to protect and enhance their business.

You clearly spend a huge amount of energy in researching and pitching to new clients. Needless to say you can't win every time. How do you cope with disappointments?

Not very well. You feel pretty gutted. If you've invested real passion and energy in a pitch, it's going to take you time to come to terms with a decision that's gone against you. It's quite difficult as the leader of a pitch, because you've got to keep the team upbeat. They may be absolutely devastated. After a big disappointment just recently, I was on my way to an industry event, and I felt dreadful, and yet I had to face people and say everything was fine, and I felt absolutely dreadful because I felt I'd let the team down because we hadn't won something that I'd put a lot into. But you do have to cut off and do something different.

It does help having a family doesn't it that you can do things with that has nothing to do with work and then you just have to rationalise what it is that might have gone wrong or that you didn't get across properly and then just redress it. There are a lot of people who are disappointed in a decision and then decide they are never going to engage with that client again because it's gone – it hasn't gone in their favour, and yet you have to remember that the decision may have been made on infinitesimally small margins and so you've just got to keep going, and usually in my experience if you do keep going, you will win it in the end.

What makes a good client?

One who also is clever enough to invest in the relationship, and one that appreciates your team and expresses that too. Then it begins to become a two-way street and the results begin to follow.

When I was a client, which I was for a long time, I would always try to be a good client. If you want the best talent to work on your account and be motivated, it helps if you treat them well doesn't it?

Yes, the good ones take the time to call me to discuss things, give feedback, share ideas. Often they'll talk about quite junior people on the team, who might not be getting all the glory points and comment on something significant we have done that has impressed them. I think that when a client takes the time not just to talk with the senior relationship lead but spends time understanding everyone on your team then that can really help other members of the team to grow. That's one of the things I think that's happened over the past couple of years. I think relationship building is key, but it has changed to be broader based with the client and the broker team.

I was going to ask you about what's changed since the early part of your career, you mentioned that at the beginning of our interview.

Well I find that it's no longer focused around one person owning the client relationship, being that lone wolf "superstar". You still see that approach but I don't think it's as effective. Teams, the complexity of business and what's required to deliver now compared to what was required thirty years ago with all the technology and the analytics and all the regulatory change that has happened in the meantime – all this means you've got to have a pretty broad team of experts to be able to deliver the perfect holistic solution for a client. We've moved from a support team that sits in the background and provides support to the "superstar" front-facing person to much more of a team of all the talents approach.

Why is that better?

I think it's much healthier for the client and much better for our own peoples' career development. It gives younger people more opportunity. I think there are still plenty of titles and status symbols in the industry but when a big client is looking for complex solutions and implementing them across a global organisation, like a BP or a Shell, they have a vast team working with them and your team face off to their team. Your team must be equally impressive in every area and in every aspect of the relationship, complement each other so that together you work like a well-oiled machine.

Any other advice you would give to a client wanting to get the best support from their broker?

As I've said, I think clients have to invest in the relationship as well. I don't think that needs to be said. Hopefully the more they deal with you the more they realise what goes in to a successful relationship. What does need to be said is that when you're recommending something and you've spent a lot of time putting a recommendation forward, that the client does actually do something about it and puts some investment into it. Each client is so different, it's very difficult to prescribe one way of doing things.

How can you best add value to a client relationship? Assuming you've done the pitch, you've won the business, you're going to deliver it at the price you've said and do the things you've promised. On top of that, where is the value-add?

Where do I start thinking instinctively? "Right, this is going to make a difference to this client?" It's always the people. It's always what team is going to be the killer asset who this client is going to love dealing with. On that big win we talked about earlier, what was key was having the right loss management person on the team, because their level of attritional claims was massive and they needed someone to help them think strategically in that area. For another client, I developed more of a risk partnership approach. Instead of just thinking of the insurance transaction, there was somebody who was the risk advisor to the client. For another client with large attrition claims it was a loss manager, rather than a risk manager, because that was where their concerns sat. Also, I just knew personality-wise it would work, and it did.

Matching people with people?

That has always been the biggest thing to get right, I believe, but across a team, not just individuals. It's partly intuitive, and it's partly knowing through this change in the way people buy now, that if you sit in front of a client and you have brilliant technical people who are all on top of their game, you could win. But if you sit in front of a client and you've got really good people who clearly enjoy working together, that complement each other's different skills and it's almost like being a family in front of the client, then you've pretty much guaranteed you're going to win it because it's a very attractive relationship experience to buy into.

Do you think about how your team stand out?

I always remember a particular client saying to me, "I have to deal with accountants and banking people, lawyers, insurers, insurance brokers, and actually everybody kind of looks identical and behaves in an identical way. Could you please try and be different? Because if you're different and you pitch to me, I'm going to remember what was different about you." And that stuck with me, but I hadn't actually selected his team on that basis. I'd selected my team on the basis that this mix of people would just work really well together.

Presumably there's been a big rise in purchasing department involvement in recent years. Has that changed the way things work?

It changes the way we have to submit reports and it also brings in an element of frustration when the KPIs or measurements don't reflect some of the things we're focused on for the client's benefit. But for the most part if it's an internal procurement department they're working for the client that is actually driving, so they need to reflect what the priorities of the buyer are going to be. Whilst as an industry we complain about these procurement teams just driving cost down, really they are reflecting what the client is prioritising.

What do you think organisations get most consistently wrong in managing client relationships effectively?

This is the most heinous crime for me, for any client relationship – overpromising and underdelivering. You've got to be absolutely certain that what you're putting forward is workable. Whilst you can be as enthusiastic as you like and over-hype it – and this comes back to having that technical grounding – the fact that when I work with people who get the real detail on loss management or analytics, it's based on science. When you get that right and you know you can deliver it because you've tested it, you've case-studied it, you've demonstrated that this could work for their specific requirement and need and then you deliver it, that is more rewarding than the win itself.

Delivering what you promise is key?

Definitely, there's an elation when you win a new client that they've trusted you enough to go with you and then you have to think to yourself - now we actually have to deliver this. For a good year or more you're still concerned that every facet that you've promised you're going to be able to deliver. If you don't deliver that then you really are in trouble. I've known clients to come back having left a broker and then move back to their original broker again because promises weren't fulfilled. I think it's a shame when I see some clients ask a broker to put all of their fee at risk, I think that's really quite an indictment that they're not entirely confident that what you're telling them as a broker is true. I've never been asked to do that, never been asked to put everything at risk, but it does happen.

What role do you think price plays in the buying decision?

You have to be quite careful. On a recent bid where we weren't successful I kept being told, "You are expensive but we know we're getting more so that's okay", and in-fact they told me what to tweak the pricing to, which was still higher than our competition, but it closed the gap a bit in order to win. You need to think about pricing and value always from the client's perspective. Let me give you an example. Often there may be a need for some extra analysis, for example a business interruption review. It could add a lot of value and you need to explain that, what you don't do is say, "We think you need to do a business interruption review – it's going to cost you £25,000. Do you want us to do the review?" No client I've ever known will say "Oh yes, I'll do that, shall we pay now?" Talk about what it is that they will get as a result of the review, where's the value?

Do you consider fee and premium costs, "in the round"?

Yes, the insurance premiums can be significant, and our job is to manage that cost for a client, so a focus on our own fee frankly is a bit of a sideshow. What I really enjoy doing is to put together for the client a journey that takes them through stages to explain how, year on year, the plan that is put in place to mitigate losses, is going to deliver improvements and reductions in their cost so that in three years' time the cost will have gone from here to there. I'm talking about the cost of insurance, not the cost of the broker fee, and then against that is the work that needs to be done to get them to that place and work with them, and the fees attached to it.

A Financial Director will absolutely buy into that for two reasons. One, you have explained a journey he can understand and he can see that they were in a position of pain but understand that you have shown them how to work out of it. Second is the science to it, a mathematician wants to see the "proof points"!

When you are recruiting client-facing talent, what are the key attributes you look for? If someone walks in for an interview, what do you want to see?

I look for stand out qualities which are more often than not related to them as a person rather than their CV.

What I look for in recruiting good client-facing consultants in our firm is intellectual self-confidence and the ability and desire to formulate a view and defend it. You see lots of clever people who can't do that.

I know exactly what you mean, I look for that too.

What could organisations do to help client-facing talent develop more effectively?

In my early career, I was very fortunate but didn't realise just how much in the deep-end I was being dropped, very young and without the experience. Despite my lack of experience I was trusted enough - within certain guidelines - to really experiment and find out what worked and what didn't work in terms of developing client relationships and what questions were really insightful and what were just a tick-box exercise. I don't think now, and maybe partly this is the regulatory environment we are in, that we're that trusting of young people, that we allow people to make mistakes in that way. That's partly it. Secondly, I don't see a career path. I don't see a career path for a young person coming in today that says, "This is where I am today. In thirty years I can do what Ailsa does and become a senior relationship officer of the firm." That lack of clarity is not attractive to a young person. What young people are telling me is that they want some guidance on how they develop. They need some – not just the training but a career framework that says, "If we do these things at this stage in our career we can then move onto the next stage and these are the expectations of the firm", we don't have that at the moment but we will be putting it in place.

How do you help them to build their commercial experience?

Where I'm not directly involved in their line management or their P&L management I always say, because it's worked for me so it's from experience, is get involved with sales. When you get involved with sales, you can rapidly learn what works and doesn't work and you can make a contribution even without technical knowledge, you can be developing your research skills and you can use those to bring some insight and some thinking to others around the table who haven't had the time that you've had to do research and think of ideas.

I think young people look at potential employers quite carefully these days. Here's something interesting: someone about to join us recently did some investigative research in advance of our last meeting. He said that he'd looked at the results at Marsh over the past few years and had compared them to a competitor's results. He'd compared the tone of our CEO and the tone of the competitor CEO in talking about those results and that it was really interesting that Marsh have grown 1% or 2% in the last five years - it's not spectacular and the CEO's townhalls and statements are suggesting that he's underwhelmed - he doesn't think it's particularly impressive, he's open to how we are going to improve. The competitor's view, whose results have gone down - sell it as a massive "success" because they're making more margin. They're cutting more and more people out of the value chain and short-term they're making more and more money which one might guess is unlikely to be sustainable in terms of client value. We need to invest in systems but most of all we need to invest in our people. Young people should join a firm with a good career path and is committed to investing in them.

Apart from investing in people, what else is key to growing the business?

What can we do to improve retention and our win rate to drive the business forward? There's an "openness" to change but I don't think we need to change too much to make a big difference. For example, the impact team I'm working with, now I've worked with them on a few bids and they've realised they don't have to stick to everything being done in a technical way and they're now really enjoying just being a bit different and really nailing that Exec Summary. Because the other thing I found when I arrived is our Exec Summaries – and to your point that a client has a relatively short attention span and first impressions do count – is key, it's often the only thing that some people in the client are going to read and it should set the tone and the key messaging that goes through the report. So we've changed the way we're putting these across and we're already seeing an uptick in our success rate in pitches.

So in summary, you could say that your ambition is to challenge a little – but constructively, encourage people to explore new approaches, train and develop people to open up client discussions more effectively and "bring the firm" better?

Yes, not a bad synthesis.

We started at the beginning of our conversation talking about your early career and aspirations, what you had learned and who had helped you along the way. I'm sure you're keen to pass on your own knowledge to benefit younger people beginning their careers today. What advice would you give to them?

The pace of change is accelerating so I would say be open to embracing change and new possibilities. Develop the ability to "listen", ask good questions, build empathy and from that position of knowledge and trust distil your analysis. From the analysis build an argument, a recommended strategy you are confident in and works backwards and forwards. Perhaps the ability to relate risk strategy to a client's business model - those skills will be more important than when I began. And as we've discussed the ability to work as a team to bring the firm even more effectively is increasingly important. Be a team player, sounds trite but true.

“

It was my first big sales call. I remember reaching down into my briefcase and pulling out the papers. I looked at him and thought, if I try to sell to him, he's going to eat me alive. I don't even know him. So I put the files back, and said, "To be honest, I need your help. The company needs me to walk out of here with a £500k order and I don't know how I'm going to do it." To my amazement he got his secretary in and cancelled all of his later appointments. At the end of the meeting he gave me a stack of orders and he said, "That should sort you out." I didn't have a calculator with me at the time, but I went back home and added it up to £750k worth of orders.

”

SIMON MARSHALL

INTERVIEWED 14TH JANUARY 2021

Simon joined Unilever straight from school in 1979 and retired nearly forty years later as Managing Director of a major Food Service Division responsible for North America. On the journey in between he was UK National Sales Director at a time when Lever Brothers and Elida Fabergé merged and ran Ireland as a market for a period. In our interview he talks about the power of a 'winning mentality', his big break as a National Account Manager and the importance of building a career which is focused on what you really enjoy.

Let's start by talking a little about your background, what your parents did and where you grew up.

I was born in Liverpool, on the red side of Liverpool I hasten to add. But when I was eight my parents moved to Sheffield. This was in the late sixties. Arriving in Sheffield with a scouse accent where the Yorkshire lads spoke very differently, I needed to adapt very fast.

What kind of school did you join in Sheffield?

A normal comprehensive school after a regular junior school. I was reflecting on that the other day, because that very experience, at a young age, of moving and having to adapt and change clearly influenced me.

How do you think it influenced you?

I needed to reflect on how people were, and to adapt myself. It's funny, I'm jumping way over now, but even in my last role, when I went to America and lived in Chicago for seven years. When I first arrived in the US, ten out of ten people that I met for the first time knew I was from England. They could just tell by my accent. By the time I left, nine out of ten people thought I was Australian. That's just a reflection of seven years of adapting to a different environment and adopting a more Chicagoan accent I suppose.

How do you think that experience of changing schools shaped you?

Well, I certainly learnt to adapt and change. I'm not kidding, I wanted to get rid of my accent pretty damn quickly, I needed to be like everyone else. To what extent that really manifested itself later in life is hard to say, but it certainly helped me when I got into my sales career because my ability to listen and adapt to what customers wanted certainly helped.

You asked about my parents. My dad was actually in business. He was an account manager for Batchelors Foods.

How did your relationships with your parents influence you?

Well, my mum, we were very close but sadly, I lost her when she was quite young, she was only 51 at the time. I miss her still. Looking back my dad had quite an influence on me, not least because he was always challenging me. No matter what I did, I could always have done better. And he still does it today.

But at school, sitting down and learning was never something that I was good at. I just never had the temperament. I never had the patience, or necessarily, even the desire. I was just so into my sports. My O Levels, I scraped through. I got six Cs and an A.

A-Levels were a complete waste of time, to be honest, because I was signed up for Sheffield United on schoolboy terms. I was playing cricket for South Yorkshire. I was playing badminton for Yorkshire. Golf, the club that I was a member at, they wanted to take me on as an apprentice. So sport was my gig. But the problem was, I couldn't focus on just one. There wasn't one that really came through to me. I was a real Jack of all trades but master of none.

Also, back then, it wasn't as if sport was that rewarding, in terms of financial security. Even being a top footballer for Sheffield United in Division One, your career would probably finish at thirty or thirty-five. Only the top players made any real money out of it. So there was never any financial stability in a sports career, though it was my passion.

My dad was very conscious about that, he kept reminding me: "At some point, you're going to have to stand up on your own two feet." I said to him, as I started my A-Levels, full of confidence despite just scrapping through my O-Levels, "I'm going to go to university." As he saw my A-Level performance start to develop, or not, as the case may be, I said to him, "Yes, I really fancy going to university," and he said, "No."

He said, "No?"

Yes. He said, "If you go to university, you're just going to waste three more years."

Being honest, were you finding the academic work difficult, or were you just not really focused enough on it?

I was definitely not focused on it. Definitely not. It's quite interesting because this is also when I learnt a little bit about myself. I got six grade C O-Levels, I just scraped through. But I got one A, which was in History. Six months before I took my exam, my history teacher pulled me to one side and said to me, "Simon, I don't know what the hell you're doing in the O-Level stream. You've been wasting my time, the school's time, and everyone else's. You realise, I've put you down for an E." That was the motivation that I needed!

But it didn't transfer to the other subjects.

No, but I was really focused on proving her wrong, and I got an A. When I saw my History teacher shortly after the results were published, she was clearly a little embarrassed but I just wanted to thank her. She gave me the kick I needed.

I got carried away with my A-Level subjects, choosing very challenging and difficult ones that would require total focus and commitment. But I didn't give it, Sport was still my passion but I still just couldn't focus on one. So, I was lost.

I didn't know what to do and I thought, "Maybe it's time to get a job." But I had no idea what I was going to do.

Your father was in grocery, was that one of the reasons that you ended up at Unilever?

I remember he had circled an advertisement and said "Look, there's a role come up as company learner for this company, Elida Gibbs. It's based in Leeds. They make products like Signal Toothpaste and Sunsilk Shampoo, so why don't you go for that?" I thought, "alright, I'll give it a go," and I applied. Elida Gibbs was part of Unilever, as was Batchelors at the time.

I applied, got an interview, and I got the job. It was difficult because for the best part of eighteen months I was travelling up and down from Sheffield to Leeds daily. The salary wasn't much and virtually all my money went on travelling. But it was nice to have a little bit of money in the pocket. Company Learner ended up being a dogsbody job, working out Reps' expenses and performance against targets, making cups of coffee in sales meetings, picking up damaged goods from local stores, that kind of thing.

But it was my first experience in sales and I really liked what I saw. I enjoyed seeing how the guys went about preparing for their meetings, how they got together and challenged each other on sales targets. It gave me an appetite to understand more about business.

By this time, you'd been there a year or so?

Yes and I wanted to move to London, to go to the Head Office. They were able to make that happen and I was offered a job as Advertising Clerk in the Accounts Department in Portman Square, I was given a one-way ticket on the train. The first couple of months I lived with an old school friend living with his parents in Tunbridge Wells and I commuted in. I later found a one-bedroomed apartment which I shared with some guy that I'd never met before, it was all I could afford.

That's how my time in London began. I was Advertising Clerk for about a year. Then I had an opportunity to join the Marketing Accountants. There were two Marketing Accountants in the business, and they had two assistants. I became one of the assistants. That was a real eye opener for me, because in that role, I was able to have a really broad look at the business. We got involved in virtually everything the business was thinking of doing. It all funnelled through Marketing Accounts. It was quite enlightening.

Were you good with numbers?

So it turned out, I hadn't necessarily considered myself to be but I actually really started to enjoy working with them. I remember a senior colleague on one occasion asking me to do an analysis. I can't remember the details of it, but I created this huge spreadsheet and this was before the days of Excel so it was a lot of work.

I had an update meeting with him, and I gave him this huge sheet of numbers. He said, "Okay, yes, I like that. I think that and that, and we need to do this." I remember being absolutely blown away with how he did that. Just his comfort with and understanding of the numbers, how quickly he could spot patterns and trends. I wanted to be able to do that.

I did develop an ease in working with and remembering numbers. In the later part of my time in that role I was also able to step in as acting Marketing Accountant when my boss left the business. I really enjoyed the increased responsibility and visibility and getting involved in some big projects. But there was a limit to what I could do as I was not interested in becoming a qualified Accountant. And then an opportunity came up for me to become a sales rep. I had liked what I saw in the Regional Sales Office and I had enjoyed working with numbers. Being a sales rep and understanding numbers and deals and discounts, how you hit your targets was bringing those two things together.

And you got a company Cortina, probably!

I got a company car, yes. The difficulty was, we were living in a small flat in Croydon by this time. The territory they gave me was the East End and the City of London, so it was a brutal commute in the car.

Your job was calling on supermarkets and corner shops?

Yes, Asda, Cash and Carries, and a lot of Independent chemists and drug stores mainly. It was a big learning for me. In the East End they either get on with you or they didn't, there was no middle ground back then. They could make you a success or a failure.

I quickly learned that whoever I called on at the beginning of the day and offered a deal to, within no time every single other person, for the rest of the day, knew what that deal was, and they wanted a better deal. I made the mistake, early on, of offering different deals. Then they would just rip you apart.

So I quickly learned that the deal you start with was the deal you had to stick to, and then you've got to hold your ground. Mutual respect began from there.

Did you have a good boss?

I would say no, I didn't have a great boss at the time. I'd love to talk to you about how things have changed… They used to call it 'man management' – the very phrase sends shivers down my spine now – as opposed to 'leadership'. It was, at best, man management: "You will do this. That's the target. Now, you get on and do it."

Did you find that you were good at the job?

Yes, I was Salesman of the Year in the first year and I won a trip to California!

What made you good at it, do you think?

Well, I think there's a little bit about being able to relate to people, to understand them and see things from their perspective. Then there's definitely something about understanding the deal, sticking with it, and perhaps most importantly developing a relationship in which customers start to trust you.

How long did you end up doing that job for?

About eighteen months.

Then what?

They offered to take me into Head Office as a Sales Planner. In that role you take the marketing plans and plan the activity for the sales force to execute it. The guy that brought me in was my old Area Manager, so he knew me, he wanted me. Unfortunately it very quickly started to turn sour. I would say that it was the one time I came close to leaving Unilever. I was not happy.

Why was that?

I didn't feel appreciated. It was as if everything that I did or wrote, he changed. So not appreciated, not trusted. To be honest, I didn't feel wanted. I was just sinking.

How did you get out of the situation?

Along came one of the best leaders I've ever had.

Talk about him.

He came to me as I was already starting to look for jobs, he came to me in my little office and said, "Simon, I've got a position coming up in Sales. It's not a management role yet, but it's a Sales Executive role, looking after national wholesale chemists. I think you'd be great at it, and I'd love you to be in my team."

I should mention the thing I was beginning to get a little bit dismayed about, which was that I joined this company in 1979, and it was now around 1986. I kept hitting this glass ceiling, trying to get into management. I knew it was going to be tough because I didn't have a degree. All the management roles, basically, were being given to Oxbridge people, because Unilever had this university graduate training programme, UCMDS, which was very strong. They pulled the best people from the best universities. It was getting difficult to see my way through. My new boss said, "Do this role for me, make a good shot at it and we'll see where it goes from there. Let's give it a go."

Overnight, I felt wanted. He trusted me and supported me whenever I needed it. I did the job for about ten months. Then another job came up - a new role as National Account Manager for regional drug stores. I was going to be responsible for four of them, my first management role! It had taken me almost ten years to get there and I was delighted.

What happened next?

Within five months of becoming a National Account Manager, all four of those regional drug stores were bought out. My job disappeared in front of my eyes! I just couldn't believe it.

They were all bought out by one large drugstore. My boss came to me and said, "Simon, I know it's disappointing." He'd obviously been working around this behind the scenes. "I know your job has disappeared, but we want you to take responsibility for the national drug store." They were now the second largest customer in the company. "It's going to be quite a challenge," he said, "are you up for it?" Of course I said I was.

The customer had a Buying Director at the time who was renowned for being a difficult person to deal with. To add to the pressure, before my first meeting with him my boss told me, "Simon, I need you to go in there and come out with a £½m deal, we need it badly."

I spent a good few days preparing, I spent a lot of sleepless nights working through my plan. I turned up at their Head Office, all suited and booted. Of course, he played it in the classic way and kept me waiting for an hour. When I was called he just looked at the chair on the other side of the desk and said, "so who are you? What do you want?" That's how it started. I explained who I was. He said, "Oh yes. Well, get your stuff ready and we'll get on with it."

You had a presentation prepared for him?

Yes, I had the works. I remember reaching down into my briefcase and pulling out the papers. I looked at him and thought, if I try to sell to him, he's going to eat me alive. I don't even know him, and he's got this tough buyer reputation.

So I put the files back, and said, "To be honest, I need your help. The company needs me to walk out of here with a £500k order and I don't know how I'm going to do it." To my amazement he got his secretary in and cancelled all of his later appointments. I walked out of that office at 6:30 in the evening. He went through everything with me, line by line.

Trying to help?

Absolutely, at the end of the meeting he gave me a stack of orders and he said, "That should sort you out." I didn't have a calculator with me at the time, but I went back home and added it up to £750k worth of orders.

How did the relationship develop from there?

When I came back from Germany some years later I sought him out because he'd left the company, he'd set up his own drug store chain. I think at the time, he was running three or four of them. I went to see him and I asked him, "Why did you help me that first meeting?" He said, "It's quite simple, you asked for my help, nobody had ever come through that door and asked for my help." It was literally as simple as that, and of course a pivotal moment in my career.

After that role I decided it would be good to get some marketing experience and became a Brand Manager for two years.

That was a really useful time, there were parts of the marketing role that I really liked, but there was definitely a lot of it that I didn't. The strategic side of it, the bigger platform side of it, I liked. Spending a load of time with people deciding what colour the label should be, I didn't.

After that I came back into sales as a National Account Controller. I actually replaced my old boss. I was responsible for Tesco, Sainsbury's and Boots.

This was a great experience for me, because I was working with three very different customers and my first experience of leading a bigger team, being responsible for a number of people, I really enjoyed that.

Before we move on, can I ask what you think makes a good salesperson?

Most definitely somebody who can listen.

The opposite of what people expect. They expect a salesperson to talk a lot, right?

Yes, but you've got to listen, then you adopt and adapt and then you deliver. I've found dealing with customers much easier than dealing with the internal organisation, actually. Most of the time people internally liked to talk a good game about customer-orientation but when push comes to shove and you've got to really align the organisation behind it, they don't respond and there is nothing worse for a salesperson than to overpromise and under-deliver.

I believe soon after, you moved to Germany?

Yes, I was offered a job in Germany to run a process re-engineering exercise. It was made very clear to me that if I was going to go to Germany, I'd have to learn the language because I would be going there to effect change in the sales organisation and the sales people didn't speak English. Setting up category management, that was my task.

I was hopeless at languages at school but I had got to know people who could speak multiple languages and had often thought "that is so cool, I'd love to be able to do that".

Corinna (my artist wife) and I were up for living in another country, having that experience. Our children Phoebe and Caine were very young at the time.

How did you find Germany?

My boss, the German sales director, sat me down on my first day in February and said, "In August we're having a national sales conference. Five hundred people will be there and you'll have an hour and a half onstage. I want you to convince people that category management is the way forward, in German and no script."

I threw myself at it, I had a new team of people. They were German but they could all speak English. I sat them down and said, "I really need you to talk to me in German." They were so good, they sat down and talked to me for fifteen minutes when it could have been done in two minutes in English, they constantly talked to me in German.

For the first few months I was on my own – Corinna and the kids only joined me once the English school year had finished. When I got back to my apartment after work, I'd just have the radio or the TV on, constantly trying to soak up German. Each day I set myself a challenge of learning ten words.

The sales conference came along and I found myself up on stage. I remember standing up, my team were down in the front row, I started and I probably got through the first ten minutes exactly as I'd scripted but before long I was completely off script. I would stop and look down at my team from time to time as if to say, "is this still making sense?".

I got through it and everybody was very complimentary. Interestingly I realised that when I went off script, I was thinking in German. That was a wonderful realisation.

What was different about doing business in Germany?

One fundamental difference was that the German hierarchy was a lot more formal. The way in which the business worked was up and down the hierarchy. Of course, process re-engineering is all about looking left and right. I'll give you an example. When I first arrived, I remember being blown away, so impressed, that every single person I spoke to knew exactly what they did and could explain their process very clearly with a very clearly defined job description. It was impressive. Not long after, however, I realised that these impressive job descriptions had brick walls built on either side of them. People really didn't understand what impact something they actioned had elsewhere.

My team would come to me and they'd say, "I've got this problem," and I started off by saying, "What do you think we should do about it?". That, in itself, was new, that I expected them to think beforehand what they thought we should do about it.

They came to know that I was going to ask that. They'd come in and say, "We've got this problem," and I'd say, "What do you think we should do about it?". They would answer and then I'd ask, "If we did that, what do you think the impact over here would be?" Literally, they'd say, "That's not my problem."

It was very old world. The 'Verkaufsdirektor', the account controllers, whenever they came into the office, you could almost feel the energy in the office change, it was like, "Oh my God, they're in". Of course, it didn't take long before they and I were having difficult conversations because a lot of what I was there to do was to change a lot of what they did.

What I didn't know at the time is that they had a bet as to how long I would last. One of the most hard line controllers retired in my time there.

You drove him to his retirement, Simon?!

Well, he invited me to his retirement event, which I was flabbergasted at. Not only that, the afternoon was a golf session and not only did he invite me to the golf, I was playing with him. On the way around he said to me, "I want you to know that you cost me a lot of bottles of champagne. When you first arrived, I didn't think you would last six months, but after the work that you've done with my client, I realised that the way in which I used to do things had gone, it was time for me to go."

You came back to the UK two years later?

Yes, a meeting was planned with the Chairman of the UK Personal care business. I was expecting to be told about another International assignment but he offered me the job of Sales Director UK with Elida Faberge.

I remember the first day I sat in my office, realising that I was Sales Director of the company where I started as "Company Learner" and thinking, "What the hell am I doing here?". Of course, many colleagues were still in the business that I had left two years earlier. It was a very strange feeling.

After 3 years in that role it was announced that we were going to merge Elida Faberge with Lever Brothers. They were two completely different businesses and cultures, primarily driven by the competitive arena. The best way I can describe it is in the personal care business there were lots of different competitors, so it was a bit more like open warfare. By contrast Lever Brothers had one main branded competitor, Procter & Gamble. So, that business was all about trench warfare, it was win an inch, lose an inch.

How did the union work out?

We brought the two businesses together, decided on the leadership team and, of course, what I wanted to do was to develop a strategy for us as a new customer development team. At the time, I talked a lot about the 'energy' of a business. Every business has an energy but with the best will in the world, a lot of the time the energy is dissipated and different parts of the organisation pull in different directions. When they're pulling against each other, the energy of the business vibrates and goes nowhere, there's a lot of frustration.

What I wanted to do with the customer development team was align the business, create forward momentum.

How did you get on with your peers like the Marketing Director?

There were two Marketing Directors, both women, and both very talented and capable. We developed a really great and powerful working relationship. In fact, the Board team that was created at that time still get together a couple of times a year for dinner and talk about old times.

At the start we got the marketing and sales teams together for a national conference and we did it abroad, so it was a big deal. We wanted to show how the departments could work better together. It came from us, it came from the three of us and we became known as 'The Three Musketeers'.

Together we created what we called the 'Winning Wheel'. There was a visualisation of this and it had a number of spokes, we talked about how we needed to align ourselves to the wheel to spin elegantly. One of the spokes was 'motivate the customer and anticipate the shopper'.

That was a time when if sales were good, it was down to great marketing, if sales were bad, it was bad sales. So, whenever there's a revenue challenge, it's sales that have to go and fix it. It wasn't like that anymore, everybody across the organisation was engaging in wanting to build the business.

I mean, the finance guys were analysing all the discount data and we had the supply chain team thinking about how we could get more stock there quickly so we can do this massive activation over here. We had marketing thinking about what activities they could put in. The whole organisation came together and it just changed the dynamic completely.

Everybody felt they had a valuable role to play. The customer wasn't just seen as the responsibility of the sales team anymore.

What next?

I got my first General Management job in Ireland running the Ireland Home and Personal Care business and after almost four years of running the UK and Ireland Unilever Foodsolutions business, I was asked to run the North American Food Service Business, based out of Chicago. It was difficult because this business had many challenges at the time I arrived. Most of the heavy lifting in terms of closing down parts of the organisation had been done. My task was to reenergise things and get the business back onto a profitable growth track.

Was the US business more like the UK than the German business?

Yes, very similar to the UK, but there were some cultural differences. I remember when I first arrived, I noticed that people often didn't take all their holidays and if they did, then it was apparent they were working just as hard and long from a hotel room. I have always felt strongly that holidays or rather taking a real break is important for your health and wellbeing and returning rested and ready for the challenges ahead was better for the person and the business. Despite leading for this by example, there was still hesitancy so I asked my HR Director "what's going on here, why won't people do this?". She explained that people are concerned that "if you can do without them for two weeks, you can do without them". But we got there in the end.

How did you manage your own work and home life balance. How did you cope with the stress of those senior roles?

I would say, on the whole I managed it fine. I definitely got stressed at times, definitely, and certainly in the sales director role, because there were some touch and go moments and difficult challenges in America, but I would honestly say that the best thing for me was Corinna and the kids. You know, Corinna being an artist meant that whenever I wasn't at work, I was either involved with the kids or with Corinna's art world. The art world is a million miles away from the world that I was living in on a day-to-day basis.

Did you talk to Corinna about your work? Was she interested?

Some of the time, more on the people side of things I would share some challenges and she would always have a great, down-to-Earth, simple insight. You know, sometimes I was overthinking things.

You were quite good at switching off?

Yes. Very rarely would it stop me sleeping.

If you were being objective, what would you say you were unusually good at?

Communication, my ability to communicate with people.

Is that key to being a good leader?

Yes but leaders also have to have a very clear vision, be able to align people to it and motivate them to go after it. When you're creating a vision it's got to be authentic, it's got to mean something to people, otherwise, you get found out quickly. If it isn't something you really believe in, people will see through it.

Did you find that you could see pictures in complex data and situations very clearly? You mentioned your early boss who could do that; could you?

Yes, you are spot on, Chris, exactly that because I think the other thing I was going to say, I think leaders sometimes get lost in their own intellectual debate and it makes everything too complex, too complicated. At the end of the day people can't understand it, so can't follow it.

Being able to distil out the few things that are really important and bring them to life for people is critical, and being able to communicate it in a way which is memorable makes a huge difference. Distil it into three words or a picture, it is really hard, but if you can achieve that the benefits are huge.

You were good at articulating a vision and getting people motivated to deliver against?

It certainly helped, Chris. I am not the sharpest, brightest, Unilever was full of incredibly intelligent people, but I think what helped me get to where I did in the end was that ability to communicate and energise people behind a very clear vision.

Did you ever feel intimidated by all the Oxford and Cambridge folk?

When I first started, yes, they could put sentences together which I couldn't even begin to understand, but in the end I turned it to my advantage because I would just say to them, "what do you mean?" and actually, they found it really quite difficult to distil.

Looking back on your career what do you understand now that you wish you'd understood when you were that 17-year-old in your first role?

Never be afraid to ask for help. There is no doubt a lot of people think that asking for help can be a sign of weakness. In my mind it is a sign of strength. Don't be afraid to ask.

Another key learning that came out for me was 'choose your attitude'. There are so many external factors that can have a massive impact that you have no control over, but the one thing that you are always in charge of, even in complex and difficult situations, is your attitude. "Do I want to 'play to win' or do I want to 'avoid losing'?" If you are in 'avoid losing' mode you are negative, finding excuses, blaming others. It is just down, down, down. But if you are 'playing to win' you are on the front foot. You are energised, you are creative, you are determined. So, just ask yourself, "Which attitude do I want to bring to this?" Decide to be 'playing to win'.

There were many times when I felt myself going into the avoid losing mode and I'd go, "stop, play to win". It is a huge psychological factor in successes.

That's a good insight. What is perhaps the best single piece of advice that someone else gave you?

That is a great question. It would be one of the things I tell people now actually, and it was something my dad said to me.

When I was getting frustrated with, "How am I going to break through into management?" he said, "Don't worry about it. Don't worry about it because you will now have an opportunity to get lots of other experiences that other people won't have, so take your time". He said, "You've got many years ahead of you to work so it's worthwhile taking time now to find out what you really enjoy." You are going to have to spend a lot of your life doing it, so take your time, don't feel you have to rush. So, if you do not already know, take your time finding out what really motivates you and what you really enjoy doing.

Very good advice. Is there a colleague or colleagues who you particularly admired?

The guy that led our Lever Fabergé challenge at the time when we brought the two businesses together, I won't mention his name, but he has gone on to do fantastic things. At the time he also knew he had challenges, he had things that he needed to develop. The way he embraced us as his leadership team to not only help us to improve and to be the best that we could be, he put himself in there too. He exposed himself in that journey and it just made it very special. We were all in it together.

I learnt a lot from that. I took that to every single leadership team that I subsequently led, thinking about how we worked together and creating a contract amongst ourselves, one where we could be open, very challenging but open. We could argue things out together but once we got outside no-one could put a fag paper between us.

Do you think young people today are very different in their goals and approach from people from our generation?

I think they are certainly more demanding and their expectations are perhaps greater but I think it's only good because with that they bring a passion and a determination, and you can channel that energy.

I would say that some are too restless. I say take your time. Use your time now to get different experiences to determine what it is you want to do.

Unilever used to have this saying: "If ever you left Unilever you've left." But in my time if people wanted different experiences that we couldn't deliver for them we'd encourage them to go and do it but say, "When you're ready, come back and let's talk again about the next thing you want to do because we might have something for you."

How did the working world change for you in terms of technology during your career?

Probably around the time I was in National Accounts, I remember thinking quite clearly that there is so much data around now, the need for relationships between businesses may diminish because data will just speak and decisions will be made.

I have never been more wrong. The role to engage with customers on a one-to-one basis is as important now as it has ever been. Those relationships are critical in any business. But the benefit is that, with better data you can elevate the quality of the conversation.

It's rare today for someone to be at one company for their entire career. How do you look back on your thirty-seven years at Unilever?

I had the pleasure of working for an amazing company, a company I am incredibly proud to have worked for because it leads on to so many things. Doing its best to make changes that can help contribute towards saving the planet, you know. There were opportunities to go elsewhere. The reality was though, every time I got itchy feet, I was lucky enough to have the opportunity that I was looking for within Unilever, so I never really had to.

I'd say you have an unusual energy and enthusiasm. Is that natural, or have you cultivated it?

I think it's natural but I need to channel the energy into something that I really believe in. Then it becomes infectious!

If I was to meet for a beer with five or six of your colleagues from Unilever and say, "tell me about Simon, what's he like?" what do you think they would say?

I think they would say, "He's got a lot of energy, a lot of passion." I think they would definitely talk about the customer-focus and my ability to communicate and engage at all levels of the organisation. I would like to think they would say I was consistent and kept things simple.

Running through all this, I think they would also say "he loves to win" which is certainly true, but winning with others is what makes it really special.

You might want to distil down some of the things we have already covered, but if you were sitting down with a group of young people starting out in their careers, what advice would you give them?

Find your passion. Find what you really enjoy doing. Not least because you are going to have to spend a lot of time doing it, but also, it's the way in which you help engage and motivate others.

And always choose your attitude, you are always in control of it so always 'play to win'.

SIMON MARSHALL

“

One of my bosses said, “You want me to tell you your problem? You are an overachiever and what that means is that unless you are overachieving at everything you do you're not happy and since you can't overachieve all the time, you are not going to be happy quite a lot. You know how I know this? Because I am an overachiever.” And I could see what he was saying. I think there is a lot of truth in that. The thing driving me and others, even if they are well educated, is the desire to prove themselves.

”

GRAHAM WHITEHAIR

INTERVIEWED 16TH APRIL 2020

Graham began his forty-year career in Finance as a trainee bullion trader in 1979, joining straight from school. He progressed to joining the Foreign Exchange team at Kleinwort Benson and by 1999 was Global Head of Foreign Exchange at Credit Lyonnais, a role he held for five years.

Subsequently he was Director of Treasury Sales at the Bank of Scotland and held a succession of senior roles at Lloyds Banking Group finally responsible for all aspects of trading and conduct risk for the Bank and a member of the Bank of England stakeholder advisory group. He retired earlier this year.

You were very clear that you wanted to go into banking. Did you know someone in that world?

My father had worked in the City, as had my grandfather.

What did they do?

My grandfather was a shipping broker and my father traded soft commodities but they were only ever in the administration/operations type areas. My father suggested to me that bankers were 'thieving wotsits' and if you couldn't beat them then joining them might be a good idea! I followed that advice. I did like Economics at A-Level, but of course like all young people I didn't have much idea of what it all meant.

You didn't know what aspect of Banking you wanted to go into?

Again, my father seemed to think that aiming to get into a trading company was a good idea.

I wrote lots of letters while completing my A-Levels at school and I got lots of interviews. I can tell you the only firm who didn't offer me a job, it was Rothschilds and I've never liked them since! I was offered a job by the Bank of England, and I was tempted by the sports centre in Roehampton, but the company that I joined paid £500 a year more than they did and I was more attracted by that!

What was it that made you so successful in your applications? Were you a red-hot student?

No, I don't think I was. I think the City of London has changed beyond recognition in the period I've been involved. A lot of boys from the local area joined straight from school, friends of mine, for example my best friend now started, when he was sixteen, I met him when I started work at eighteen and we're still friends.

Where did you grow up?

Where I am now. I grew up in Wallington, which is in Sutton.

I had good enough A-Levels to go to university, and I was the only one who didn't, who said, "no thanks, I think I'll go and get a job instead".

Your parents didn't advise you to go?

My brother went. I was one of four kids under one salary, I don't think my dad relished the idea of financing me. I would say I wasn't an academic superstar but I was a confident young man in the rugby team and the cricket teams, a prefect and all that sort of thing.

Was your dad a big influence on you and are you like him as an operator?

Yes, he has been and he's still here at ninety-one. He was always a strong influence on me. As I've told you I am one of four kids, my older brother is four years older than I am. He was working for Arthur Anderson.

So which Bank did you join?

I didn't actually join a Bank. I joined a company called Sharps Pixley which was a bullion house, trading Gold and Silver.

What did you do when you first arrived?

I lucked out big time! On the first week I was there, I met my now friend Paul in what was called the Bullion Transfer Department. They were playing a football match that week and he asked if I wanted to play. I got a lift to Eltham from one of the guys on his motor bike. He proceeded to crash it but fortunately not badly! I was most upset that I might damage the suit my father had bought me but I managed not to put any holes in it. He wasn't so lucky, he came off his bike and he broke his wrist.

In my second week I was put in the deep end making the bullion transfers in place of the chap with the broken wrist, which meant debiting the account of the chap who sold it and crediting the account of the person who bought it. He was off for a while, I managed to get more right than I got wrong and was noticed as having turned up and been useful. I only spent six months in the Operations department before there was an opening in the Trading room and I was asked if I would be interested to go and be a dealer's clerk, and I said yes! If you were trading and I was your clerk, you would write in your book 'sold ten' and I would write in my book 'sold ten', it was a check. Later in the day we would go around and check all the deals, tally the totals and make sure we both had the same information because if we hadn't it meant somebody had missed something and we'd have a possible out-trade.

You were eighteen at the time, did you have any views or aspirations in terms of what you wanted to achieve in your career?

At the very early stage I was just pleased to get a job and my suit. I landed in a world that was very much 'work hard, play hard'. If I skip forward a little bit, my twenty-first birthday, I was taken to the pub and had twenty-one vodka and orange juices and then went back to the office, it was a different world.

You didn't have a view of what you aspired to achieve in particular?

I think I did, but on arrival I was keen to earn some money. I met my wife when I was sixteen. She was working for Barclays in a local branch while I was doing my A-Levels and we got engaged at twenty and married at twenty-one.

I've got three grown up children now. My adult son is interviewing for roles right now and he's got three interviews and eighteen online tests but that's not how it used to be. You'd get a job through a mixture of cheek and persistence, and once in you'd get noticed for working hard and playing hard. I knew I wanted to get-on but I didn't know what that looked like.

How did your career unfold early on?

Once I made it onto the trading floor, the view then was that traders would be burned out by the time they were thirty-five. I definitely recall going to meet my friends that had gone to university and I noticed they seemed to have more disposable income than I did because I'd quickly bought a flat after we got married. By the time I had paid the mortgage and bought a washing machine, I had nothing. I went to Leicester to see my friend and he wanted to go to a concert, and I wasn't sure I had the £20 to do it, he was a student and he had. I was driven by need really, the need to provide and a desire to achieve.

Tell me about your early days on the trading floor.

A dealer's clerk was the bottom rank, sitting next to the traders, scribing, a bit like a bookmaker that takes all the bets but he has someone else keeping the notes. I was in the right place at the right time. I was working long days, we kept losing staff because there were only five broking houses including Rothschilds so they seemed to want to keep me on.

I had a senior trader next to me. I was doing the clerking, the guy that was number two to the chief dealer left to join JP Morgan, so I was asked to have a go at that. There was nowhere to go to replace lost staff, so they had to train their own, which was to my benefit. I kept on getting pushed into new roles because they needed someone to step up.

Was all the training on the job?

All on the job! I made trades on my own when it was quiet.

You said at the time there was a strong lunchtime drinking culture. Were you confident that the drinking wouldn't spoil your judgment?

Bear in mind I was a young man about twenty-three or twenty-four, I took risks that I didn't realise I was taking. Had I known I wouldn't have taken them. I'm not saying it was clever, but that's just how things were.

It sounds like it worked.

If you were roaring drunk and stupid you would have been sacked. There was a book, if you were going out for a long session you put your name in it and wouldn't do much in the afternoon unless you had to get back and it was really busy. It was like a rota. It was a bit like a rugby club, if you did well in a rugby club then you would do well in trading, because they had a similar sort of laddish culture; being liked, being efficient and being accurate. If you put it into today's language, they weren't going to suffer fools gladly. If you were making mistakes you wouldn't survive.

Do the same attributes work for the people in those jobs now? If not, is there a reason why that has changed?

Yes, it's changed in many respects but not fundamentally. If you are comparing it up to today in the now sanitised city, drinking is forbidden during work and sometimes after work. Laddish behaviour is not happening and the skill sets are changed because you don't have the same interaction with other firms and individuals, you don't have two phones in your ear, everything is pretty much on an electronic keyboard. But the fundamentals underlying trading don't change.

If you were recruiting someone now, would you look for a good sportsman, good socially and confident?

You can teach most things, if you have the right raw ingredients. When I started you couldn't join the trading floor if you had a degree and we've moved to a situation where you can't get into a bank without a degree in almost any role!

Why would it preclude you in those days if you had a degree?

Because it was a zoo. A lot more traders were required after the deregulation by Margaret Thatcher. When the Americans came, we stopped having beers for lunch, we stopped going to lunch, started having lunch at our desks, we brought in lots of graduates and then the industry moved to only taking Mathematicians. You might argue that's one of the things that went wrong with financial markets. When I joined we had a very diverse community.

For a long time in my career I suffered from inferiority, not from race or colour or sex but of educational standard. Because I ended up sitting next to Oxford and Cambridge graduates that thought they knew it all but there was a balance of background across the firm which seemed to work well.

How were all of the traders diverse if they were all sporty confident types?

I don't like the word diverse because generally today diverse means ethnicity or sex. But yes, it was a lot of white males that played rugby and football and if you were a woman trying to make it in that environment it would have been difficult. I agree, maybe diverse in that sense wasn't the right word, what I meant was diverse in background. There were people like me from grammar schools sitting on the trading floor next to Oxford graduates.

With your industry today, to paraphrase, only employing graduates and mathematicians, do you think they have the right mix?

No, I don't think they have. We continued down the mathematical genius route and people are promoted because they need to be intellectually satisfied, but like every other industry, people reach a level of incompetence. You may be a good trader and get promoted to become a manager, but you're not necessarily a good manager. Those skills are not intellectual but about character, decisiveness, energy, courage even.

Did you become a good manager of people?

I believe so.

What else do you think makes a good manager?

Empathy and empowerment. In a team working out people's strengths and weaknesses is crucial and playing to those strengths. I think my biggest skill is being approachable, then letting people have credit for their own work and profiling people.

If you think back over your career, what's the single best piece of advice that anyone gave you?

I don't listen enough and will dominate the conversation and one of my bosses taught me to prioritise the two or three asks of him that I had. Another person said I was extremely verbose but when a person is really on top of their topic they tend to be very precise. Take time to work out what you want to say. I have tried to become more precise.

What colleagues have you most admired?

I don't think I can pick one. Different eras present different answers to that question. When I started, the chief dealer that put me onto the trading floor, I had a lot of admiration for his ability. I had no formal training and information used to come from him really easily. The answer to your question in the macro is, people I've learned from have been the people I've most respected and the ones I wanted to work for. Out of the people I have worked for, and there are a lot, there are only two or three in that category. I'm extremely straightforward and it has been to my detriment as well as often a strength. Going through the list of attributes most of the people like that even if you're firing them. Honesty is a powerful tool, people may not like it but they tend to respect it.

One of my bosses was a very hard task master, very difficult to get anywhere with but there was a graduation. Once I had earned his trust and demonstrated that I could take on the task that I'd been given, all of a sudden there was a switch and we began to get on like a house on fire. I worked for him for four years. The first two were terrible and the last two were fantastic. He could be very aggressive and overly demanding but once I demonstrated my worth, we got on famously.

When I first started my bosses, the trader types, were very forgiving. I once lost a lot of money and was worried that I would be sacked. I now understand what I thought was a lot of money they didn't because they had already lost a lot more than that, so your perception changes as you progress. They all had different styles, I worked out the strengths and weakness of the people senior to me and tried to add some of the skills and behaviours which I admired, I never changed to my detriment, although I think it's fair to say that I would have had more senior roles if I were willing to be more orthodox or less outspoken, more accommodating.

How do you feel about that now that you are retired?

I lived a very successful forty years, unusual to survive that long. All the time I would say to people, "when I look at myself in the mirror, I have to be happy with what I see". If I've compromised myself or my opinion in what I've said or how I've acted, then I can't look myself in the mirror.

What do you wish you'd understood at the start of your career that you understand now?

For a long time, I had an inferiority complex in terms of academic background but I came to realise you can't survive forty years without being good at what you do, so my relative lack of education was much more of an issue in my own mind. I've always used the professional football analogy. There's always going to be someone coming to take your spot and I now realise to have held my own in amongst people that went to Cambridge and Harvard, I can't be as stupid as I look. I could have gone off and done an MBA, but I didn't have the interest in doing that,

It's interesting, most of the successful people I have interviewed have given a similar answer. I think there's truth in that 'grit in the oyster' analogy. Perhaps it's the anxiety, the feeling of needing to prove to yourself, which drives very successful people.

I think there's truth in that. One of my bosses from the French Bank I worked for said, "You want me to tell you your problem? You are an overachiever and what that means is that unless you are overachieving at everything you do you're not happy and since you can't overachieve all the time, you are not going to be happy quite a lot. You know how I know this? Because I am an overachiever." And I could see what he was saying. I think there is a lot of truth in that.

The thing driving me and others, even if they are well educated, is the desire to prove themselves.

In your early career you had a very hard driving style. Did you find a way to manage yourself physically and mentally to keep yourself from burning out?

I used to play for the bank's football team until my eldest son was born and I didn't have time to go trekking across London to get to the grounds but I have manged to remain relatively fit, innately. I think having had kids at twenty-four, my outlet was family and it very quickly brings you back down to earth regardless if you had a good or a bad day. I obviously had more good than bad, if not I wouldn't have survived. But I remember bad days and getting home, the kids don't care, they want you to read them a story and give them a bath. So it helps you realise that there is more to life than your narrow business fixation.

Did you speak to your wife much about work life?

No, it's interesting. I was glad my wife stayed home for twenty-five years to bring our kids up, but it's unusual today. We managed to stay married, it's our thirty-ninth wedding anniversary in October, that's also not so normal, a lot of people don't manage that. Unspoken, she was not interested in Finance or Banking, she only ever heard about it when I had friends over that were in the business but then she would get bored and want to talk about something else.

There was quite a significant detachment between us in terms of work and non-work. Although I was responsible for one-hundred-

and-twenty people in twelve countries when I was at my peak, I would normally be home at the weekend. I might have flown in from Singapore to be there. I can remember flying back in from Singapore, landing at 5:30am and being on the football pitch at 9:30am taking training for the under-tens. Now if I was to fly back from Singapore it would take me a couple weeks to work out the time zone I'm in. When you're a bit younger you can get away with it.

Did you become good at switching off?

No, never.

When you went on holiday, were you still thinking about work?

Always. Before mobile phones became prevalent I would look at the markets on my pocket watch all the time. It only bothered me occasionally, when things weren't going well. But not knowing where the markets were, the positions and things like that; I found that stressful. As long as I knew, even if it was negative, I could manage better.

I'm the type of chap that would be emailing all day, all night because it's a twenty-four-hour business, it never stops. You wake up in the morning and you speak to Asia, then you go into London, do your day and New York starts ringing you up at eleven. When you go to bed someone is ringing you at two in the morning.

I didn't always cope, I had periods. When my brother came to see me some years ago, he said, "I'm taking you to the doctors and getting you signed off for stress". I told him I knew it was a stressful time, but I thought I was on top of it and he told me, "we don't think so and we're getting you signed off". Actually he was right, I had a break and a rest and came back refreshed.

Could you always sleep okay?

Yes, even now.

If I was to ask some people who had worked with you to describe you, what do you think they would say?

Talks too much but cares, understands, driven and helpful.

What would you say you are most proud of looking back over your career?

The people I've helped.

You described yourself as very driven, how are you finding things now that you are retired?

Psychologically I knew I couldn't do it forever. I told you when I started, thirty-five was it. I don't think my career will be repeated, because I started on the trading floor at twenty-one and I finished when I was fifty-eight, I was on the trading floor the whole time.

How do you think tomorrow's successful organisations might be different from today's?

A lot of my views are based on my experience, when I joined the French Bank it made a significant impact on me. In an Anglo Saxon organisation the top down management kind of works and the management criteria largely is, if you do a good job I'll promote you, if you do a really good job I'll promote you and I'll pay you a lot and if you do a bad job I will fire you. Upward and downward motivation is very clear, but in a French bank the marginal tax rate for an individual is 75%. You couldn't really motivate anybody with money because they get precious little of it. You couldn't fire anyone because it's heavily unionised.

So in that situation, prestige and status took on a completely different complexion. The work of tomorrow will be more like that, I think. How do we motivate people other than with money? I think it will be harder to find the driven people, because people aren't necessarily going to strive to own their own home. They come out of university, heavily indebted, they take out a mortgage and are then supposed to save for a pension, they're never going to get anywhere. Compared to me, I came out of school and got a job, bought my house, did my holidays, paid for my kids' education and have a few quid to show for it. Actually, it's not repeatable. We need to find a different way to motivate and careers will take on a different pattern.

What motivated your French colleagues back then?

I have never had a thirst for knowledge for the sake of knowledge, I describe myself as a 'need-to-know' person. If I need to know something, I shall find out. But other people are hungry for knowledge because they find it interesting, it's what drives them. You need to work out what it is that drives people.

What I'm seeing in my own children makes me think about the businesses of the future. I read a book by Bill Gates called the 'The Road Ahead'. He argued that the things people will value in the future are property and a nice location because people wouldn't need to be in their offices, as demonstrated by Covid-19. He gave foreign exchange as the first example of frictionless trade, matching buyers and sellers electronically, as we now see with eBay and everything else, so markets were becoming more perfect. Perhaps in that context the 'human factor' becomes less important. But I think it will always be important. If AI can take care of the mechanics of business, people will step into the 'added-value' areas and there will always be a need for strategy, decision-making and team building.

I believe that 80% of equity trades today are driven by artificial intelligence. I've got the same view of artificial intelligence that I had of two standard deviations in the analysts' models, they don't work! The people who wrote the option formula, Fischer and Black, set up a fund to trade and it went bust. People don't apply psychological or human thinking and it's increasingly the case now. A very senior person at the bank called John I remember had a stutter. Why? Because his brain was three seconds ahead of his mouth, so intelligent. The divide between supreme intelligence and stupidity isn't very wide I've noticed. And that is why the diversity question has some validity – we need diversity of thought, checks and balances, particularly in banking.

To me, football is a wonderful analogy. If you put all of your best players on the team, will they be the best team? I don't think they will, because they are missing what we need you to have which is a blend of talent and character. Have we worked out the strengths and weaknesses in our team? It's easy to blow teams up, just work out where the weaknesses are and pick on them. It will take me no time at all to blow up your team. To make a team successful it's much more difficult, it's the reverse. We have to work out what makes people tick, what they are good at. Give them more of what they are good at and less of what they are not good at and you'll be surprised at how effective they can be!

How are you finding retirement?

Surprisingly good, I figure I'm resting. I'm puffed out after forty years. I want to rest, I'm not hankering after the next success and it all goes back to the questions you first asked me, what aspirations did I have when I started? It was easy, earning enough to pay my mortgage, then earning enough to pay a bigger mortgage, have a colour telly, go on holiday, educate the kids, running fast around the hamster wheel. Once I got to a happy place, where my kids were educated and standing on their own two feet and I paid the mortgage, I was working because I liked it. That was a very odd feeling.

You feel like you're resting now, you deserve a rest?

Yes, but I know people were worrying about me packing up, not the least my wife! Someone said to me you're going to be a different kind of busy because you won't be able to not be busy, you can't do that. I like that and I think that's right. I'm going to be busy but I don't know how yet, I don't expect I'll be sitting in the rocking chair just rocking away though!

If you were to sit in a room full of people starting out in their careers today, what advice would you give them?

Perhaps surprisingly given my own experience I'd say first go and collect your platform ticket.

What do you mean?

You must get your GCSEs, A-Levels, degree, you might need your CFA. If you don't collect your platform tickets opportunities close down on you. Will the sky cave in? No, people will find a way but if you can keep your opportunities open, why wouldn't you?

It's interesting, you asked me earlier what I judge success by. It's the people I've helped. And who do I have a lot of respect for? The people who helped me.

You are a good observer of other people. How do you perceive yourself?

When I look in the mirror, what do I see? I've never knowingly screwed anybody over, I'm in competition with people because I'm in a competitive environment. There will be people that I can introduce you to that think I did, but in my mind, I made very reasonable judgements of who I had to fire, who I had to promote. I tried to be transparent and explain to people. I said to my team, be careful what questions you ask me because I'm likely to answer them. My reputation is that I am going to answer you and it's going to be straight. I get accused of being hard, but I want to be fair. I want people to succeed. My starting point is how do we find those strengths in individuals and play to them, if they haven't got a strength then we need to find them a new role.

What do you think drove the success you managed to achieve in your career?

Actually the truth is that I spent all my career worrying about losing my job. I rationalised that the reason I was well paid in my youth was because I wasn't going to have a job when I was thirty-five. If you're a football player and you're earning a decent amount, you're going to finish when you're forty. You and I know that you're going to need an awful lot of money to see you through your old age. I initially thought I was well paid because I had a life expectancy, but I managed to keep on the merry-go-round. The syllabus is constantly changing and you have to remain on top of it, it's hard to remain up-to-speed, there is a new thing that's come along and somebody might be better at it than you are. Remaining relevant has not been easy.

I wasn't driven because I wanted to succeed or to be the next great thing, I simply didn't want to lose my job, that drove me all the time. Until it didn't happen anymore. I got to a happy place five to six years ago. You asked me what I wish I knew; realising I was good enough would have been helpful. Having faith in my own ability, I think it would have been nice if I got that sooner in life.

Actually I think the idea behind success is a book of its own. From my point of view staying married and having a strong family unit has been a big success in itself. I've worked with hundreds of people in the course of a long career but there are only a handful of people that I am close to; I think that's a lesson in life, everybody wants to be liked by people but perhaps the people who count are relatively small in number, so value them. My advice would be, be successful on your own terms and look after the people that are important to you.

GRAHAM WHITEHAIR

“

The people I've seen that are the most successful are the ones who seem to have time. It's a bit like football. They've found a way of working where they don't seem hurried and rushed, they focus on their priorities and they bring people together around their ideas. Whereas the less successful try to constrain things or narrow them. The best leaders broaden things, give people space and act with a quiet confidence and poise.

CARL JOHNSON

INTERVIEWED 17TH JANUARY 2020

Carl is Director of Organisational Development and Learning at the support services giant Interserve (now Mitie). The firm had approximately 50,000 employees working across a broad range of industries and government departments. Carl and I first met in 1999 when our consultancy began working with the team at Bluewater, the then revolutionary new Retail and Leisure Centre in Kent, UK. Carl was on the team.

Tell me about the early part of your career, Carl.

Well, I wasn't especially great at school so going to university wasn't really on my radar, at school age. I was under the false impression that I would be a professional sports person and I convinced myself that was going to be the case.

A footballer?

Yes, this was before there was big money in it, when most footballers finished their career and then bought a pub.

Or went into insurance.

Yes, and I think Neil Webb is a Postman now. Anyway, as any young kid would, I thought that's going to be me (a footballer, not a postman!), it's just a matter of time. In the meantime, I'll go to school. I did okay but not great and University wasn't the obvious next step for me.

So, you had some interest from football clubs?

I was playing county standard when I lived in Germany as a schoolboy, I wasn't a bad player, but at the time you needed to get on a Youth Training Scheme contract to play football after leaving school, that was the way to get in at a professional club. If you didn't have a YTS in those days, you wouldn't play football, it was that simple and I didn't get one. I tried to figure out what else I could do. With little else to consider I managed to get a job at the local Charlie Brown's Auto Centres, which is a bit like KwikFit but in Yorkshire. I had no idea what to expect, I just turned up to my role as a Trainee Manager, which in a sense it was, but also a bit of a dog's body, but they called it a Trainee Manager and I really enjoyed it. There was never a dull moment and all the lads that worked there were fantastic.

Just out of interest, I know your family is very close and your parents are important figures in your life. Were they happy for you to do that or were they trying to persuade you to go to university?

At school I was deemed to be reasonably bright, I passed my eleven plus which meant I had a choice to go to grammar school, but the grammar school in Doncaster town centre didn't play football, only rugby.

I remember we went to the interview for this school and when they said they didn't play football, I said to my dad, this is not for me,

I'd rather go to the comprehensive school near where we live, and there was no argument, no discussion. He said fine, I know you love playing football and they don't do it there. There was no 'we think this is good for your education', there was no pushing me down that line and they've never said anything about it even to this day. I have to say the local Comprehensive was a great school with very strong educational outcomes, I didn't know that at the time, but I'm sure they did.

Your dad had been in the forces I believe?

Yes, he joined the Royal Air force as a "boy entrant" when he was fifteen and a half, my mother also joined the air force when she was a little bit older, seventeen or eighteen, after school. They met in the air force, got married and had my sister and me. We travelled around the world as forces kids; one of the benefits of that is it makes you quite happy to adapt and quite nomadic at heart I think. You grow up believing it's normal to move every 3 years, but when we spoke to people in Doncaster when we settled, they found it all a bit odd as many of them had known their friends from nursery age.

Just a thought, it's unusual that you've worked in this company for a long time, over twenty years. Do you think it's in any way a reaction to that period of constant change in your life?

I don't know. I think that's a good point. Certainly the company has altered a great deal in that period, we've grown and changed so much. The shape and the size of the business is very different to when I first joined. It hasn't really felt like the same company throughout the 22 years, it's been quite an evolution to be honest.

Tell me about that first job.

I was at the auto shop as a Trainee Manager but that generally meant I had to do whatever needed doing. All the dirty jobs! That said, I really enjoyed it, it was great fun but it wasn't particularly stimulating mentally. Then someone came in one day and as I was interacting with them they said they wanted to offer me a sales job and that I would make a lot more money.

The first time you met them?

Yes, they were just there to get their car sorted out. I do remember that they had a very nice car and that probably influenced me at that age! And I was always stony broke.

They were impressed with your conversation?

I suppose so, I didn't think much of it at the time but afterwards I went and had a chat with them, and I ended up becoming an Account Manager selling personal accident insurance. It was a bit weird to go from car repairs to that, quite an unusual transition, and I was still very young. Until very recently I was still in touch with my manager from that job, all these years later.

You were obviously a good salesperson.

Not too bad, actually they sold a lot to sports people, so it helped to have an interest in sports. I then went from doing that to becoming an

Account Manager at a Capital Equipment company selling commercial leases for things such as vending machines, mail sorting equipment. I was on the road selling those products for close to five years.

A few of my friends went off to university during that time and when I visited them thought I should really have done that too. While still working I went back to college at night and did a couple of A-Levels so I then had the choice of going to university. I thought 'I'm going to give this a go' and at the same time I'd started playing semi-professional football on Saturdays. I had gone back to playing football a little bit because I'd stopped playing seriously after I didn't get on a YTS contract at a professional club, I was so disappointed I just didn't play much for a few years. I got to a point when I was about twenty-four, I had my two A-Levels, I applied to do a Business Management course at Derby University and was accepted.

Full time?

Yes, but I was also playing plenty of football. The university was in a great location, an equal distance between my folks and my maternal grandparents, I'm very close with that side of my family. It was perfect! I left the world of commerce behind and went off to university to see what it was all about. Ultimately, I realised I didn't just want to work on the road selling capital equipment for ever.

Is that why you chose to study Business Management at university?

Yes, it's a course with a broad base. I thought the wider curriculum course would whet my appetite and introduce me to different specialisms. When I first got there, I thought law would be my main focus as I could feel the social injustice building up inside of me quite often, as it does with student types! I thought the legal route would be a good way of exploring that, but it wasn't until I got into it that I felt it wasn't for me and I got much more enjoyment from Marketing and the people side of business management.

Was that because there was a particularly charismatic lecturer or because that was what you found really interesting?

It was what interested me the most. I was very lucky, I had great people around the university to learn from. Those topics were the things that I was interested in, much more relatable to me. I began learning about why people behave in different ways. If you think about it, I came from a sales and marketing background, my whole four or five years at work before that was an experience in how and why people behave the way they do and how you can influence them.

Was there anyone who influenced you particularly at the time?

Steve Duffy. He was the Managing Director of the company I worked for, a proud Scot, who lived up in Leeds, and he was terrific. He gave me books by Napoleon Hill. Back in the day he gave me tape cassettes that you put in your car by these people who were sales trainers. Loads of motivational stuff about behaviour and I found it to be incredibly powerful.

W. Clement Stone - you may have heard of him? These guys were talking about what drives people's behaviour and how positivity is important, the PMA [Positive Mental Attitude] effect and such. I was always really interested why people with the same level of intelligence and the same opportunities in life - why some are more successful and some less so? What's going on? That's what drove me to take an interest in organisational and individual behaviour. I found that to be an endless trove of interest for me. While I was at university I did my football coaching badges too, I've always felt like I've been a bit of a coach at heart really, and it's a large part of what I do today in reality.

Were you older than most people at university since you'd joined later? Do you think that affected your experience there at all?

Absolutely. I was club captain of the University football club and so was generally relied on to get things done, and I got ribbed for being few years older of course. I think I was expected to organise everyone. Even to this day, twenty odd years on, we have a football club reunion each year, and although the lads all have kids and a bit of grey hair and I'm still in the middle of organising it all! They still called me "gaffer" on our little group page, which is quite funny. We've all gone on to do different things now of course, and you get on with life, but you're still seen as ancient, even though I'm only four or five years older, it's too good an opportunity for them to take the micky!! Fair enough I think. I had a house in Doncaster at the time I was at university as well, so I was a landlord as well as a student, which meant I probably had a little bit more cash than your average student did at the time, and I was a bit clearer about what I wanted to do after university than perhaps most of the other students I knew.

Were you still hoping you might become a footballer even after university?

No, that was definitely a long-departed dream... and I also knew by this point why I hadn't become a footballer, because I had played with some really great football players. When I played semi-professionally, we had some people drop out of the pro leagues to play with us and the difference was just mind-blowing - the strength, the speed, the touch, the vision... it was very clear to me why they had made it to the professional level and I hadn't. But that's life!

Did you begin to think about applying for jobs as university drew to a close?

Yes, but the thing is that I had worked for three summers in a row in the USA coaching football for Major League Soccer (a bit like the Premier League here) in the University holiday periods. They would fly us out there - we all had our FA football coaching badges, and we coached young footballers, in a different community every week. We would turn up in a town on a weekend, set up everything, teach the kids all week and then go on to the next community.

What was wonderful was that each week was so different. Sometimes it was good, sometimes not so good, but it was always different. We were paid like professional coaches. The local media would turn up sometimes - we'd be in a little town in upstate New York for example, we'd be the only English people they ever saw, every year, and they'd look forward to it. The bars in these small towns would often have photos up of the coaches from previous years! It was great.

We were treated like mini celebrities! In my last year there when I was finishing University, I applied for a Marketing job with them, went for the interview, was offered the job. The condition was that you had to change your visa and then come back again. It was about October or November. When I came back to the UK that December, a friend of my dad's, John King, was at Bluewater and he knew my dad from many years previously. He also knew me a bit, he'd met me a few times, and he'd obviously been talking to my father who'd said I was back in the UK. He said, "Do you think you could come and give us a hand in delivering some training programmes? You must be an expert coach after coaching hundreds of American youngsters!" He wanted me to work for a few months, so I thought that would be perfect! I went down to the site and became a "hosting excellence trainer", training the operational service teams in readiness for the opening of Bluewater, at the time, the largest shopping centre in Europe.

This was not long before I met you?

Yes, 1998. And I was just going to do the trainer job for December, January and February, get my visa sorted and go back to the States. But when I got to Bluewater, I really enjoyed it. I met Paul May, Heather Ward-Russell, terrific people who I am still close to today. We had a really tight team, it was really long hours and hard work but great fun. Obviously, Bluewater is a fantastic project to be associated with, a great, globally recognised, brand.

How long had it been open then?

It hadn't opened yet. It was opening in March 1999 so we were there for the mobilisation and pre-opening phase, which made it all the more interesting.

At the time, people were coming from all around the world to see it because it was so different. It was beyond shopping, it was more about the whole customer experience.

You would call visitors guests rather than customers as I remember.

Yes, everyone who visited would be called a guest and we were there to 'host' them, much as you would a guest to your home. There was a very strong ethos about it.

Who had developed that philosophy?

It was this larger-than-life chap called Eric Kuhne, the architect who designed the centre. His vision was to create a unique retail environment. It was more than just the building, it was also the experience and how it felt to be there. The team working there were part and parcel of developing and delivering that unique experience. I didn't realise it at the time of course, but we were being handed a blueprint and a vision for what a retail centre could be like, and a model that people around the world were waiting to see.

Tell me about what made Bluewater different at the time.

If you look at the design of the centre it was completely different to anything else in Europe, even the retailers were asked to be different in their store design. As you can probably imagine, most retail centres say we want JD Sports, Next or John Lewis, all the big names, and they would approach the retailers and say here's the retail unit, it's X foot by X foot with this much frontage, you will pay us X amount in rental, please put your standard store fit-out in. For most retailers, that's how they operate – they just turn up with their standard fit-out and drop it in. But Bluewater didn't ask for that in this new set-up. They went to the retailers and said we want you to do something different from what you would normally do, we want you to innovate your retail space, make it new and exciting – more engaging.

I remember reading that Eric Kuhne had never designed a shopping centre before?

No, I don't think he had and we'd never run a shopping centre operation before. The service delivery team I was part of came from critical process management in the car manufacturing industry. I think the whole point of that place was to bring people in who'd not been in the industry to increase the chance of there being an innovative, fresh approach.

One of the other ways the Bluewater owners thought it could be different was to train all the people working there to be hosts, and treat the visitors as 'guests' would be treated in a five-star hotel. Whatever role a person had in our team, first and foremost they were a host. It made them feel special themselves, created a sense of pride and the guests noticed the difference.

What was your role specifically once you'd decided to stay and not go back to the US?

At that time, prior to opening it was 'Special Projects', because they couldn't really find me a specific job role. I wasn't meant to be there, so I wasn't on the organisation chart. The role required me to keep all of the training going, do some coaching of the hosting team and do whatever else was needed in a very dynamic 24-hour 7-day a week operation. Soon I was given the external areas to look after, as there was 51 acres of parkland to manage and all of the roadways and car parking, and then over time the internal operations came to me too, so basically everything apart from the engineering team. For me, one of the biggest attractions of the role was working with Adrian Wright, the Bluewater CEO. He was a very inspirational figure, and he was so willing to offer guidance and support, we all learnt a great deal from him. It was really hard work, a seven-day-a-week operation, and I was working very long hours, quite often six days a week, but it was incredibly entertaining. You felt like you were doing something important and within a very short period of time I was entrusted to join the Duty Manager rota. So, on a Saturday and Sunday, I would have full responsibility for Bluewater operations. I felt very grateful to be trusted to perform that role.

How many staff were you responsible for?

There would be about circa 300 of our directly employed colleagues and I was also responsible for operational contact with the retailers and for security protocols in partnership with the police and other emergency services. At the weekends and holidays the police would come into our control room because all the road networks around Bluewater were important. If we caused the queuing traffic to tail back onto the motorway an incident could be potentially fatal. As such, they would always want to know what we were doing to keep the traffic flowing, to get people into the site and get them parked up.

After that time at Bluewater you switched to a group role in MacLellan (the service delivery partner to the centre) itself and took on a broader role. Tell me about MacLellan.

They were a Midlands-based business which grew up working for the car manufacturers in the north of England maintaining the car spraying booths. When you spray paint cars, they have to be incredibly clean, because if there are any flaws in the paintwork it would need to go right back through the whole process again, which was a very expensive thing to do.

MacLellan became very good at cleaning paint booths and making sure that cars were immaculate when they came out, ensuring that the paint work was always perfect. They worked with Aston Martin, Toyota, Bentley, Mercedes McLaren and many more of the high-quality car manufacturers. Essentially MacLellan formed part of the client companies' critical process management community on site. They had to understood lean thinking, the whole six sigma approach and how to constantly iterate and improve service delivery standards. They branched out from the spray booth capability to look at facilities management as a whole and then moved into multiple sectors beyond automotive.

Later they started to look at Total Facilities Management (TFM). They were looking at TFM before TFM became a popular concept, they were really at the forefront of it at the time.

What is TFM?

For a long time the Facilities Management (FM) market worked in silos. As a client you'd buy your security from one company, your engineering from another, your catering from a third company and your cleaning from yet another supplier. You were managing a complex number of suppliers and that could be an expensive and time-consuming way of doing it. We began to offer them the whole package - a one stop service delivery contract. One company, one service agreement, one invoice. The customer didn't need to worry about all the people issues, we would cover all of that and they could focus on their core business. The idea was that if you were running a business where customer engagement was critical, culture was key. You have a far better chance of everybody being unified in their approach if they all work for the same company than you would if you had eight different organisations working to their own agenda. A unified culture would deliver a better customer experience. That was essentially the idea. We give clients one invoice, we can do all of it and we can do it at a lower price too, because there are economies of scale for us. And the client could reduce their own overhead because the team they had managing all those suppliers now just needed to manage one! That's what we did at Bluewater.

The MacLellan Managing Director John Ellis liked what we were able to achieve at Bluewater. He asked me if we could build similar service cultures elsewhere. He said, 'do you think it's possible that we could do it for our whole organisation?' At that time we had about 3000 people working at MacLellan which meant a tenfold increase in scope, headcount wise, if I took on the challenge. I would be working for the MacLellan HR Director to create a business culture similar to the one at Bluewater, creating a culture of service excellence. Could we do it for MacLellan? That was the ask, and I said yes, I think so.

I know that a great culture was created at MacLellan, you diversified aggressively and grew exponentially. How many people were there when the business was acquired by Interserve?

About 13,000, we grew year on year and acquired several businesses over that period.

Most acquisitions don't work in terms of adding value and they don't work because of the culture factor, not because the numbers don't add up. Tell me a little about the experience of being acquired and what you learned from it.

Well, I've been in that situation where we were bought. I've also been the person who turns up representing the acquirer because Interserve were and still are very acquisitive. You turn up in a room with a group of people from the organisation that's just been sold by their holding company, they're all sitting there with their arms folded. Some of them not so pleased to see you, some are very proud of their own brand and your business has just acquired them. And so now I've been on the other side of the equation where we've been acquired, and someone comes in the room and says "Welcome to Interserve".

From a practical point of view, I believe that you buy a company you should try to create the space for people in the acquired businesses to explain how they feel about what's happened, but also genuinely let them share what they have done in their organisation to share best practice, because quite often the thought is 'we've bought you and therefore we're going to tell you what to do'. That can be an unhelpful approach.

And it goes hand in hand with a temptation to standardise processes, doesn't it?

Quite often the driver of an acquisition is to buy yourself a bigger share of the current market and the expectation is that you will strip away cost as well. You keep the market and remove costs, sounds perfect! One of the common downward cost drivers is standardising and simplifying processes.

My observation is, in the course of that change customers can lose out.

Yes, very much so. That is often the case.

Because they're caught in-between the coming together of the two organisations.

Absolutely, they're watching from a distance. And certainly, in our sector, your customers will know your new colleagues better than they know you. They may have been working with them for many years, so they will want to see a swift, seamless integration, keeping all the people they have come to trust over the years fully engaged, and have all the benefits of the acquiring business quickly folded into the service delivery model! That is a very tricky path to navigate during integration.

What would be your advice to organisations who want to integrate acquisitions most effectively?

The main thing I think that I've seen work well is to move quickly. The more you delay getting things done, even with the best intentions, the more challenging it becomes. Alongside this, making decisions that are backed by data as much as possible, it makes building the case for transformation stronger and more readily accepted.

Does that include confronting issues?

Yes, you have to face things as quickly as you can but have a clear plan before you start, have a really ambitious deadline for getting it done and take people with you in terms of pace. That doesn't mean you don't consult, and you don't spend time with people, that's part of the plan. People need to see that you're going to go from A to B swiftly, that you're not going to drag it out. Move with pace and confront things in a very open way.

The second thing is what I was saying earlier, you have to find a way of genuinely taking the best of both organisations. You need to create the environment where you can have the "best of breed" conversation and not expect that to happen automatically. It won't. Human behaviour is 'I'm going to defend what I've authored' and there are many creative ways of doing that I've discovered!

And the third thing?

I remember it quite vividly, it's more psychological really. Realise that it will be difficult. Set the expectation that everyone will have to work together to get through the integration and it is going to be tough, it will not be plain sailing regardless of how good the plan is.

Is there a financial side to that? Often acquisitions are made to keep the city or investors happy and management will be hungry to deliver the cost savings. Some of the things we've discussed will take time, is that an issue? Getting senior management to understand that things won't be delivered as quickly as they'd always like?

I'll give an example. When companies do "due diligence" in advance of an acquisition, they have an area where data is kept. A data room. The data is looked at, but in a separate way from how the day-to-day business operates and the intricacies of how it really works. Quite often it's very senior people or consultants that are trying to evaluate the target business and looking at that data in something of a vacuum. Usually the financials look good and they make certain assumptions. They're already evaluating it and trying to look at the reality of mobilising the integration but the analysis is based only on flat, cold data. When you actually get into the business you find that the data story is not quite what had been expected. The data was probably incomplete and then lining up the real data streams can be challenging. You begin to figure out where their servers are or where the data is held, security profiles or licensing agreements need to be accessed and sorted. Then you start to get into the complexity that the accountant or the M&A expert is not going to get into. Everybody has to sign an NDA when these happen, all the people on the inside get to see the data but they don't get to talk to the people running the business at the front line. As soon as you've bought a business and it's live, you then go and talk to the people running the systems and processes, that's when you get into the reality! This is where you bump into the things that are going to be more difficult than you thought, that is why you should manage expectations upwards accepting that the plan is imperfect by definition. Being clear about what it's going to take to do it and make sure those who looked at the numbers pre-acquisition realise that it might not be the same as they initially thought. Integration costs are likely to increase from the baseline assumption and extracting the projected cost savings may take longer too.

You're a big believer in the value of trust in organisations. How does that play in this scenario?

Well, when you buy an organisation there can't be that level of trust initially, the relationships are all new. Quite often when you've been acquired, you probably have a low level of expectation in terms of how that's going to work out for you. Immediately trying to build some level of shared trust is part of the challenge actually. In organisations generally, the level of trust becomes apparent very quickly in terms of how people are with each other at the human level. When you turn up to the building, the way people engage with you will give you an indication of how well trusted they feel. If they are open and expressive and happy to engage then the chances are they feel safe, they feel like somebody's got their back and they will be supported.

You see that a lot and sometimes the opposite even within teams, the way people show up day to day is a fairly strong indicator of how far they feel trusted by the business and how they give out their trust as well. You can't just expect it to happen by chance. Humans are very aware of their environment and our life experiences come into the environment. We all 'read' people, when we go to meetings and everybody is tense, you might not say it out loud, but you might think 'what's going on here?'. You can cut the atmosphere with a knife and you feel it. Organisations have a sense of this and that's what Culture and Climate is all about in HR terms and I think trust is a massive part of creating a healthy culture.

You're now a leader in your organisation and therefore your own actions are key to creating the right culture. Remind me of your role and responsibilities specifically?

Director of Organisational Development and Learning. My role is in three parts. The first part is delivering the training and learning interventions the organisation needs. The second part is equipping the business for the future - what the talent agenda will look like, what the organisational development actions are to help us deliver our strategy and the third part is the recruitment of our new talent. Part of my remit is the hiring of all the salaried roles into the business, we hire about 2,600 people a year right across the UK, so it's a busy team.

We're talking about your role in leading in a complex organisation. You need of course to take people with you in different situations. What do you think makes an effective business leader?

The people I've seen that are the most successful are the ones who seem to have time. It's a bit like football. They've found a way of working where they don't seem hurried and rushed, they focus on their priorities and they bring people together around their ideas. I'm sure you know people like this and I've worked with people in the business who have that special quality. They are the people who always find time for other people, always find time to deal with their priorities and always seem as though they are not being rushed by externalities. That engenders confidence in other people. Back to the trust - they give it out in a way that less successful people that I have worked with don't seem able to. It's an abundance mentality I think, where they believe there's something for everyone. 'I can give you all the space you need to get things done because there is plenty of space to go round'. Whereas the less successful people I have seen have always tried to constrain things or 'narrow' them. The best leaders tend to open things out, give people space and inspire confidence in others.

Giving instead of taking oxygen?

Yes, people want to work for people like that because they are given the space to work and the trust and confidence given suggests that the leader believes in them. That ability to instil belief in others is a defining factor in successful leaders in my experience.

What do you think people would say about you as a leader if I were to ask them?

I certainly try and emulate the things I admire in others. I try to give people my trust and tell them I believe in them and give them the space to do great work. I would hope they would say I've tried to create as much opportunity for them as they can handle and trusted them to get on with it. Whenever things have not worked out, I've been able to help them move past that and find a way to succeed. The only evidence to say that worked is, there are a lot of people who have worked in my teams who have gone on to do pretty well. They've stayed with us and moved up in their roles and done well for themselves. Paul May, my old boss at Bluewater, always used to say he wanted to one day work for someone who had worked for him, that's an admirable goal I think.

You mentioned Paul as a person you admire and have learned from. Are there others?

If you were to take out hierarchy, some of the people I've worked with, some people who have been specialists I really admire. Like Health and Safety people with a great passion for their work and capability in their specific role, their dedication to it is phenomenal. They're not especially senior or necessarily making massive decisions around the business but their ability to do their job and the commitment to making it work well is incredibly impressive to me. Quite often we look at the super high achievers and the celebrity CEOs. Whereas I prefer the ordinary team members, the people who turn up every day and do a brilliant job, support their team and are proud to do it.

You mean that?

Yes, for example we have a cleaning team leader in our London office who is fantastic, and if I'm working late, we'll have a quick catch up on life and work. She has a family in the Caribbean and has never had a day off in twenty-five years. Overall, she brings enormous enthusiasm and humour to her work and does a great job. I think there's a huge amount of dedication shown and nowhere near enough credit given for the people that actually do the job that earns the money that pays all the wages.

There's something noble and admirable about people wanting to provide for their families and maybe their background or education wasn't as privileged as others or they might be first or second-generation migrants building a life in a new country, whatever it might be. The personal effort and focus required to do that job brilliantly is not that much different to a CEO. It's a different skill set of course, they apply a different set of capabilities on a day-to-day basis, but we've got the data on this and their engagement levels can often be much higher than people getting paid ten times what they're earning. They often care more about the business than people who get paid much more. I believe strongly in respecting the application and effort given by all colleagues, regardless of where they sit in a hierarchy.

What's the best piece of advice you've been given so far in your career?

One of the best pieces of advice I've had in life has been from my dad and grandad and has been really useful to me. They say, "Don't worry about things you can't control." You can spend an awful lot of time and energy just worrying. They would say, can you do anything about it? If the answer is no then don't worry about it. If you can, then do something about it!

To compartmentalise things in this way in what is an increasingly cluttered world is useful. There is an unending amount of stimulus coming at us that could stop you from doing the things that are worthwhile. It's very easy to become over-active. I think one thing your organisation has always been very good at, Chris, is trying to simplify complex things, and why shouldn't that apply to people's lives? Try and focus on things you can affect and don't waste energy worrying about things you can't affect.

We have spoken recently about our research into the idea of psychological capital. One of the things at the centre of it is resilience. People who endure, whether they are in a humble role or CEO, must have that. Any other learning in that area?

The people that I think have the most resilience, the ones that I've tried to learn from, tend to be people who seem to apply a perspective to things that others struggle with. I see people get highly emotional in a work environment, very up and down and that is exhausting for them and quite likely exhausting for people around them. The people I'm talking about have much less fluctuation, they've found a way of keeping steady, they are more emotionally consistent, and the people around them pick up on that stability and it creates calm and focus.

Karl Bevan is another person who has been a huge influence on me, he has delivered our leadership training for many years now. He uses a really neat example when we do training on resilience. He describes it a bit like a 'spring', remember in the old days when you would measure your vegetables on a hanging spring scales? Essentially if you have a strong spring, it's going to stretch a little bit when stressed and if you have a weak spring it's going to stretch a lot. The metaphor is your spring is your own capacity for resilience, your ability to deal with the weight of life when it comes.

What is the key to keeping your spring strong?

That's up to the individual I think. For some people it's exercise, some people meditate and for some it's their family unit. My sense is to just try and make sure your "spring" stays strong because the load is definitely going to come, some days it is light and some days it is heavy, but it will definitely come. This could be in your personal life or at work; things will try and pull you down and stretch you.

It makes good sense to me, good advice. Do you use that in the company to teach people?

We use that exact model.

And do you train everyone in that or is it part of a performance review? How does it work?

We included it as part of our leadership and management training programme but I know many of the participants on that programme then shared the learning with their teams. Here's the thing, if you accept that the spring is a metaphor for your own wellbeing, you need to know yourself and use that knowledge to keep it STRONG. I don't know what you need but I know what I need. The common ways to keep it strong are a good whole food diet, good sleep habits and some regular exercise. The evidence for better mental health is closely linked to good overall health.

I suspect that most people don't think about managing their 'spring' without help?

People often think, 'I'm the finished product, my spring is my spring', whereas people who are resilient know that is not the case and they decide what they need to keep it strong. It might be intellectual stimulation, it might be a better diet, it might be time away, it doesn't matter. When the spring is strong, you're more prepared and you can handle issues, the dial doesn't move much. When you're not strong and you're struggling, you feel terrible, you're perhaps snapping at people. You beat yourself up and your self-confidence dips, and it's hard to recover from that. What we try to say to people is that there are a lot of benefits to being conscious of your own spring. Mental health is the biggest problem in the workplace today and a lot of it is because they aren't attending to their own personal needs for resilience. We're constantly putting that heavy load on people in life. I think it's a massive thing in organisations today and as you're probably aware the biggest killer in men under thirty-five in the UK is suicide. We all need to be much better at helping people manage their mental health and their resilience. Having a good level of resilience in the people working across your organisation is a key measure of organisational resilience overall. It can help the business stay strong, focused and effective when a shock comes like we've had with COVID-19.

Can you see your training helping people and them changing? Do you think the training works?

I think it's better for some than others, I think it's also a timing thing, some people are ready to listen, and others aren't. One of the reasons I love the work I do is that we are focused on trying to create an environment in which people can explore what they are capable of emotionally and physically in any situation.

I still see people who worked for us, people now outside of the organisation who remember the training that we did. There's one guy who started off as an engineer in a van and now he's a Regional Director. He's very generous and says he wouldn't have managed to achieve that if it wasn't for the training we provided for him. Actually, he did it, we didn't. But we try to create the environment where people can flourish. I think it's like the old adage about opportunity and preparation meeting each other. We're trying to give people the preparation they need so they are ready to take the opportunity when it comes their way.

I notice the impact particularly with women in the workplace. They often don't think they can do things, whereas men will give it a go, learn on the fly. My observation is that women very often need to be confident they can do the job before they even apply sometimes.

What do you wish you had understood at the beginning of your career that you understand now?

This is a personal thing, but I always thought everybody was going to be much smarter than me because I didn't have the classical education route into business, and it turns out they are just the same as people who didn't go to university or those that came up through the ranks. We tend to put very senior leaders on a pedestal and they are just the same as everyone else in a human sense, we just need to appreciate they make mistakes and worry like the rest of us.

You're smarter than you think?

Ha ha, no, not at all. I get by. I've done enough aptitude tests (as you would in my role) to know exactly where I sit on the bell curve and I've got enough intelligence to operate, but I've also had chance to see that people who score very highly on intelligence tests are not always successful. I just think people should believe in themselves a bit more and understand that the vast majority of people in the workplace are of a similar capability, but it's how they apply it that makes the difference.

Interestingly when we talked about leadership you emphasised the importance of calmness, and you don't need to be a genius intellectually to have that, do you? You probably just need to be sure of yourself.

Yes I agree, and clear about what your priorities are and what you need from your team. I think the thing that I know now is that it will be okay. I probably undersold myself a bit and I wasn't as confident in my own abilities in the early days.

It's often labelled as "imposter syndrome" and it's not a nice feeling. I've since realised we're all in it together, nobody else thinks they're all that smart either. I think they are, but they don't, so they're on the same journey.

No one has all the answers. That lack of confidence can lead to the stress. It's born probably from a certain level of insecurity or feeling like they should have all the answers.

I suspect it encourages a lot of defensive behaviours.

Yes, you see that a lot in organisations. If you're not sure of yourself, you put up a defence, you try to keep people further back from you.

I suspect if I asked the people who exude that confidence and calm that I admire as leaders whether they've come to a stage in their lives where they know they don't have to have all the answers and don't need to be the smartest person in the room. The answer would be that they've been on that same journey of self discovery and are emerging on the other side.

Can we change track a little and talk about strategy? What do you understand by strategy?

I have this drawing that I do [laughs]. This is a specialist area of yours, Chris, so I'll just speak about how I experience strategy as well as how I understand it. For me it's about how you take the resources you have and apply them in the most effective way to win in whatever environment you are in. With strategy, clarity is key but often execution is the hard part. You can get a board to agree with your strategy but how can you get the organisation to pull in that direction? That's much trickier. If everyone was brilliant at it we would get it right all the time, but we don't. One of the things that I've noticed is when it's done well the leadership in an organisation is consistent to the point to which it's almost dogmatic – "This is what we're doing and why", "This is what we're doing and why", again and again. For your strategic intent to become engrained in the culture there needs to be a constant drum beat in the organisation.

You've seen a lot of changes in the way business works over the last twenty years. Looking forward, how do you think successful organisations tomorrow will differ from those we work in today?

I hope their agendas will be broader. It worries me that the financial imperative is always so consuming and always will be. The ability to see how the business has been impacting its environment, paying tax properly and being held to account for the contribution to the communities that they're serving is still really poor in my view. I'm hoping this will improve in the future and you're seeing a bit of it already. Amazon for example are being looked at in terms of their tax contribution in the UK as a percentage of its UK earnings, and it is woeful. Is that going to affect their ability to do business here in the long term? It will only be effective when people stop using them as a result of their lack of overall social contribution. That is my hope for business in the future, they will realise that you have to present your credentials in terms of your impact beyond the balance sheet in order for you to remain competitive.

Apart from that I think the biggest change in the last ten years has been the language around disruptive technology which was a phrase that wasn't heard before. Organisations are very aware that their business might be disrupted by AI or something else from the technological spectrum. They are asking themselves – 'are we the sort of sector that could be blindsided by technology?' In the future I think the pace of disruption will accelerate, so organisations will need to be very responsive and agile. They will need a clear and consistent strategy, a strong culture built on trust and be adaptable to the opportunities and threats which technology, a pandemic or other shocks to the system can deliver.

Your sector is vulnerable, isn't it? In the simplest terms, you have an awful lot of labour doing things which could be done more quickly by machines?

We are a labour-intensive sector and no doubt robotics will be a part of the future in our sector, I do believe there is still a very strong case for outsourcing as a service, and the best FM providers will just add that capability to their offering and more technical jobs will emerge to support that drive to automation. Also I think in our sector if you can collect and leverage data more effectively you can move up the value chain and perhaps improve margins by delivering more strategic insight on client property portfolios, allowing them to make better investment decisions.

If in time more work is done by machines and AI, what are the implications for today's employees?

I believe work will be more flexible, less nine to five, perhaps with career breaks and other types of flexible arrangements like job sharing.

People might scoff at this conversation if you are thinking about some of the less wealthy developing countries. The idea of a three-day working week to them would be unthinkable. They might be thinking 'I am struggling to find food to feed my family and I have to walk 2 miles to get water' - how does a flexible working week make sense to them? But in advanced industrialised economies, there is a definitely an opportunity to change the way we interact with work and create value. We can't ignore the fact that we are only a small part of the world's community in our privileged environment, this room has coffee and tea to hand. In much of the world the opposite is true, they are struggling to make ends meet and they perhaps don't have the environments with easy access to healthcare and education.

Perhaps expectations around work are evolving faster than we think. Are millennials different in their thinking in your experience?

I don't think so at a human level, I think their environment is different and therefore their response to their environment is different. We talked about 24/7 connections when we last met, the 'always on' culture. Young people always seem connected to stimulus, whether that's social media, workplace software, their friends or online games. We weren't "always connected" when we were younger, so there's very little space for being alone if you're a young person today. Their environment is driving their behaviour differently but I think they're the same as we were underneath. Same basic hopes, fears and needs.

I can imagine if you sat down with someone from the punk era (1970s) for example, like Chris Packham from Springwatch, who has recently been interviewing people from the punk era, he was a punk when he was growing up and their parents were looking at them thinking – what is wrong with them, what's with the anarchism? We look at it as quite quaint now, it's just a phase they were going through. A lot of those anarchic punks have become successful businesspeople. One guy he knew was in a punk band and now he's the Vice Chancellor of Southampton University! Today's young people are still as idealistic as we were I think. They perhaps just have different way of expressing and articulating it, but as they move through life and they are given responsibilities and perhaps have families they will no doubt be more like their parents than they think, but appropriate for their new environments.

How do you balance work, home and leisure, and how important has your family been to the success you have achieved?

Having the support of family members is really important when you spend so much of your time at work, often more of your waking day is spent at work than at home. You might struggle to work at the pace the business requires of you in a senior role without strong support from your family, whatever that looks like. From my personal point of view, if you have a strong sense of purpose at work it's easier for your family to support that. My niece just started as a nurse in ICU and she's really passionate about her work. The biggest lesson I've learned on how to manage your work life balance is to set aside time for your family and if you say you're going to do something with them, do it. Stick to your promises even if it's for a limited amount of time or not as often as you want to. If family and friends are going to be generous with their time and allow you to work hard, give you that space and permission almost, then you've got to turn up to the things that you're committed to do with or for them; it's easier said than done sometimes but a maxim worth striving for.

Apart from spending time with your family what else do you do to refresh?

My spring! It's exercise. It helps me feel more resilient. If I don't play football or get out on the bike once or twice a week, I feel sluggish. And as you know my diet has changed in the last couple of years to make that easier as I've gotten older, but as soon as you get pass thirty-five it all gets a bit more difficult. I also love reading, as you know. I've always got a few good books on the go.

How about listening to podcasts?

Yes, more recently I've really started enjoying podcasts. I've got a few favourites that I go to across work topics or social interests.

Where do you listen to them, on the way to work?

It depends, my commute is an hour and a half each way. Not many people want to talk to at 6:30am. If I know my boss is driving up to the office he'll get a call because he drives for two hours too, so I'll ring him! I can get an hour talking to him whereas in the office

I'll only get fifteen or twenty minutes. If we have something to talk about, we can have a good long conversation. If I have to make calls, I'll make my calls. If not, I'll listen to a podcast on my way in. I tend to choose things that are work related, organisational change topics, behavioural psychology, that type of thing. So I come into the office with my mind on that track but on the way home I try to listen to things which are more entertaining to relax and unwind a little.

So you use that hour and a half at the end of the day to decompress?

Yes, it's two things. One is, when I used to work in London I would work on the way into the office, but on the way back home I'd try not to work. I prefer a paper when I'm on the train and I would just sit on the journey for the last forty minutes reading about something that interested me personally. Which means I finish my day's work and by the time I've arrived home I'm switched off, and in that way I feel better for it.

Do you talk to Lesley, your partner, about work?

No, not a huge amount.

Do you purposely not?

Not especially. If there are unusual things happening at work, we'll talk about it. If it's things that will affect us, we will always talk about it but not for hours on end, just enough to make decisions and be clear on what we need to do. I'd much rather spend time talking about what we're doing on the weekend, what holidays we have planned, what are we going to cook, stuff that's not work related.

Have you become good at switching off?

Yes, not bad. I've never had a big problem switching off, but I know people do. The times that I do struggle are at night if I go to bed with a lot on my mind and then I wake up for some reason, when that happens I do I find it difficult not to start churning through things in my head. I look at my watch and think 'it's 3:30am, I'm up in a couple of hours, I'm not going to fall back to sleep' so I will work through the problems that I'm going to have to deal with. I've gotten better at it, and actually I've found listening to a podcast or an audiobook can be quite an effective way to get back to sleep, if it's something easy to listen to, nothing too taxing!

We are close to the end of our time, Carl. I've really enjoyed the discussion but let me ask you one last question. If you were sat in front of a group of young people, perhaps at school or university, or in the first days of their first job, what would your advice to them be as they contemplate their journey as adults in the world of work?

Do the best job you can on any task you are given. That might sound a bit simplistic but, in my experience, senior people who rise up through the ranks or business owners who build their companies successfully share a common factor - their willingness to tackle any challenge with maximum effort and enthusiasm. All of the senior people I know have navigated a winding and sometimes unexpected journey to the top. You just never know who is watching your progress from a distance, so commit to delivering at your best every time. Having overseen many talent reviews in organisations over the years, I know that senior management are always looking for exciting new talent, so if you've got it they'll see it, but talent and commitment go together.

“

There is an emotional and intellectual resilience that is required to keep on pushing ahead when you're faced with resistance. Build your allies, set clear goals, create energy and excitement, share knowledge and power – and go for it anyway!

”

HELEN HUGHES

INTERVIEWED 31ST JANUARY 2020

I first met Helen when she was Director of Strategy and Change at the Alzheimer's Society, a client of my consultancy at the time.

Born in North Wales and from a family of schoolteachers, Helen decided on a different path. A passionate campaigner even as a student, she has forged a career in the public and healthcare sectors. Her career to date has included a senior role in the World Health Organisation and within the London Development Agency working with the Permanent Secretary at DCMS in the 2012 London Olympics bid.

Now Chief Executive of Patient Safety Learning she is passionate about improving patient safety outcomes, a passion which has shone through in every one of her roles in a very varied career to date.

Perhaps you could start by telling me a little bit about your current role?

I'm the Chief Executive of Patient Safety Learning. We are a small, highly ambitious charity founded in November 2018. An independent voice helping transform healthcare to make it safer for patients and staff.

Was the charity your idea?

No, it wasn't. I've always been passionate about patient safety and I engaged with two people, James Titcombe and Jonathan Hazan, the organisation's Chair, about how we could make a difference. Jonathan had an idea for a new charity and asked me to join as CEO, which I did. I have tried to bring some of the skills I have to bear in strategy and marketing.

I'd like to return a little more to learn about your work at the charity but I'm really interested to understand where your interest in this whole area began. You're a psychologist by degree, I believe?

Yes, I studied Psychology, but I wasn't a particularly active student, I didn't quite know what I wanted to do when I graduated. As a student I was a campaigner, I supported small charities campaigning on education and feminist issues. Career wise, I really didn't know what to do. Most of my family were primary school teachers, so I thought I'd do that. I tried it for about six weeks and realised how awful I was at it!

Were you qualified to teach?

No, completely unqualified. Emotionally I was too immature and after six weeks I left, they said they wanted the grant handed back! So, I got a temporary admin job in the NHS. All my psychometric assessments, because I was quite numerate, said I that I was well suited to become an accountant, something I was most keen to avoid. But I began working in a finance department, just to pay the rent while I worked out my grand life-plan. Fairly soon the Deputy Director for

Finance said, "You're too smart to be doing this, why don't you train to become an accountant?" I was not convinced, but he explained that there was a new graduate financial training scheme where you could learn about healthcare as a business and that's what I did. I found I loved the area and the work and became a Finance Director before I was thirty.

My first provider jobs in SE London were in a non-acute service organisation providing mental health, community health and services for people with learning disabilities. Keen to make a greater impact, I moved up into commissioning and became Finance Director at a Health Authority in London.

Having been unconvinced that you wanted to be an accountant, you found out that you quite liked being a Finance Director then?

Yes and I turned out to be good at it which helped. I gained a good business understanding and worked with accountants who were much better than me at doing the technical stuff. What I really enjoyed was the financial management side, supporting organisations to use their resources more effectively. We were trying to develop new models of care to support people closer to their own home with improved primary care services and more investment in prevention and community-based care. Planning care pathways to deliver safer and more cost-effective care so that the money wasn't always being sucked into the acute sector. It's a challenge that still exists today well over 20 years later. I really enjoyed working with clinicians and managers, contributing to financial management, service planning and improving organisational effectiveness. I discovered early on that I was definitely more of a strategist, people and general manager than a technical accountant.

What was your next career move?

Well, a big report came out called "Organisation with a Memory". It was commissioned by the then Chief Medical Officer, Professor Sir Liam Donaldson, and looked in detail at the issues around patient safety, ensuring that health care was a learning system. Up until that point the broad assumption was that if people in the NHS were good clinicians, then care would be safe. It put a lot of responsibility on individual professionals. At the same time, you had people like me supporting corporate governance, risk management and organisational effectiveness agendas, but it felt to me that there was too much of a separation between clinical delivery and the actual running of the organisation. Reading the report was a massive 'lightbulb moment' for me. I can remember exactly where I was sitting, the room, the desk when I read this report. It introduced insights from other safety critical sectors like the airline industry which had changed their approach to one of system safety and achieved a big impact. It was encouraging the application of human factors and ergonomics and how best to design health care organisations and systems for safety, valuing the importance of how people work within systems. If you don't have the right culture, if you don't have the right leadership, if you're not learning from things which go wrong and where there is good practice, then you won't be fixing the flaws in your system and patient safety will be compromised. I felt those lessons were essential.

What did you do?

The leadership team I was working in had an idea to offer our team to help set up the newly established National Patient Safety Agency. We applied as an entire management team to run the agency. They didn't go for that model, but they did appoint the Joint Chief Executive and I became the first Director of Operations there. We achieved a lot in the first few years, but it didn't feel to me that we were getting a health care system-wide approach to what we were doing and there were risks that we weren't addressing. I felt there was more we needed to do but some of my ideas weren't prioritised and I became a little frustrated.

In the event for a period of time I moved out of healthcare and joined the London Development Agency (LDA). It was fascinating and I learned so much. I was joint Accounting Officer with the permanent secretary at DCMS for the 2012 Olympic bid, the Executive lead for Equality and Diversity, exploring initiatives across the GLA group as well as being the responsible officer for LDA's economic and business regeneration.

Who was the mayor then?

Ken Livingstone. I remember him for his encyclopaedic knowledge and commitment to London. That focus and zeal didn't always go down well with the then Blair Government, especially in discussions on the Olympic 2012 bid.

What did you learn from that experience?

What I saw first-hand was politics in the raw. You had the Greater London Authority, made up of the Mayor's office, the GLA's 'civil service' of officers and the elected members - and often these three constituent groups were not aligned on small and big P politics. We had to work with all parties, and we were accountable not only to the GLA but to the government office for London and the Department of Trade and Industry. The government office and the Mayor's office weren't in sync and the tensions related to multiple accountabilities and different regulatory frameworks were a huge headache and often got in the way.

I learned that in order to make good things happen you have to work with all parts of the chain, and you must work the politics effectively. Particularly in terms of the Olympic bid, the relationships between the GLA and central government were fascinating. I learned the importance of governance and in particular outlining very clearly what is acceptable and what is not acceptable, what leeway you will allow your Board or other organisations to take on matters of significant financial investment.

Did you learn positive things about playing the politics?

The shortest distance between two points isn't always a straight line, you need to be agile to achieve your goal. But, if you have a clear goal, do things well, engage effectively with other stakeholders and have luck on your side, you can make good stuff happen.

What did you learn about negotiation in that context?

Work out what the other party wants to get out of a situation, how you can help them achieve their aims whilst achieving your own aims too. Definitely the value of win/win.

Did you find that you were good at negotiation?

I was quite naive when I started but got better at it. I like making things happen so administering a system is not what floats my boat. I learned a lot about managing change in a complex environment and the challenge of working with different people with different motivations. Anything that involves people involves negotiation!

What's key to that?

You have to know what it is you want to do specifically and be able to articulate very clearly why it's a good idea, you need to get good people on board, understand what allies you need, consider the barriers and how you overcome them.

As you've become more and more senior, do you train your own team in how to do that?

I try to lead by example, help people understand how to influence people in a positive way.

Do you always try to lead by example?

I think it's important, I try to explain why I'm doing things, though I probably don't do it often enough. I often 'leap in' because I want to make things happen NOW, but I'm getting better at being more structured at it; ultimately it's important for leadership to be about the heart as well as the mind.

Looking back, what do you wish you had known at the start of your career that you know now?

I suppose it's less about knowledge and more about my own sense of self-worth because I was never particularly confident, I didn't have a great deal of self-esteem as a young woman. I have recently chaired a charity that supports victims of domestic violence and there are personal reasons why I'm motivated to support work in that area. The burdens of a difficult childhood can cast a long shadow.

I wish I had a clearer sense of where I was going as a young woman. I would have had a plan to make it happen, plan my career around that but my career evolution was less planned than that. I didn't push myself for senior jobs, it was always people saying, "why don't you apply for that?". There's a statistic that says women look at a job description and if they can only hit 80% of the requirements, they think maybe that's not the job for them, yet many men look at the same job having 20% of the attributes but say, "I'm going to go for it anyway". That general difference in confidence and sense of self-worth between the sexes was something that didn't work in my favour, for sure.

Here's a concrete example. In my early thirties, I was thinking about applying to become a Chief Executive in the NHS. I distinctively remember the Chairman of our organisation talking to me, I was saying I wasn't really sure, and they were actively encouraging me to go for it, but I was scared. I wasn't sure I could do it, so I didn't take their advice. If I had done that, I might have progressed faster but ended up in a much more conventional career. So, I'm actually glad that things didn't happen that way, but who knows what I might have achieved had I had more support at the right time.

It is very common in these interviews for people who become successful to share the fact that they lacked confidence early on in their careers. It's a common thread.

Yes, imposter syndrome.

There's a lot of research which shows that people's effectiveness is hugely impacted by positive feedback, not just in a general way, but specifically pointing out to people the impact they have. It can transform them and that is something that I actively try to do with my teams.

I remember early on a Chief Executive when I was working in Southeast London highlighted an article written by the National Finance Director which said that we needed to move our financial professionals in the NHS into a different mode. They wanted their financial professionals to become contributors to organisational development and leadership rather than just number crunchers. They outlined the future for Finance Directors and the Chief Executive sent the article to me and said, "you're already doing this"! I knew that I was good at my job and was breaking the mould certainty in terms of seniority and my gender, but to get affirmation by a senior leader that I respected was amazing. Makes me feel good even now.

Having that kind of feedback made you more confident?

Yes, and also because over time you prove to yourself that you really can deliver and achieve things.

Is there any specific advice you've been given which has helped you in this respect?

When you're at the start of a piece of work, be very clear about what you want to achieve. If you're not clear, it's going to make it very difficult for the people you are working with and it's up to you to show everyone the path that you are following. I learned that from Dame Julie Mellor, she was Ombudsman at the PHSO. She taught me about the importance of simplicity and clarity and the value in having an articulated purpose.

She sounds like a great influence. Have there been others in your career?

Yes, Sir Liam Donaldson who I mentioned earlier. I found him an inspiring visionary. He had a very clear sense of what he wanted to achieve for safer care, globally, and also that his way was the right way. At the time I worked with him, he had to make decisions about what was right and what was politically expedient. It was a fascinating journey.

You admired him because of the clarity of his vision?

Yes. His vision was to create an international patient safety movement and organisation, which eventually became the World Health Organisation Patient Safety flagship. It was his drive, his vision for improving patient safety, his tenacity, his ability to create partnerships with amazing people and his kindness as a human being, which brought that about in the large part. Though very clear and driven, sometimes impatient, he had a great ability to listen and learn from others, including patients. I feel that he genuinely put patients at the heart of his work.

You have worked in some quite high-powered teams. What have you learned about teamwork?

The biggest thing for me is making sure you've got the best people around you. A great team of people with a diverse range of knowledge and experiences can always produce something better than an individual no matter how committed that individual is.

I've seen in my career people not being appointed because they might challenge the person that's appointing them. Always appoint the best person, support them and encourage and praise them when that praise is warranted. It's been a constant effort for me to follow that advice because I'm quite task focussed, I like the outcome and sometimes forget that someone has been up half the night because their two-year-old has a toothache. Setting clear goals and gathering the right resources, showing understanding and emphasising the importance of everyone on the team and supporting them is a key leadership skill, I believe. You need to stop to consider the impact and contribution of everyone and take people with you so that they feel they're involved and contributing, even if sometimes you are just itching to push things along as fast as you can.

In some of the situations you've been involved in with the kind of political landscape and obstacles you've discussed, you must need to be incredibly tenacious to make things happen when obstacle after obstacle presents itself.

Tenacity is certainly a necessary attribute. At Patient Safety Learning we are challenging the system. We have huge support from leaders, patients and patient groups, but there are people in senior roles who seem to be threatened by what we're doing because it changes their power base. We're asking questions and saying, "Can we do it in a better way?" Sometimes responses can be, "Who are you to challenge the status quo, we're doing fine?!" There's an emotional and intellectual resilience that is required to keep pushing ahead when you're faced with that kind of resistance. Build your allies, set clear goals, create energy and excitement, share knowledge and power - and go for it anyway!

Tell me a little more about what Patient Safety Learning does.

The actions needed to address avoidable harm are not being properly addressed by the health and social care system in the UK and globally. They're not being brought together or implemented quickly enough and the worrying statistics of over 10,000 avoidable deaths annually persist. There used to be a National Patient Safety Agency in the UK that oversaw many patient safety initiatives, but it was closed down with the resources dissipated.

The health care industry isn't operating as a Safety Management System in the way other industries do. We want to kickstart changes to ensure that patient safety is at the heart of healthcare. At the heart of what we do is the hub, a platform to share learning for patient safety. It offers a combination of tools, resources, ideas, case studies and good practice to anyone who wants to make care safer for patients. It started as a UK-focused resource but in only three years, over 40% of our users are global.

Rather astonishingly, there are no organisational patient safety standards that have to be achieved. So, we've developed them. We are also developing an accreditation model to formalise and promote improvements in the area.

You have set yourself a big challenge which sounds like it will be all consuming. I wonder, thinking back on your whole career, not just your current role, how do you try to achieve a healthy balance in your life?

I like being busy and the temptation is to dive from one thing to another because it's quite fun and I like juggling a variety of things. Having structure and clarity around priorities is key though.

It important to have enough time to develop policy, set strategies and deliver. In a start-up organisation it's about getting the balance right, setting ambitious plans and being able to demonstrate impact by delivering and taking people with you. I try and divide my time between planning and delivering and effective governance.

How do you manage your work life balance?

When I had my children I became fundamentally much more effective because I couldn't let work drift into the evenings in the way I had previously. For me, work fills all the time I've got if I'm not careful. I've been lucky to have roles that are much more than 'just a job' – roles that are values based and vocational. When I started a family, I had to be much more disciplined about things. I would try to be home at least three times in the week at a reasonable time to have supper and be there for the children's bedtime. I didn't want to be a mum that just saw my kids at weekends. My ex-partner was a schoolteacher, he was always there so it would have been quite easy to over-rely on him especially as I was working internationally with the World Health Organisation for some of that time. I learned the discipline of having lines that I wouldn't cross.

In managing a healthy balance and maintaining energy and freshness, fitness is important to me. My husband and I got into running and long-distance hill walking. We talk as we run, it's a chance to chat and reflect on things if we can catch our breath!

When you look back, has your career been more challenging as a woman?

Certainly, it has, though things are getting better. That doesn't mean that sexism doesn't exist today, people just have to be a bit smarter about it now because it's much more exposed and less acceptable both legally and socially.

The first big conference that I went to as a Finance Director, I went with a close colleague. It was in Brighton, not long after the Brighton bombing, so there was intense security and my colleague's briefcase was checked. I went to have my own checked and the security officer said, "No, we don't need to check secretaries' briefcases." I was astonished. I don't think that would happen now. Society is changing but still there are too many glass ceilings. Access to affordable childcare, secure employment and equal pay is perhaps a challenge for far too many women.

Has it forced you to be tougher?

I think so, tougher and more focused. Discrimination forces you to choose how to respond, do you go along with it or fight it? I've been fortunate that I've had personal support and have worked in organisations that are actively trying to address discrimination. As CEO of the Equality and Human Rights Commission, I helped steer through the Equality Act in 2010, to give legal protections to those that need it. Seeing the impact that discrimination can have on people just strengthens my resolve. Sometimes that involves 'speaking truth to power'. That's not always a comfortable place to be but I've not been afraid to promote change.

When I talked to one of my colleagues about the challenges of being a woman in business, she said the challenge starts at home. Do you agree?

Yes, and I think back to that time when I was considering applying to the graduate recruitment scheme in the NHS. The deputy Director of Finance who encouraged me said, "you will have a harder time as a woman," and I asked him why. His response was that if you have kids, you'll be expected to do everything at home as well. "I can do what I can do but my wife works part-time, and she is the main caregiver to the kids, so it will be more difficult for you." At the time I thought that what he'd said was outrageous, but he was right. One of my friends had kids before me and I said to her, "Me and my partner are going to share everything equally." She laughed and said, "There's always one of you that knows if there are clean socks." I did have it lucky because my then-partner was able to help with the pick-ups, drop-offs and being around for the long holidays. If I had a partner who was doing a similar kind of job, I don't know how that would have worked.

Do you talk often to your husband about your work?

Yes, but sometimes more than I want to because I want to switch off, and he's very interested in what I do! He works in a senior operational role for a mental health organisation and is intrigued by the work we do. And then other times, I don't stop talking about it!

Many of the people I've been in conversation with have said they don't really talk about work with their partners because they think they would be bored!

People work in charities or the public sector often because it is aligned to their broader purpose in life. I think what is interesting about charities is that people work for them because of their values, how they want to improve society, perhaps less motivated by money.

This stuff matters to them. I've worked most of my life in healthcare or social justice and care about making our society fairer and better. It's also important to my husband so we talk long and often about our work, our plans and how to overcome any frustrations. I'm not sure that if we were working in just commercial organisations that we'd have such in-depth conversations!

So far, what do you think you are most proud of in your career?

Essentially, making a difference.

If I can indulge with two examples, one tactical and one more strategic.

When I worked in the World Health Organisation one of the things that we wanted to do was to create a global programme but the WHO didn't have any secure funding. It had contributions from nation states based on what they contributed the year before, but most countries didn't deliver on their pledges, which meant the WHO was always struggling for money. When Sir Liam proposed a World Alliance for Patient Safety it needed funding, and he asked me and his then Deputy Chief Medical Officer to find a way to do it and we did! We had to be rather unconventional and creative about it, but we managed to secure funding of five million pounds a year for five years from the Department of Health. I'm very proud of that, my role in helping the WHO Patient Safety programme get started.

Strategically, I'm very proud of Patient Safety Learning, what we've achieved in three years as a campaigner, influencer and in developing and sharing knowledge and resources to improve the safety of care. There is much to be done, but we are creating a sustainable organisation in the UK and globally.

You are a very purpose driven person. Can you imagine retiring?

Well, I'm of the age where some of my peers are retiring. I see what their lives are like without work, and I don't like the look of it! Their horizons narrow. I suppose that is part of the aging process, people can step away from the frantic-ness of life when they retire.

There will be ways of making my contribution to the causes I believe in, whether it's remunerated or not. What I would miss about work if I were to give it up would be the people and helping to make good things happen.

I do have a hankering for designing and building a Japanese garden. I need to be able to find time for that!

How do you think successful organisations tomorrow might be different from those of today?

Well, healthcare is an interesting one because it's old-fashioned in so many respects organisationally, based so much on tradition and precedent. If you were designing healthcare now you wouldn't start where you are now because healthcare is full of tribes, managerial tribes as well as clinical tribes. There is a delineation of roles between doctors, nurses, OT, etc. whereas if you started afresh, would you have multidisciplinary teams as you do now or would you have multi-skilled professionals doing things differently? The idea now is for patient-focussed care pathways enabled by digital interfaces.

How can the information age support patients and their families help navigate their care path to ensure everyone gets the right support, at the right time, from people with the right skills and experience? There's a really fascinating sense of how that might impact the existing power relationships. Information sharing, rather than professionals having knowledge and passing it out to their patients in an almost master / servant type relationship; patients as partners in their care.

Have you ever walked away from a work challenge?

There was a time where I walked away from a role because I felt like it wasn't working, one I mentioned earlier. The night before I left, I literally sobbed because the organisation was so important to me. I thought I had a big contribution to make but I didn't think they were making the right choices.

I'm quite proud that I made that decision. It would have been much easier to have stayed. I didn't know if I had made the right choice at the time, but I've enjoyed the career I've had immensely. I've had the opportunity to learn, see other cultures and contribute to some good causes, so it worked out fine!

Walking away from a challenge is not something that sits well with me, but I'm pragmatic enough to realise that sometimes the barriers to change mean you might have to.

What will you be most proud of when you retire?

That I put my energy into causes which were important to me and made some impact in a positive way. That I have set good standards and encouraged those I've worked with to do the same. I hope that I have learned along the way and become a more effective leader and perhaps a better colleague. I hope that I've made the most of the talents I have and of the experience I've gained to pursue the things I believe in and move the needle a little on the dial towards a better and fairer society.

“

All of the senior people I know have navigated a windy and sometimes unexpected journey to the top. You just never know who is watching from a distance, so commit to delivering your best every time.

- Carl Johnson

”

POSTSCRIPT

No two people are the same, even successful ones. We are all on an adventure in life which is unique. A fact amply borne out by the eclectic mix of experience and achievements catalogued in these interviews.

I hope you have found their stories interesting as I have and perhaps been prompted to pause and reflect on your own life and its lessons as you plot your next few chapters.

In today's madcap world we sometimes forget to make time to pause and reflect on things. It's always worthwhile.